" The Idea of a University
by Cardinal

THE IDEA OF

A New University

An Experiment in Sussex

EDITED BY DAVID DAICHES

André Deutsch

FIRST PUBLISHED 1964 BY
ANDRE DEUTSCH LIMITED
105 GREAT RUSSELL STREET
LONDON WCI
COPYRIGHT © 1964 BY R. J. BLIN-STOYLE, ASA BRIGGS
J. P. CORBETT, D. COX, DAVID DAICHES, BORIS FORD
JOHN FULTON, GRANVILLE HAWKINS, M. G. HUTT
BASIL SPENCE, W. G. STONE, MARTIN WIGHT
ALL RIGHTS RESERVED
PRINTED IN GREAT BRITAIN BY
EBENEZER BAYLIS AND SON LTD
WORCESTER AND LONDON

CONTENTS

CONTENTS

ILLUSTRATIONS

DAVID DAICHES

Introduction

The founding of a new university is always an exciting and a challenging task. And this is particularly so when the university is founded at a time of rapid expansion of higher education and of equally rapid development of fruitful new ideas about the way such education ought to be conducted. Those who have been concerned with planning the University of Sussex responded from the beginning to both the opportunity and the challenge and have tried hard to map out a scheme both for the arts and the sciences, as well as for the relation between the two, that will at the same time provide a promising solution to some of the problems which universities now face and deal seriously and honestly with the academic content of the education provided. But it is not only those who are professionally interested in university teaching who have been involved in getting the University of Sussex under way. This symposium includes contributions from those who have been concerned with planning and designing the university in all its aspects and will, I hope, illuminate some of the problems with which anyone concerned with developing a new university in our generation will have to be involved.

One of the difficulties in producing a collection of essays of this kind is that the situation was changing rapidly even as the essays were being written – and is changing now as I write these words. There is bound to be an element of experiment, of trial and error, in the first years of a new university, and certainly all the academic contributors are very much aware of the difficulty of discussing a university which has only just completed its third year. Nevertheless, it was thought helpful both for ourselves, who need to examine carefully and justify before public opinion what we are doing, and for others interested in higher education to set down at this stage the steps by which the University came into being, the ideas and principles which underlie its curriculum and its general planning, the way of living as well as of learning that it plans for its undergraduates, and its hopes and intentions for the future.

The views adopted by the University of Sussex are not presented here as representing a new academic orthodoxy which we wish to impose on other universities. Far from it; we are very conscious of the need for different institutions to improve old methods and pioneer new ones, and we welcome the fact that the other new universities are each developing their own ideas and techniques. The University of Sussex offers its principles and practice as one contribution to the body of knowledge and understanding of the nature and function of a university in this period of history.

SIR JOHN FULTON

1. New Universities in Perspective

The ante-natal history of the University of Sussex was, as Mr Stone
will show, a long one. This is in accordance with the laws of the
natural order which prescribe for the most long-lived animals a
correspondingly long period of gestation. As the university is a
perpetual corporation, it has done very well to get itself delivered at
all. It was first registered as a limited liability company under the
name of the University College of Sussex: but it received its Royal
Charter in August 1961, as the University of Sussex. The date of
the Charter is the official birthday of the University: but the records
will show other no less important early landmarks. The appointment of the Academic Planning Committee in 1958 was one such.
The University owes a great debt to Sir James Duff and his colleagues for their work which Mr Stone will describe in some detail:
most of all for their decision to recommend that the new university
should organize its academic courses in Schools of Studies. This
decision emancipated the university from the restrictions of the
departmental system and ensured for those who were to plan and
provide its courses the maximum possible flexibility and freedom.

In using that freedom the University depended on the goodwill
and encouragement of the University Grants Committee. It was
always forthcoming. Sir Keith Murray, his successor as Chairman,
Sir John Wolfenden, and their colleagues have played a memorable,
if self-effacing, part.

The next stage was the appointment in 1959 of the Vice-Chancellor and the first permanent administrative officers of the University; these were followed soon afterwards by the first academic
appointments. From then on theirs was the main responsibility for
planning and carrying out the University's development. They
shared that responsibility with new colleagues as they came; they
received, and continue to receive, the most generous and firm support from the University Council and the Academic Advisory

Committee as well as from the local authorities and the wider public of the region and the country at large. Indeed, the friendly interest in the new university shown by sister universities, the schools, professional bodies and the press, both national and local, came as something of a revelation of the changing role of universities in our society. To this aspect we shall return shortly.

The next landmark was the arrival of the first undergraduates and post-graduate students. They came – a small company some fifty strong – in 1961 instead of 1963 as had at first been intended. The change of timetable was in itself symbolic of the change which has taken place since the war in the public 'image' of education and of the new attitudes which encouraged the foundation of the group of seven new universities, of which Sussex is the earliest. In our own country it was not only the rising birth-rate and, in particular, the enlarged age-groups born in the years just after the war (the 'bulge') which were emphasizing the need to enlarge the number of university places. Even more significant was the 'trend', the increasing proportion in each successive age-group staying on beyond the age of compulsory schooling to prepare for entry to higher education. Overseas – for example, in our former colonial dependencies – the same process was at work in an even more explosive form. In the eyes of these newly independent peoples education – particularly education in science and its applications – holds the key not only to the defeat of poverty and the human suffering that goes with it but gives access also to the secrets of Western affluence. Affluence has its tempting fruits: but independently of these, the spread of education among the peoples of the world seems to the underdeveloped and underprivileged the best hope that the relations between men, between nations and between races will be progressively based on reason rather than on prejudice, fear and passion. Whereas at the end of the war of 1939–45 there was in British Colonial Africa only one College teaching for degrees, there are at the time of writing no less than sixteen. Most of these came into being before independence with the help of capital from the United Kingdom and with extensive help from the universities of the United Kingdom, which were in the main the source of staff; what is true in Africa is true also of former British territories elsewhere – Hong Kong, Ceylon, Malaysia, the West Indies: and true also of the entire underdeveloped parts of the world. These institutions, then, are the contemporaries of the seven new universities being founded in the decade of the 1960s in the United Kingdom. No such upsurge has been known in the past. Its consequences are certain to be commensurate with its gigantic scale.

It is important in describing the challenge presented to the new universities to remind ourselves – not for the first time – of the contrast between the conditions of their birth and those of their predecessors. As University Colleges the latter began their existence academically dependent on another institution. They taught their students according to the syllabus of that institution and prepared them to take its degrees externally. Their prospect of growth was uncertain because there was no rising demand for student places. They had no assurance that the necessary capital for site, buildings and equipment would be forthcoming; it had to be raised by private subscription. Grants for recurrent expenditure were small and chancy. Small wonder if the outlook over the first quarter or even half-century appeared daunting for the pioneer staff of these institutions. The conditions in the 1960s are very different. Capital for basic needs is assured; maintenance grants for suitably qualified students ensure that the rising demand for university education will allow numbers rapidly to expand in new as well as in existing institutions. Above all, the new universities of the 1960s have been allowed their academic independence. From the start they have been granted the right to confer their own degrees (including higher degrees), based upon courses of study of which they themselves are the authors. This improvement on the conditions under which universities used to be born does not of course in itself assure the new ones of success in attracting and retaining staff of high quality: but it has removed the most serious obstacles to their early progress and offers them the opportunity, if they can take it, of influencing the course of higher education during the present critically important years.

This then was the setting in which the small group who were first given responsibility for planning the new University of Sussex came together. In what follows there are set out some of the chief issues as they presented themselves. Many of them are dwelt upon at length in other chapters of this book. Here no detailed discussion will be attempted. We believed that we saw answers to some of our problems. For the answers to others we knew that time was essential. We recognized some of the issues only imperfectly at the beginning and have become aware of their fuller implications since. We are indebted to the experience of the University of Keele in ways too numerous for separate acknowledgement. And we have learned much from the discussions which have marked the progress of our six sister institutions.

The present book, which is intended to restate the main problems of a university at its beginning and to recapture some of the attitudes of mind in which the answers were sought, inevitably fails to present an up-to-date record of recent developments. Conversely, although the University is less than three years old the presence of over one hundred and ten members of faculty and nearly a thousand undergraduate and postgraduate students makes it difficult to think oneself back into the time when there were few colleagues, no students, no buildings and all was to plan for. Therefore the writer of the present chapter may be permitted to quote the notes of an address he gave on the subject of new universities at the Home Universities Conference in December 1960.

'The question of what the new universities should be like must raise many questions about *all* universities and the influences to which they will be subjected over at least the next forty years. Some of these questions are:

a) Will the universities have a monopoly of the nation's talented youth?

b) If they share them with other post-school institutions, how?

c) How many students altogether?

d) How big should individual universities be?

e) The balance of studies:

   i) Will they become more vocational e.g. moving towards an American pattern?

   ii) Will they, even if they are non-vocational in the strict sense, reflect changes in the country's social and economic structure, e.g. towards a service economy?

   iii) Will they reflect changes in the structure and balance of international (and inter-continental) politics and trade e.g. African and Asian Studies?

f) How will they teach?

g) How residential and what sort of residence?

The most immediate of these questions as they affect the *new* foundations are:

1) Where should they be?

2) How big should they be?

3) What should they teach?

4) How should they teach it?'

Let us begin with the first of these last four questions. There has been much public argument in the last five years about the choice of sites for universities. Should they be in new towns or old towns; in large industrial centres or small 'cathedral' cities; in the heart of towns or on their outskirts; in places whose existing cultural amenities would support a new university through its infancy or in culturally underdeveloped areas needing the intellectual stimulus of academic missionaries? Those who have to plan and organize the life of new universities have generally no say in the choice of site. That has been settled at an earlier stage. But the issue of the argument deeply concerns them. It would be perverse to argue that the quality of the academic staff of a new university is wholly determined by the choice of site; but it is only realistic to recognize that the choice of site does exercise an important influence. Is it culturally rich or barren? Is it near the great libraries? Are London and the learned societies within fairly easy reach? Are there good schools for the children of the university teachers? The answers to these and similar questions may well tip the balance for men of great academic talent between accepting or rejecting the challenge to new adventure. In these respects the University of Sussex has enjoyed singular good fortune.

But behind this question of site lie other profounder issues. Are universities to be national, regional or local? Post-war policy in this country has favoured the 'national' answer. That is to say, maintenance grants have been payable to enable a student, if he so chooses, to live away from home in lodgings or in a hall of residence at any university at which he has been accepted for a course of study: and very many students have chosen to go further afield than the university nearest to their homes. The locations of the seven new universities were clearly chosen on the assumption that this practice would continue. Few of them could grow to a substantial size if they relied solely on students living within daily travelling distance. They must expect therefore to recruit students from the country as a whole. This in turn presupposes either a plentiful supply of lodgings or an appropriate programme of residential building. Sussex has enough lodgings in Brighton to provide for its students during the first stages of its growth. But its site is four miles out of the town. One of the conditions for starting a new university in the 1960s was that it should possess a site of some 200 acres, which is likely to be available only some distance out in the country. Thus a new form of the old problem of 'nine-to-five' was back with us, at least temporarily; the best (though not the only) means of overcoming it would be to have a reasonable proportion of undergraduates (and postgraduates) living on the site in University property. To build residences, whether conventional or as blocks of student flats, is, however, what the new universities may not do with their initial capital grants from the public purse. It is to be hoped that this restriction will be removed before long. The appeals of the new universities to private benefactors have been in large part for residential buildings. Sussex is building two halls from the proceeds of its appeal. These will take it some part of the way towards its desired objective of offering all its students at least one year's residence out of three.

Controversy over the siting of new universities rests in part on the competition between one kind of town with another and also raises the question of the social cost of higher education with and without 'residence' for undergraduates. In both these matters there is surely room for diversity. One has only to consider the splendid and fertile relationship between the ancient University of Glasgow and modern Clydeside, the place of London University in the capital or again, the relationship of the University of Cambridge to its own immediate environment, to see the great and rich diversity which is possible. Again, the proportion of 'local' to 'national' students in each university need not be traditionally uniform but should in each place grow out of local choice and tradition.

But behind all of the discussion there lies the profoundest issue of all – the relation between university and society. There is the view – I suppose it could be called the North American view – that taking the campus to the state must bring the state to the campus, and that the result will be to the benefit of both. This view rests either on straightforward utilitarian considerations – the advantage of applying, let us say, the biological sciences to the problems of agriculture; or on the ideal of an educated democracy in which the citizen is raised through contact with the man of learning to a higher level of personal development. On the other side is the view that in the last resort the scholar is a man apart and – subject to his acceptance of the high responsibility he bears – that he ought to be so. His world and his values are not the world or the values of the here-and-now in which the 'doers' live. He is engaged upon problems for whose solution another perspective, another time-scale is needed. It is his business and his duty to attract young people in sufficient numbers from each age-group to concern themselves with his perspectives, his time-scale, his probing beyond the appearances of things to their ultimate nature and the laws of their behaviour. If he is to succeed in this he must be able to draw them for a few years aside from the distractions of the here-and-now. Some will take to the scholarly life and remain in it. The rest will take into the everyday bustle of affairs an enduring experience of the other kind of world. This view involves the inevitability (and desirability) of a healthy tension between the two worlds and the two sets of values. Here is an issue of the first importance about the relation between the university and society at large. Every university, new or old, whether placed in the heart of an industrial city or in a rural environment, must come in some measure to grips with it. Its verdict will be reflected in many facets of its academic and business policy. Will it be content for its students to spend thirty weeks of the year at the university and then merge themselves with the rest of society during vacations by taking employment unconnected with their studies? Will it choose to fill its residences in the vacations with its own students or those from sister universities so that they can engage in private study? Will it prefer to increase the number of its students in residence during term by profitable letting of residential accommodation to outside bodies during the vacations? These are some practical every-day forms of the larger issue.

We may turn now to the question of size. How big should a new university plan to be? And at what rate should it grow? These questions are – for reasons already mentioned – quite new in the history of the foundation of universities in the United Kingdom; and for the new universities of the 1960s they are inescapable. In the first place the total resources of men and money are limited; to spread them over a large number of small institutions would be manifestly un-economic. Even more urgent is the question, 'what is the smallest size of university which can achieve academic quality sufficiently high to attract and retain men of distinction in their subjects?' There is, of course, no precisely determinable answer. As the first of the new seven, Sussex had to give itself the best answer it could. Accepting that a reasonable spread of subjects must be provided for – but excluding professional schools – the University felt that not less than 350–400 members of faculty would be adequate to provide impetus for scholarship and to maintain the teaching services. As new subjects (including the coming together of subjects formerly distinct) vindicated their claim to inclusion the number of teachers and researchers would have to grow. But assuming a figure halfway between the limits indicated – 375 – the 'supporting' student population calculated on a staff-student ratio of 1:8 would be 3,000. This objective was first set in the speech already referred to which was made by the present writer at the Home Universities Conference in 1960. In the course of that speech he prescribed a period of ten years within which the aim should be achieved. No evidence which experience since 1960 has provided suggests that the estimate of number was far out; the timetable on the other hand seems likely to be shortened from ten years to six. Although there was a good deal of scepticism as recently as 1960, there is already a consensus of view that the rewards of growing rapidly (relatively to past experience in the United Kingdom) far outweigh the difficulties which it causes. To create a sense of community among faculty and students when a great proportionate increase in numbers occurs year by year is not so difficult as some pessimistic critics asserted that it would be. The newcomers are not conscripts: they have chosen to join the university on the basis of what they know of its academic aims and objects. To have them sooner rather than later is to build upon a broader and stronger base. The advantages, on the other hand, of growing fast are incontestable. Distinguished scholars can be offered the opportunity of experimenting without forgoing for a long and indefinite period the resources which accompany reasonable size. Able undergraduates will choose universities where there are distinguished scholars at work. Thus rapid growth is a necessary condition for achieving high academic standards; it is not their enemy.

One final word on growth is worth saying. A static or slow growing university has to pay very heavy prices; its resources remain the same, or increase only at a very slow rate. In such circumstances resistances to new subjects of study are inevitably generated. New resources, when they come, have already been claimed by existing academic interests; if they are diverted to new fields of study they may well be thought to have overridden the claims of established and thus more deserving disciplines. And so rivalry and contest replace what should be co-operation in the work of scholarship. In new universities the steepest curve of growth is at the beginning.

The sting is removed from inter-subject rivalry because, with rapid growth ahead, unsuccessful claims are thought to be postponed rather than surrendered. It is of course true that in this period of rapid build-up irreparable damage could be done to the future balance of the university unless there were a clear academic pattern or 'shape' controlling the allocation of resources. But, provided that there is a conscious shaping of the university's development towards an agreed academic pattern, there is overwhelming advantage in having as many aspects of scholarship as possible represented as soon as possible. It is regrettable if scientific subjects are introduced even a year later (as was the case at Sussex) than those in Arts; if applied science comes after pure science; and so on. If we must fall short of the ideal – a university born full-grown like Athene from the head of Zeus – then let the arrival on the academic stage of the chief and the lesser actors be as nearly simultaneous as possible.

The third and fourth of my questions, 'what to teach?' and 'how to teach it?', are dealt with separately and in detail elsewhere. Something, however, may properly be said of their relationship to the wider purposes of the University. Those who believe, like the present writer, that education is 'making the future' must ask the question whether the 'future' is to be a tailor-made society whose features are clearly imprinted and pre-determined by men's decisions in the past or laid down by present authority. Alternatively, is the teacher's responsibility for the future discharged when he has done all that can be done to raise the powers of the individuals committed to his charge to their highest capacity, in the confidence that, if they have been so prepared, the future which they shape will be the best attainable? The second course seems likely to be more congenial to a free society. Even so, it will not be possible completely to avoid seeking to discover the shape of the future which has to be built upon the foundations of today's education. If our present society could look forward with assurance to a long period of stability – of which history shows many examples – the character of the education appropriate to it would be one thing: but for a world of rapid change – technological, social and political – it must be another. Thus whether we hold to our traditional educational practices or whether we change them, we are, in either case, saying our say about the future. Within the limits of human foresight we must see that what we choose is relevant to the needs of the long-term as well as to those of the short-term future.

It would be difficult to trace the sequence of ideas out of which grew the definitive proposals for new academic courses; and where so much sprang from the give-and-take of discussions it would be impracticable to recall the details. But of some things one can be sure. All the participants shared the view that when a university was founded it was admitted to membership of a company which recognizes in its dealings with the world of scholarship no frontiers of race or religion or politics: to be born into such a society is to accept as final the arbitration of human reason together with all the implications of that acceptance. But common membership of a family should not mean entirely to sink one's individual identity in the group. A new institution must make its own contribution in its own way if it is not to be a merely sterile replica. It was also accepted by all that it was the duty of a university to ensure that its studies involved exacting, disciplined work. Whatever varieties of courses might be introduced, they must all have in them disciplined study in depth. There was acceptance too of the view that over the next half-century change would be even more rapid than in the past fifty years; so that flexibility of mind would be a necessary condition of a fully effective intellectual contribution by the graduates-to-be. It was accepted that such flexibility would be encouraged and sustained if a main discipline studied in depth were accompanied by cognate, 'minor', 'contextual' subjects which would naturally illuminate and be illuminated by the 'major' subject and by one another. It was agreed also that there would be great educational benefit if subjects were held together (as they were in Oxford's Classical Greats) by virtue of being aspects of a single civilization. These tests were applied to all the proposals for degree courses. From the discussions there emerged projects for Schools of European Studies, English (and American) Studies, Social Studies, African and Asian Studies, Educational Studies; on the Science side Schools of Physical Science, Biological Studies, Applied Science and Engineering Science. Discussion of individual Schools will be found in the appropriate chapters. All that need be said in general is to record the striking degree of willingness to exchange the narrower dominion of the single-subject course for the freedom to contribute from the angle of one's own subject – whether it might be history, literature, philosophy – to the understanding of a more complex whole. Such an approach to academic work clearly commands sympathy from university teachers of ripe scholarship as well as from undergraduates and applicants for places. Two examples from among many may be quoted. First, the exhortation directed at new universities from a number of most distinguished biologists to 'integrate' in a new unity what are presently rigidly divided aspects of biology. Second; in the field of developmental social studies, the demand for the co-operation of the psychologist, the sociologist and the economist in solving the problems of the 'economics of growth'.

So much for the fundamental studies in Arts and Science. These must necessarily remain the primary responsibility of the university as far ahead as one can see. The new University must give its first attention to them. But if we look forward into the long term future it is probable that the growth points of most decisive importance will be technology and the applied social sciences. The rate of technological development and technological change is certain to increase rapidly over the next half century. And the stresses and strains set up within the technological society will require a great extension of the 'welfare' services (in the broadest use of that term) to overcome them. The University of Sussex has nailed its colours to the mast about the nature of its courses in fundamental arts and sciences. It is now planning its courses in the 'applied' fields. Their importance is bound to grow with each decade that passes.

The last of the challenging questions is 'how to teach?'. The university committed itself at a very early stage to the tutorial rather than the lecturing system. This does not mean that all teaching is done in tutorials (one:one) with no lectures. On the contrary, lectures – though voluntary – play an important part in teaching, as do small classes also. What the University holds to be of prime importance, however, is that a strong element of individual tutorial teaching (based on undergraduate written work) should be part of the experience of every student. This has three outstanding virtues. First, it makes the pupil active and forces him to measure his own identifiable work against that of a professional in the particular field of study. Second, it prescribes that such activity should be regular (week by week) and not spasmodic or belated. Third, it offers the possibility (not unerringly but largely with success) of a special and valuable relationship between teacher and pupil.

So much for formal teaching. Beyond it the process of education should be continuous. Education of taste (the architecture of the new university; its landscaping, furnishing and decoration; the pictures on the walls, the musical life of the place) is a responsibility of the university as a whole; and each element within it – young and old – has much to give and to take. Partly because it recognized this (and partly because of the need, already referred to, of avoiding the 'nine-to-five' danger) the University deliberately chose to put up, as its very first building, Falmer House, the social and amenity centre shared by the student body and the faculty in common. It also warmly welcomed the benefaction of the Gulbenkian Trust to establish fellowships for practising artists in the creative arts. It is intended that the holders will live for a few years as members of the university. Their studios, practice rooms, workshops will be in an Arts Centre in the University Park. As they work they will be able to transmit something of their own creative quality in exchange for the intellectual stimulus which the academic community will offer them.

But beyond formal education and the education of taste there is a further task. How to organize the life of the university so as to ensure for its undergraduates the fullest development of their whole personalities on which their effective membership in the future of the free society depends. First, they should be so selected that they will form a richly diverse body, stimulating the whole university through differences of social origin, of educational background, and of vocational motive; with appropriate proportions devoting themselves to the different disciplines, and appropriate proportions of men and women, overseas students of different races and so on. Secondly, the university should provide for them an orderly framework of tutorial and other teaching within which they can enjoy the maximum freedom for personal intellectual development. Thirdly, the working framework must be flexible enough to allow for a considered choice of course (and in appropriate circumstances for a change of course); closely related to the student health service and to the arrangements for guiding the undergraduate's choice of career; and related also to a humane and satisfactory examination system. Under these conditions the undergraduates should be able to contribute through the diversity of their talents, backgrounds and experiences to a university society marked by its insight, liveliness and vitality; and from their association with it emerge armed against the encroachments of uncritical uniformity which are the result of the modern mass media of communication and entertainment.

Finally, there is the challenge facing all universities, new and old, to vindicate their right to autonomy. University autonomy, properly understood, is to be defended not for the sake of academic privilege but on the ground that it is essential to the health of society as a whole. If it is withdrawn or forfeited, society's way of life must suffer a profound change. Much has been heard of late – and discussion will certainly continue – about the response of the universities to changes in the character of the larger society. Each university has to give its own answer, recognizing that that answer is bound to affect not only itself but other institutions as well. Those that are new have perhaps a special opportunity to present what they offer in a clear and unambiguous pattern. So long as the initiative in making new patterns and modifying those that already exist rests with the universities themselves their autonomy is assured; and so long as their different individual patterns, taken as a whole, fulfil the needs of the present and anticipate those of the future, in exercising their autonomy they are beyond reproach. The price of failing in this would be sooner or later to have a pattern imposed from outside.

Patterns or shapes can be discovered or arrived at in different ways. It matters greatly to capture the imagination and the minds of all the academics on whom rests the task of turning patterns into working reality. The inventiveness of the individual member of faculty must be used in the evolution of the primary academic pattern through to maturity. No new university is in a position to claim achievement in this. Time must pass before progress can even begin to be measured. But whether or not they succeed will weigh heavily in determining the final verdict upon them.

2. *Opening the Mind*

I

The art of teaching at a university is, to a great extent, just like the art of teaching anywhere else. All teachers have to invent ways of putting important points with clarity and force, to discover what it really is that students find hard in a given topic, to consider what personal difficulties are holding a particular pupil back, to maintain interest during studies that are indispensable, but dull. The university teacher, however, faces special problems that arise from the peculiarities of university work. While he must spend much time ensuring that the elements of his subject are mastered, he must always remember that some of his students will go on to make fresh contributions to knowledge and that as many of them as possible should leave the university, if not with the power to do original work, at least with some idea of what original work is like and of what is happening at the frontiers of their subject. This the teacher can only do if he keeps in touch with the advancement of knowledge. The special problems of university teaching stem from these facts.

Although people outside universities often fail to see it, the fact that the university teacher has not only to teach but to contribute to research imposes a considerable strain upon him. Research is exacting. It demands not only time, but sustained concentration. It is an activity hard to start and stop, and therefore to combine with any other. The personal problem of the university teacher, even if he can free himself from administration and other cares, is always therefore how to combine his own work in his own subject, on which his reputation and success equally depend, with the work of teaching. He can only teach well if he does research; but if he does research, it is difficult for him to give his teaching the attention it requires. Plainly, there can be no perfect solution to such a conflict. A compromise is the most that can be achieved. But the need to find a compromise by which teaching is made at least compatible with, and at best conducive to research, is fundamental to the design of any university.

The fact that universities are places of research not only sets the teacher a personal problem but deeply affects his task in teaching. It is essential here to keep in view the different categories of students, in point of immediate academic ability, with which he has to deal. There is always a minority of academic adepts who present no problems. They soon find out where they want to go and how to get there, under any system. They have only to live in a university in order to absorb its values and methods and make rapid progress. The real problem of teaching begins with those students to whom the values and methods of higher study are strange or alien or repulsive, whether because their intellectual capacity is relatively low, or because their previous environment, at home and school, has failed to bring it out, or because, for the moment, they are just not interested. Such students, numerous even in universities as selective as the English, are not incapable of studying well, but cannot do so without much help. If the university is to give them a respectable command of a branch of knowledge, with some understanding of the process of research and of the significance of its current achievements – and the university can hardly be content with less – then it must carefully consider by what means, in the circumstances, that can be done. This consideration, though trite, deserves emphasis; for university teachers tend to forget that the art of inquiry is often as mysterious to their pupils as it is familiar to themselves, and tend to suppose that that art, merely by existing in themselves, will be automatically transmitted to those who come in contact with them. One result is the view, frequently acted on and even sometimes confidently stated, that the form and manner of a lecture are unimportant and do not need to be studied as carefully as its content. These are illusions. Some automatic transmission of intellectual attitudes and skills does certainly occur. The inspiration of particular teachers and the gentle force of imitation do a great deal. But whatever these spontaneous influences may achieve, there is much that they do not; and if anyone doubts that methods of teaching must be studied he has only to consider the needless dreariness of many university lectures. There is thus, undeniably, a problem of university teaching: the problem of so organizing matters that the teacher is helped, in every possible way, to bridge the yawning gulf that runs right through the university between the bewildered first year student on the one hand, and, on the other, the latest brilliant contribution to the learned journals.

To decide how this gap can best be bridged, one thing to consider is what causes students to be bewildered by university work. They may, of course, be so incapable of it intellectually that there is nothing for it but to move them to an easier course; and since procedures of selection are very inefficient there are bound to be many such students in every university. Their number, however, is often exaggerated, for they are difficult to distinguish from students who are intellectually capable of the work before them but who, for one reason or another, cannot bring their powers to bear upon it. Very many factors, some profound, some trivial, from neurosis and personal anxiety to bad habits of reading and taking notes, interfere with the development of intellectual power. These circumstances vary not only with the individual student, but with the society to which he and the university belong. Much obviously depends upon academic experience in the last years of school, but there are other influences less direct but not less real. A society, for instance, in which differences of wealth and privilege are very marked and clearly reflected in student life and in the student's expectations of his subsequent career presents quite different personal problems to the individual student than those, perhaps as difficult, that are presented by more egalitarian conditions. Each type of society produces its characteristic tensions which, according to his temperament, encourage or inhibit the intellectual growth of a particular student. But whatever the particular circumstances may be, students are always struggling with more than purely intellectual difficulties, and it follows that if the university is to get the best from them it must devise a teaching system that not only is efficient intellectually but makes it possible and natural for teachers to take account of these other difficulties and do what they can to overcome them.

In devising a strategy for university teaching one must therefore attend to the personal problems of the teachers and the taught; but equally one must attend to the demands of particular subjects. Different methods are needed for teaching literature or philosophy than are needed for teaching physics or mathematics. Arts subjects are, and doubtless will always remain, controversial: they have indeed a factual basis that can and must be learned, but differences of opinion are the normal thing on all the main topics with which the student finds himself concerned. By contrast, while differences of opinion do exist in the most advanced fields of the exact sciences, there is in those subjects a much greater area of indisputable and essential knowledge that has simply to be mastered before those fields can even be approached. It is natural to suppose that different methods will be required for teaching subjects with such different logical structures.

These are the broad principles that must be borne in mind when devising a strategy for teaching in a new university. In applying them to the particular problems faced by our university we do not claim to have invented any new forms of university teaching; we only claim to have combined the traditional forms in more profitable ways. These forms are the lecture, the seminar or class, and the tutorial.

Lectures, we think, are rather less valuable than is commonly supposed; but we give this point a different force according as to whether, to take extreme examples, one is dealing with mathematics or with literature. The great merit of the lecture is that it can present, in the simplest form, the essentials of a subject. For this purpose a good book may be even more efficient, but books that do successfully simplify a subject are often hard to find, for a speaker can repeat and illustrate points to an extent that would be intolerable on paper. In addition there is always the advantage that a group of students can acquire by means of lectures a common framework for their studies. Lectures are therefore particularly useful in the exact sciences, where there is such a large amount of uncontroversial knowledge to be imparted, and tend to be less so in the arts and social studies, where questions of interpretation and attitude arise so quickly that the student will get a false impression of the subject if he is not exposed at once to the conflict of opinion which lectures so easily conceal. We do not think that this implies that lectures in arts subjects have no use at all; but our intention is to use them mainly as an aid to other methods, their function being to provide an introductory framework, to fill up gaps in the available literature, and to permit the exceptional lecturer to exert his talents in that way. In the exact sciences, on the other hand, lectures will play a more important part, and will provide a comprehensive framework for all other teaching. But whatever use is made of lectures we do not think that students ought to spend a large part of their time in listening to them, and so be led to suppose that this is the main part of their education; for unless the lecturer is extremely skilful, and this inevitably is rare, lectures tend to encourage students to adopt passive, rather than active, attitudes towards their subjects, to write down the thoughts of others rather than to write up their own. The student straight from school, in particular, needs every encouragement to escape from that mechanical attitude to knowledge which is produced by long preoccupation with elementary examinations. For this fundamental purpose the lecture, except in rarely skilful hands, is badly suited; and we have therefore decided, though rather more in arts and social studies and rather less in science, to throw the main burden of teaching upon methods of other kinds.

One consequence of the kind of curriculum that we have adopted is that we shall make much use of classes or seminars of a special kind. Our curriculum is designed to encourage students, while still undergraduates, to reflect upon the relevance of one branch of study to others from which, traditionally, it has been divided. While, for example, a work of literature stands in its own right and may indeed be read and enjoyed with the help of little or no historical knowledge, to study a work of literature is one way of studying the society from which it sprang, and to study that society is to learn much about the work that would otherwise go unperceived. The French Revolution and Romanticism were interacting movements of society, and need to be seen as such. In this, therefore, as in many other similar cases, we propose to make much use of seminars held by two or more teachers whose different interests and skills converge on a particular topic. We believe that seminars of this kind will not only be very stimulating to students but will provoke fresh thought amongst those who conduct them. We are all to some extent prisoners of the academic classifications in which we are placed; it does us good to have to move outside them.

In addition to this use of seminars we shall naturally also use them in the normal way for advanced teaching of both undergraduates and graduates, but we do not think that this method is suitable for more elementary teaching for the first degree. Its defect is that it allows the student who finds the subject difficult, or who is prevented by shyness from entering into the discussion, to play an entirely passive role. On this point, however, we recognize that English experience may differ from that in other countries. English undergraduates – by comparison, for example, with American undergraduates – are reluctant to speak in front of even a small audience; consequently, a method of teaching that may work very well with young Americans is ineffective in this country. Our intention at Sussex is therefore to make the tutorial, rather than either the lecture or the class, the main means of undergraduate instruction. This is a drastic departure from the practice of modern English universities, though not, of course, from that of Oxford and Cambridge; one can indeed say that what we are doing is to adapt the principle of a tutorial system, as developed in Oxford and Cambridge, to the conditions of a modern university. By tutorial teaching we understand an arrangement under which each undergraduate attends one or two sessions each week with a tutor in groups of not more than five members. The size of the groups that we propose varies between subjects. Since scientific subjects are relatively uncontroversial and have a relatively settled form there is less room in them for individual approaches and individual difficulties; tutors find in practice that there is a great similarity between the obstacles encountered by the members of any group of students, and therefore that individual attention to them is less important. In the arts and social studies, on the other hand, where the subject matter is less definite and more controversial, individual attention is indispensable. Most tutors find that these subjects are best taught to students either singly or, at most, in pairs. So soon as one teacher is asked to deal in the course of one hour with more than two students he finds it very hard, perhaps impossible, to adapt his treatment of the material to the particular interests and difficulties of each. In spite of these differences, however, there is a substantial similarity between the teaching in such small groups in subjects of either kind, and the reasons for adopting the method are the same.

The first reason is that, by contrast with the lecture, this method of teaching is a powerful means of obliging the student to adopt an active rather than a passive attitude to learning. He is given a task each week; in order to fulfil it he has to make use of books whose style and method, and perhaps whose assumptions and conclusions, will be diverse; he is compelled to come to conclusions of his own by having to produce some written work for his tutor's criticism at their next meeting. The system therefore counters perhaps the greatest enemy of intellectual progress amongst undergraduates: the passive collection of unanalysed material. Far from being, as it is sometimes said to be, a system that makes things easy for the student, it is one that demands the greatest effort and initiative from him, but demands it in such a way that is within the reach of all. The ablest student, who will analyse and organize on his own initiative the material that he collects at lectures, in seminars and in the laboratory, needs to be led on to deeper issues; the weaker student finds the task of analysis too difficult and needs to have the problems simplified. Whereas the lecture or the class is bound to go too slowly for some and too fast for others, the merit of the tutorial system is that it enables the teacher to adjust the pace of learning to individual need. However, we consider that tutorial teaching should succeed during the first year or two of the undergraduate's course in teaching him the values and methods of higher study, and that for the remainder of his course less personal methods of teaching should generally be adequate. By relying more at this stage upon the lecture and the class we hope to save teaching time that can be devoted to beginners. The crux of our strategy is, in fact, just the reverse of what is practised in most universities; we think that the main teaching effort should be devoted to students who are just beginning their course rather than to those who are concluding it. We feel that this is the only way in which students can be saved from wasting a great deal of time before they learn, if they ever do, what university work should be.

This process of learning the essential values and methods of higher study is promoted by another aspect of tutorial work. When a teacher is working with a small group, whose members he therefore gets to know personally, he can teach in a less formal way than is possible in the lecture theatre or even in the class. Thus, when a difficulty has been suggested, he can think about it aloud and let his thoughts rove freely over the possible ways of dealing with it. He can admit, in a way that would be awkward with a larger audience, that he is not sure how best to handle the matter; he can take down books from the shelf and consider what they say; he can try out one method and then another. This informal thinking aloud about difficulties is of the greatest value to the student. It enables him to see how a more experienced thinker handles the sort of difficulty with which he is constantly confronted and so conveys to him, by suggestion and imitation, something of the knowhow of inquiry.

Personal contact between the teacher and student is not, however, only useful from this intellectual point of view. It is, we think, the only really effective way of ensuring that when students run into difficulties of whatever kind some teacher knows about it immediately and is placed in a position in which he is encouraged and enabled to give help. Under a lecturing system, weeks, terms or even years may elapse before it comes unmistakeably to the knowledge of any teacher that a particular student is so much at sea in the subject that he is really wasting his time. An immense amount of talent is thus wasted. But under the tutorial system such waste is much less likely. No system, of course, can prevent it altogether. The tutor, besides being a bad teacher, may lack interest in people; short of that, he may not get on with a particular student. In such cases personal contact of the kind that the tutorial system involves may even do more harm than good. Experience suggests, however, that they are rare, and that on the whole, when teachers meet their pupils in groups small enough to permit friendship, they not only notice but care about, and not only care about but tackle, the difficulties that their pupils meet. The truth is that where these difficulties are not so much of an intellectual as of a personal kind they can only be quickly brought to light on the basis of personal friendship between the teacher and the taught. That is not to say that students do not have many personal problems that are beyond the competence of the teacher to handle; nor is it to say that tutors should be always thinking about and inquiring into their pupils' lives. Universities need a psychiatric service, and undergraduates, like the rest of us, need to be left to their own devices. But nobody is better placed than a teacher who sees his pupils weekly to notice when something is going wrong and to make a first assessment of the trouble. Sometimes he will discover quite soon that the difficulty is one that requires the expert help of a doctor or psychiatrist; but very often it will prove to be something that he can deal with by himself. Students, like other mortals, are often shy and lonely; they work badly because they are afraid to meet another mind. When that is so, a teacher's genial response may be all that is needed to ease away the inhibiting emotion. It is on these grounds, just as much as on grounds of intellectual efficiency, that we think that the tutorial system is to be preferred as the main method of instruction.

Once this system of instruction has been adopted, interesting consequences follow for the observation and control of each student's progress. Personal methods on the one side of teaching imply personal methods on the other. Apart from the preliminary examinations, to be taken at the end of the second term, we intend to hold no university examinations or tests, in the strict sense, before finals; and the purpose of our preliminary examinations is merely to discover which students appear to be quite incapable of working to our standards. We feel that the decision to send students down for this reason must be based upon a university examination, since to base it entirely upon the judgment of tutors would be invidious; and we are holding the examination at the end of the second term from entry in order that this decision should be taken at the earliest possible moment. But, with this exception, we shall rely entirely upon the judgment of tutors for observing, recording and controlling the progress of each student's work. Informal examinations will be held from time to time in order to stimulate and verify the amount of work that students have done during the vacation to consolidate their studies of the term before, but these examinations will be considered as a transaction between each student and the tutor concerned and their result need not be officially recorded. One favoured method for taking cognisance of each student's progress is for the results of such examinations, taken together with all that the tutor has observed about a student's work during a given term, to be reported at the end of it to the Dean of the student's school, as a rule verbally, and in the student's presence. Some of our Schools attach much importance to this occasion, which gives the Dean the opportunity to bring to the notice of each student the impression that his recent work has made on those most competent to judge it. Another favoured system is for the Dean of a School to discuss privately with each student once a term the written reports that his tutors have submitted. And while it is possible for us at the moment, being as small as we are, to use a whole School as the unit for this and kindred purposes, when we get larger we shall no doubt subdivide each School amongst groups of tutors in such a way as to preserve a proper balance between, on the one hand, continuity of teaching – and therefore of observation and control – and, on the other, the authoritative watch of the university, through its tutors, over its students' work.

Finally, we believe that these methods will enable us to deal effectively with the problem of wastage. At Oxford and Cambridge about 5% of students fail to complete their course; at other universities in England and Wales the average is about 14%, and this average conceals figures falling as low as 3% and rising as high as 30%, as between different universities and departments. We consider that the national average is too high, that figures of 30%, or even 20%, are absurd, when taken in relation to the size and quality of the university population in the country, and that the figure of under 5%, achieved not only by Oxford and Cambridge but by some science departments, is a reasonable target. The first set of factors through whose operation we shall, we believe, be able to hit that target, is the flexibility of our admissions requirements (which we have reduced to a minimum), and of our curriculum. Exploiting that flexibility, we give every encouragement to students to change their course of study during their first year; in the Arts and Social Studies Schools, for example, we expect on past experience that some 15% of our students will change their main subject of study as between the GCE and finals. Given that many students are thoroughly dissatisfied with the choice of subjects that they made at school and that this certainly hampers their progress at the university, this should greatly reduce the size of the problem of wastage, and we think that our present methods of teaching and supervision will do the rest and keep our rate safely under 5%. This, admittedly, is still a claim, and not a fact, but we shall be surprised if the claim fails and would regard its doing so as a serious criticism of our work.

This whole system of instruction and control has so far been considered with respect to the advantages that it affords the student; but it seems to us to be no less advantageous to the teacher. In the first place, as we have established, it does not entail excessive teaching hours. Given a ratio between teachers and students of the order of magnitude that prevails in the United Kingdom, the system only requires that each teacher must be prepared to do up to 12 hours' teaching, of all kinds, in the week. This means that more time is spent in actual teaching than is normal with a system based upon the lecture and the class, but less in the preparation of lectures and in the marking of papers. Teachers who have had experience of both systems seem to agree that the tutorial system is less burdensome and more rewarding.

But this is not the only way in which, we think, the use of the tutorial as the main instrument of teaching can improve the teacher's lot. We are deeply concerned with a difference between the ancient and modern universities in England about which much has been said but little done: the difference in respect of the independence of the junior teacher. Universities have to be organized; organization leads to hierarchy; but hierarchy is inconsistent with what, after all, is the most important fact about university teachers – their equality before the truth to which their lives are dedicated. This conflict presents the fundamental problem of university government, and we at Sussex, though still unsure about the practical steps to take, are deeply concerned to establish patterns of university organization in which that fundamental equality will be more faithfully reflected. The fact that we have abolished departments and that our curriculum requires that many teachers will work in more than one School will, we hope, carry with them the advantage that the individual teacher will be less subordinate to any one professor, and therefore more independent, than in the usual modern system. Tutorial teaching reinforces this tendency. When a teacher, however junior, carries the prime responsibility for a number of students he acquires automatically a certain independence of the university hierarchy. He alone knows how those students are getting on; he alone can and must take important decisions about them. There is no doubt that these facts help to give the young teacher in the ancient universities some of the freedom he enjoys; and although of course it is not possible without the collegiate system, which depends essentially on private finance, to give the young teacher the kind of independence that a fellowship provides, we hope that we are at least beginning to open up new possibilities of academic democracy.

Thus the main principles on which we are tackling the teaching problems are these: the first emphasis should be laid on the teaching of undergraduates in their first years, because this is the period during which time and talent are wasted by the failure to communicate the essential attitudes and procedures of higher study; and this teaching effort should be made in very small groups rather than in classes and lectures, because it is through such small groups that the quality of higher study can be most effectively maintained and imparted.

II

Some of these points are strikingly illustrated by the special problems of teaching philosophy.

A plausible consequence of our rearrangement of the curriculum is that this subject should play an unusually large part in undergraduate study. Philosophy concerns itself – at least – with the most general and pervasive questions about the logical character of other kinds of inquiry and about the ways in which they fit together; hence, from the moment that you make it a main principle of higher education to get undergraduates to think how their major study is related to others, it seems inevitable that philosophical questions should be raised and desirable that they should be thoroughly investigated. And, in fact, all undergraduates in our Arts and Social Studies Schools will take one philosophy paper in their preliminary examination, and at least one, and in many cases more than one, in their finals; and while our plans for the Science Schools in this respect are still incomplete, philosophy will certainly play a leading part in the programme, to which the University is committed, of opening up to science students the possibilities of systematic thought in other fields, and by other methods, than those of science.

That this programme is likely to present unusual teaching problems is obvious when one compares it with the role that philosophy plays in most English – and other – universities. The standard pattern is for philosophy to be taught as a recondite special subject, whether alone or in conjunction with one other, to a small minority of undergraduates; Oxford, where all who study ancient history or modern society, and most who study psychology, do so together with philosophy, is the sole, though great, exception. With what justification, then, and by what means, is this kind of inquiry, both celebrated and notorious as it is, to be brought home, not just to the small minority who have a special inclination for it, but to a much greater proportion of undergraduates than even Oxford has attempted?

If philosophy is conceived as the attempt to depict all reality – in the manner of an Aristotle, an Aquinas or a Hegel – then this programme would certainly be not merely paradoxical, but absurd: the ordinary student, as opposed to the rare devotee, would have neither time nor taste for such an enterprise. But if philosophy is conceived, in the Socratic manner, as the relentless probing of assumptions, come then what may, there is a strong case for the view that it is both possible and desirable to give it a central role in the education of undergraduates: possible, since the time needed for the purpose is not long; desirable, since doing so lets light into recesses of the mind which would otherwise remain in darkness.

But what assumptions should be subjected to Socratic probing? Just those, as our rearrangement of the curriculum suggests, which characterize the special studies of each student, so that the young historian or physicist would be invited by philosophers to apply his mind to the methodology of those inquiries? There is something to be said for that, and the presence of philosophers in a university should certainly give rise to vigorous methodological inquiries; but when one considers how well historians and scientists can get on, in both research and teaching, without making such explicit inquiry into their own procedures, and how seldom philosophers do in fact contribute to methodology in a manner that commands respect, it is plain that the case for giving philosophy the part it has at Sussex must rest elsewhere.

People ordinarily take for granted not only their particular moral convictions but also some general procedure for dealing with unusual situations in which those convictions conflict with one another or do not apply. For some it is then natural to appeal to tradition; others invoke their moral sense or insight; others look to a political or religious authority; others again, the utilitarians, feel that the only sensible thing to do, when their normal beliefs have got them into difficulty, is to ask what action or what principle of action is most likely to increase human happiness or to diminish suffering. The first thing that the teacher of philosophy has to do here is to force his students into the recognition that particular moral convictions often do prove inadequate to the demands of action, and that the more fundamental notions or procedures to which appeal is then made are startlingly different from person to person, and vary with religious and political belief. Once these simple facts have been clearly recognized and openly admitted the first and most difficult task in teaching ethics has been accomplished. The student sees the point that has exercised moral philosophers from Socrates till now: that men differ not only in their particular moral convictions but in their notions as to how these differences should be settled. When one person thinks that a grossly deformed baby should be killed, and another thinks that it should be kept alive, they will probably disagree not just on this immediate point but, more profoundly, on whether the issue should be resolved by consideration of the suffering or happiness that will attend the different decisions or by appeal to a postulated superhuman law. By considering such cases the student is forced to dwell upon these differences of attitude, to consider whether his own are clear and tenable, and to ask, with a full sense of the practical importance of the question, which he should now prefer, and why. With that, he has become a philosopher, differing only from those who claim the title by the amount of time and effort that he puts into the inquiry.

As with personal conduct, so with social systems. In the world today there are not only particular differences of policy between the great powers as to what should happen in, say, Berlin, or as to how nuclear arms should be controlled; there are intellectual differences concerning the whole nature of this struggle. These underlying differences of view exert great influence upon the concrete policies that governments pursue. Thus the particular policies of the Soviet Union are profoundly influenced by the Communist conviction that the social system of the Western powers is no longer suited to the times and will slowly but surely die away, while the Soviet social system is uniquely able to develop and control what communists believe to be the dominating forces of the epoch, and is therefore bound to triumph. It is this conviction that they know the long-run destinies of human society and that they are on the winning side that gives communists the power to act with that combination of inflexible purpose and flexible means that makes them very hard for anyone else to handle. Dialectic is not for them a text-book notion; it is the very stuff of life. So anyone who is going to live in the same world with them and, as graduates must, either take or at least intelligently support the initiative in dealing with them, needs to understand this point of view. An essential task of higher education in a liberal society at the present time must therefore be to shock students out of the uncritical acceptance of the political ideas and values of their society, and to get them to see that other societies, in our case particularly Soviet society, look at social questions in a different way. It is not primarily the business of the university teacher to say which of these social views, any more than which of those moral views, is right; his business is to see that students realize that these profound conceptual differences exist, and start to think about them for themselves. But, in the one case as in the other, this is philosophical work. The communist conception of man in society is very general. It involves a certain way of looking at history, science, morality and politics, and can only be appreciated if one takes in all of these. It is therefore the philosopher who must disengage the general issues and make students see them in their full scope and significance, if anybody is to do so.

Thus the case for giving philosophy the part in the education of undergraduates that it has at Sussex ultimately rests on the view that they – or as many of them as possible – should concern themselves not just privately, but as part of their academic work, with these grand differences of human outlook in which, as moral and political beings, they are inevitably involved. But this view rests in turn upon the view that is taken of the function of the liberal university. Should it be a forum where the resources of trained intelligence are applied as keenly to men's ultimate convictions as to the atom or the cell, or a cloister where people take refuge from such contentious issues? Perhaps the deepest implication of our rearrangement of the curriculum is that we have opted, even if more by instinct than by deliberation, for the former course. In particular, by confronting our philosophers with the mass of students we have placed them in a situation from which they can only extricate themselves by playing to the limit the Socratic role. They must bring all faiths and assumptions into the open. They are there to challenge, to provoke, to raise doubts and difficulties, to prevent thoughtless acquiescence in current assumptions, to awaken students to that sense of the precariousness of human thinking that should always inform and enliven advanced study and research, and to do what can be done to awaken in them that critical sympathy for men's diverse convictions that is the stuff of civilized life.

If this is how philosophy and its service to the university should be conceived, our general views about the value of the different forms of teaching apply to the subject with particular force. Lectures can serve to raise the great philosophical problems at an elementary level and in a simple and dramatic form, so that a large body of students may start weighing and discussing them in common. But when the student has got beyond the first shock of recognizing that there do exist fundamental issues of the kinds with which philosophers deal, and before he has reached the stage of wanting comprehensive knowledge of how philosophers have proceeded in the past, the lecture ceases to be useful. What the student then needs is to learn to raise philosophical questions for himself: in relation to his own life, his own assumptions, his own intellectual habits, his own values. Philosophical questions that strike one person as clear and urgent can strike another as obscure and trivial. To one it is essential to decide whether religious thought and language have real significance, or should be rejected as so much sophistry and illusion; to another the issue of religion is curious but inessential, while those of political freedom or of social progress are all-important. Even when all members of a group feel that one such issue matters, their attitudes towards it and therefore the best ways for them to start to think about it may be quite diverse. Thus, since the teacher must always base his work upon the interests of the taught, philosophical teaching must be personal. And equally telling is the fact that philosophy is essentially an argumentative subject. Here the amount of established knowledge to be handed on is minimal; what has to be cultivated is the art of disentangling fundamental assumptions from the concrete material in which they are normally embodied, and this is something that can only be acquired by constant practice. After he has taken his first steps into the subject the student does not gain by hearing a lecturer raise and tackle philosophical questions; he must be obliged to raise and tackle them himself. He must be stopped in his tracks by steady questioning and only permitted to go forward when he is prepared, on these matters of profound conviction, to take his intellectual fate boldly into his hands. This it is that gives work in small groups, ideally, indeed, the tutorial that each student attends alone, its particular importance in philosophical teaching.

III

This essay strikingly illustrates the logical predicament that besets all attempts to think out questions of personal and social policy. In order to get anywhere it has had to make assertions about human dispositions and behaviour; but the concepts that it has used for the purpose are too vague to serve it properly. 'Open-mindedness', 'passive' and 'active' attitudes to learning, 'the art of inquiry': without such concepts it would be impossible to frame any educational policy at all. We have to think in some terms, and no others are to hand. A moment's reflection will however show that the criteria for the application of these concepts are so numerous, diverse, and uncertain, so complicatedly and perhaps inconsistently related to each other, that the statements in which the terms occur cannot be taken to have a clear and settled meaning and so cannot be regularly confirmed or refuted. Any two people may well disagree both as to whether a third is open-minded and as to how that first disagreement should be settled; the validity of an educational policy that relies upon the term is therefore dubious in the extreme. A further moment's reflection, moreover, will reveal that 'open-minded', in this society, is a normative term, as precise in expressing the favourable attitude of the speaker as it is vague in evoking the human qualities on which that attitude is focussed. This makes confusion worse confounded, since any attempt to sort out and define the term's criteria of use is likely to be distorted by the sentiments that it conveys. Thus the prudent logician emerges from a bout of policy-making not only with the sense that he has been talking prejudiced – and prejudicial – nonsense, but also with the sense, still more alarming, that there is nothing else that he can do.

But this conclusion goes too far. Given the premise as to the vagueness and bias of the terms in which, perforce, our policies are framed, the right conclusion, especially for an institution devoted to research, is that no effort should be spared to make them more respectable. Psychologists and sociologists are striving to refine the crudities of common language with respect to intelligence, attitudes, groups and classes; the right course for a university is to enlist their help in subjecting its educational policy and achievements to scrupulous investigation. This, naturally, is easier said than done. University teachers, like other mortals, prefer to beat the big drum of their convictions than to consider what they mean and what they do; they are also quick to take refuge from expert scrutiny behind the pretext that since psychological and sociological analysis has often failed to reach reliable conclusions it may be indefinitely disregarded. But we at Sussex hope at least to check these furtive habits and to start inquiries going into our own educational work which may help to clarify its fundamental concepts, to provide us with a relatively unbiased record of our achievements, and so to keep our policies realistic.

Thus our attitude towards our principles is pragmatic, tempering zeal with scepticism. We are well aware that they are somewhat platitudinous and that, while they point usefully in the directions along which we have to work, they need much interpretation before they can be used to guide particular decisions. Educational writers often content themselves with repeating such platitudes, and pretending without more ado that something useful has been said; the real problem is always as to how they should be interpreted and applied. What we have tried to do at the University of Sussex is to bring these broad principles to bear upon the particular circumstances of England now; but it must be insisted that our conclusions are tentative, that we have had hardly any time to see how they stand the test of experience, and that they are conclusions that we have drawn, not for universities in general, but for one particular new university in England at this point in time. They may have a more general significance, especially for other English universities; but in such uncertain matters there is room for great diversity even in a single country, and it would be very rash to apply them to universities in other places, whose social and intellectual conditions are unlike ours.

It is equally important to avoid the common error of educational writers who suppose that when they have described the advantages that may accrue from a particular system of teaching they have described the system itself, and are therefore led to give an unduly roseate picture of the situation that has resulted or that may result from the adoption of its principles. Thus we know very well that whatever the merits of the tutorial system it also has its defects; and common prudence assures us that, transplanted to fresh soil, it will develop new characteristics, both good and bad, that have not been foreseen. While then we believe that our principles mark out the lines on which we ought to start, we do not suppose that their adoption will carry us at once to our goal, the effective teaching of undergraduates of all ages and of all levels of ability. Even to approach that goal we shall surely have to reject some of our principles and adapt the rest to circumstances, in many fresh ways, under the constant pressure of research into the results of working on them. But to have a plan, and yet to know that it will have to be modified, perhaps drastically, under the pressure of events, is the delightful secret of creation.

MAURICE HUTT

3. *Undergraduates and their Problems*

In October 1962 there were some 400 undergraduates reading for their first degrees in the University. About 240 of these were aged 18 when they arrived; another 120 were 19. Nearly all of them were, at this stage understandably, British, indeed English – which was not, by definition, the case with the 5 'occasional' students, nor the case with 6 of the 26 graduate students. About 20% had been to independent schools, 10% to direct grant and similar establishments and 55% to county maintained schools, the figures being similar for men and women. As for social class, the information available at the time of writing suggests that (to use the Registrar General's classifications) the parents of about 50% are in professional or intermediate occupations, 30% in skilled or partly skilled, and 20% in unskilled occupations. In terms of age, therefore, they are like the undergraduates of any British university (European students tend to be at least three years older) while in terms of schooling and class they are in no way abnormal[1] – again by English standards, for on the continent working-class students are very much rarer phenomena. Our students thus being 'normal' we can rely on the experience of other universities to give us pointers to some of the problems which our undergraduates face, and this knowledge can help us take in advance what seem appropriate steps to deal with them.

The three or four years undergraduates spend at the university are critical years in the process of turning from adolescence to adulthood. Of course their university must, to employ a UGC subcommittee's phrase, 'treat them as adults that they may become

---

[1] In these two respects they correspond most closely with students of the University of London, about 20% of whom are of working class origin and of whom 18% (in 1955) went to boarding schools and 58% to LEA secondary schools.

In universities other than Oxford, Cambridge and London roughly 70% of entrants in 1955 came from LEA schools and 10% from boarding schools, while about 30% came from working class families.

more adult', but it would be ostrich-like to ignore the fact that when they first arrive they certainly are not fully adult but are in transition, a transition which may perhaps by careful provision be made more smooth than it might otherwise be. Adjustment at this stage involves, it has been suggested, four things: emancipation from the family, the establishment of intimate cross-sex relationships, the achievement of peer group acceptance and participation and that of economic independence. These apply, of course, to all late adolescents, but certain aspects of this transitional process are made more difficult by the fact of being an undergraduate – while others may, if due attention has been paid in advance by the university, be made much more easy. An example of one difficulty exacerbated by his undergraduate status is that relating to economic independence.

Elspeth Huxley tells the story of an elderly professor who was asked to compare his early days with the present and comment on what he missed most. 'Undergraduate funerals' was his reply. Certainly malnutrition due to poverty has disappeared, but affluence is rare. At the moment a student on a local authority grant has his fees (some £70) paid and also receives £290 (I quote the figure for students in hall or college at universities outside Oxford, Cambridge and London). The grants are subject to a means test: if, for example, the parents' net income is £1,000, the child will receive £258, if £1,500 £216, and the £32 and the £74 respectively are considered due from the parent. (Although precise evidence is lacking, it is, incidentally, clear that there are considerable discrepancies in parents' reaction to such demands). The rent for a shared room with bed, breakfast and week-end meals in one of the guest houses (this term will be explained below) is £3 12s 6d. Rents in lodgings are comparable, while those in flats, finding all their meals, are paying about £2 10s 0d per person per week. As the University is some three miles out of Brighton about 7s 6d per week tends to be spent on fares. For those in guest houses and lodgings at least 35s 0d may reasonably be allotted to heating and to meals taken in the University or elsewhere – making, in the case of the former, £5 15s 0d per week. There are 30 weeks in the University year. Thus £172 of £290 is unavoidably committed, leaving £118 plus £30 vacation allowance to meet all the remaining expenses of the 30 weeks of term and all those of 22 weeks of vacation. If only for this reason (and there are others) the undergraduate must therefore take a vacation job – or live off his family. Generally most do both, 'the central problems [being]', to quote an acute observer, 'to bridge the gap between their grants and the costs of a reasonable degree of independence and how, in addition, to raise the money for the books, travel and other items necessary for a liberal education.'

The crucial word here is 'independence'. More and more identifying himself with his age-group outside the university, the student nowadays is, to quote Klingender, 'zealous for economic independence as few students have been in the past'. The upper middle class undergraduate of the past came from a milieu in which economic dependence until early adulthood was the accepted rule. But the working class undergraduate's fellows are more or less economically independent at 16 and, furthermore, contributing to the family budget. Nor is this sense of forcing sacrifice on one's family by not earning confined to working class boys. It is significant that in a group of working class and lower middle class students, 25% of the latter had, like 30% of the former, contributed to their families part of their earnings from the holiday jobs they had done as schoolboys. Clearly, the less 'bourgeois' the student community, the more will more of its members feel uncomfortably aware of the sacrifice their families make. They are 'uncomfortable' because they have a conscience and also because they are in the process of becoming emancipated from the family and find it all the more galling, therefore, to remain, as a good two thirds of undergraduates have to do, partly dependent on their parents for their means of living.

Money also poses another type of problem. 'The process of maturation implies learning the value of money' – and yet often it is only after coming to the university that students come to control incomes and expenditure of more than a weekly pocket-money size. Once again the changing class structure of the undergraduate population is relevant.

If the old-style bourgeois student was financially dependent he was at least, thanks to a nanny and a boarding-school, already well on the way to being psychologically weaned from his family by the age of 18. But further down the social scale close involvement with the family is infinitely more frequent, and the shock of having independence thrust upon them is undoubtedly very considerable in the case of many undergraduates. How great the shock is depends, of course, on the degree of independence which parents have already encouraged and it is difficult to provide any firm evidence of the extent to which parents are wise or foolish in this respect. There is, however, one interesting pointer. One survey shows that only about half the undergraduates at one university had earlier spent periods of more than just a week or two away from home (and in the case of the working class women, only a quarter had done so). To this one may add 'impressionistic evidence'. At the start of their first term many undergraduates simply squander wonderful hours going round the shops, buying Nescafe to brew, biscuits to eat, materials to entertain because they have never entertained before. Some undergraduates have never previously bought their own clothes, many have never paid for their own meal in a café – let alone a girl friend's. Just as over-disciplined children run shouting, tumultuous out of school, so carefully segregated young people either become intoxicated with the sudden availability of accessible members of the opposite sex or, if their conditioning has been powerful enough, shrink away in embarrassment and confusion. Then there is the new delight of staying up late, to tire the moon with talking. Nor is the daytime unduly crammed with formal commitments. In the School of Physical Sciences freshmen are advised to put in five or six hours of laboratory work and to attend some nine or ten lectures per week, while in the other Schools attendance at three or four lectures seems to be the general pattern. Together with two tutorials, this is hardly a crushing burden. But this is to look at things the wrong way round. What is burdensome is the very lightness of this load, and whether or not it is relatively easily shouldered depends in part upon the way the student has been taught (or rather shown how to learn) during his last year or two at school.

Sudden new freedoms, then, dance before the freshman's eyes – while round him circulate hundreds, even thousands, of other young people few of whom are known to him. At school he was a prefect, captain of tennis or known as 'a swot'. Even if he was not a Somebody at least he was somebody; he had his niche in society, status, even if lowly, within his group. Now he is back in the ranks again – and, worse still, everyone is and there has to be a general sorting, scrambling, re-alignment before this inchoate mass differentiates out into the hierarchies, interest-groups and friendship circles which make up undergraduate society. And simultaneously with having to adjust to his unfamiliar social environment he has to tackle new studies – while rather more gradually trying to come to terms with the demands of 'total' university life. 'To accept the idea that university standards should influence their whole personality, their range of interests and their social being', notes a sub-committee of the UGC, 'requires a revolution of mind and attitude'. The university as a place you are 'of' not just 'go to', a community not just a processing plant – this can be a strange and not necessarily welcome prospect to the schoolboy rigidly bent on being taught what he needs to know so that he may get his 'qualifications'.

Social adjustment and intellectual adjustment, both necessarily attempted in an unfamiliar environment – these are the problems the undergraduate has to face, and facing them, at a time when he is in any case involved in the emotional stress of late adolescence, can be painful. This is common knowledge, but just the same knowledge which a new university does well to keep in mind. Why? First and foremost because the University is concerned with the overall education, with the whole humanity of its undergraduate members, not just with getting them through examinations; secondly, inasmuch as there are examinations there to be passed, it is overwhelmingly clear that among the reasons for failures are many which are connected with problems of adjustment; and thirdly because armed with this knowledge the University can do something to help.

Those adjust most easily who feel secure, and there is nothing the University can do except hope that most of its undergraduates will come from homes which have fostered this sense of security and which have wisely encouraged their children to grow increasingly independent, self-reliant in their teens. The student must be prepared to live a life of his own, and if he has had some practice the demands of the university world will not be quite so strange. But then too the University must make an effort to see that, en route to full independence, the student does not feel utterly isolated in his strange new environment. The tutorial system is, of course, preeminently important in this respect. So too is the question of where students live.

Unless government policies and/or students' attitudes change radically, the university will continue to need to find accommodation for the vast majority of its undergraduates. And clearly it is unrealistic – even if it were desirable – to expect to be able to build, at a cost of four or five millions, study-bedrooms for three or four thousand students. Besides, given the resources of a seaside town, building on this scale would be quite unjustifiable in what even the

sober Robbins Report terms the current 'emergency'. And fortunately these resources are not only considerable but also in large
part of a type which enables us to offer an alternative to lodgings.
For no matter how comfortable these may be, lodgings have some
great disadvantages, a fact clearly recognized by students, 70% of
whom have, in various surveys at other universities, expressed a
preference for other forms of accommodation.

One of the four elements, it has already been suggested, in adjustment during late adolescence is the achievement of peer group
acceptance and participation; but if this group is very big, and if
the undergraduate is alone, he is much less likely to penetrate into it
and come to belong to the larger community than if he has 'allies'
in his friends. The importance of the informal, loose-knit friendship
group can hardly be over-stressed, for it is 'by participating in a
variety of . . . peer groups [that] . . . the adolescent finds himself in
a familiar and meaningful universe made up of similarly situated
people from whom he may derive motivation and sympathetic
support'. Such groups 'satisfy the wishes for response, recognition,
security and new experience [and provide] the closest equivalent to
the family' during the awkward process of adjusting to a novel
social and intellectual world. Their formation is thus essential to
learning and living at the university. What conditions favour their
formation?

It is clear from the work of Eden, Thoday and others that the
place of residence is far and away the most important factor.
Laboratory work, tutorials, sometimes seminars and even lectures
can help but, contrary, perhaps, to the expectations of many
observers, it seems that the Students' Union does not itself encourage
the formation of acquaintance groups. Of course some of its societies
do bring together devotees of particular interests, but perhaps their
main importance lies less in their role as 'group-creators' than in that
of 'group exercisers'. For such societies, it has been found in other
universities, 'function largely through the control of informal cliques
within them'. Such informal cliques are in fact not merely essential
to the running of societies but to the very existence of a satisfying
and manageable undergraduate life, the undergraduate wanting
independence wisely seeking it '[not] in solitude but in the company
of congenial spirits'. In 1961 half the students at one university and
at another one third of the men and 60% of the women lived alone
or with just one other student. Such lodgings clearly do not help the

student to find 'allies'. Halls clearly do, and so does the less formal arrangement whereby bed-sitters are clustered, in groups of six or eight, round kitchens – a Scandinavian conception which has already attracted several British universities. And so too, we believe, can guest houses.

Guest houses and small private hotels abound in such a resort as Brighton, but their presence does not automatically solve the accommodation problem. To begin with, 'the season' begins at Whitsun and undergraduates in lodgings in seaside towns are heavily outbid by, and therefore might be ejected to make room for, summer visitors. Besides, the summer visitor seeks an unheated bedroom, whereas the student needs a study where he can work through the winter months too. On the other hand, guest house proprietors normally have to carry various overhead charges through the six dead months. There was thus the possibility of some large-scale arrangement, and negotiations between the University and the Brighton Hotels and Guest Houses Association have led to agreements being signed with various proprietors by which they reserved for the exclusive occupation, in term time, by undergraduates of their rooms from early October until mid June. In October 1962 312 were housed in this way in 19 guest houses, in October 1963 520 in 31. The University pays the proprietors a contract fee and the undergraduate pays to the University a standard rent. The rooms (about half of which have two beds) all have washbasins, a desk or table surface to work on and – vital to the avoidance of disputes – metered heating. In each house a common room is made available. Of course such provision is not perfect, but it does do more than merely solve the critical problem of sleeping space. Such an arrangement positively encourages the formation of acquaintance groups and if as living-units they are somewhat on the small side – 10 of the 31 hold less than a dozen undergraduates – it may be noted that most of the guest houses are, naturally, grouped along the sea front. With the extension year by year of the scheme that area will perhaps become a sort of experimental 'Latin quarter' of the type which Halsey has suggested may well be 'the most attractive solution to the conflict between collegiate ideals and technological pressures under modern urban conditions'.

By making appropriate arrangements about housing, by giving each undergraduate one or two tutors to work with each term, the University has, of course, only provided those conditions which, it seems from past experience, are most conducive to the under-graduate's settling down to mastering his work and to coping with his new environment. But this environment is the university, and the university is more, far more, than just an assemblage of under-graduates. His fellows provide the phalanx amid which the under-graduate advances into the mass of the university, but just the same he and they need to have the purpose, function, nature, peculiarities of that mass explained to them, interpreted to them; they need to be exposed to its influence at many points, in many different ways; they need to be caught up by the university, exposed to its values by becoming involved – by being 'of it' and not merely 'going to it'. Here again the University can, by making appropriate arrange-ments, encourage such involvement.

The best interpreters for the undergraduates are, of course, his elders in the university – undergraduates senior to him, graduate students and lastly, tutors. It is important here to recognize, and counter, pressures naturally dividing students into 'years'. Societies can be important 'bridges' across this gap, but once again the vital role is played by the place of residence. That in October 1963 nearly 170 of the second year chose to live in guest houses not only pro-vides an interesting testimony to the scheme's attractiveness, but also made the guest houses that much more valuable to freshmen. And the first two halls, generously donated, coming into use in the winter of 1964–5 will, of course, have a four or five year 'spread' of students in residence. There will also be some members of the faculty living there – as in the 'study-bedroom village' which we hope eventually to build. But many pressures nowadays militate against the notion of a fully residential university. In any case the problem of bridging the gap between undergraduates and faculty can never be solved by merely arranging for them to live in contiguity. There must be a sense of shared interests and purposes.

The best opportunity to bridge this gap derives from the facts that undergraduate and don are both students and that they work together in tutorials. It is not my place to enlarge upon this, but clearly tutorials as instruments of general education, as the means of transmitting values, outlook and attitudes, are the more important the larger and the less residential is the university. 'As the universities get bigger' (I quote from the National Union of Students' memoran-dum to the Hale Committee), 'we fear that the difficulty which the student has in identifying himself with the rest of the university community is going to become more severe. It is essential, therefore, that every effort is made to counteract this tendency and we feel that tutorials have a valuable contribution to make in this respect.' At Sussex we would wholeheartedly agree – save that for 'valuable' I myself would substitute 'invaluable'.

If the tutorial system is the chief means of throwing undergraduates and their seniors together in a semi-formal way, other arrangements need to be made to 'support' the informal relationships which can be thus engendered. Of course their respective reasonable needs for privacy on occasion must be met, but privacy and the legitimate distinctions conferred by age and responsibilities must not be allowed to 'justify' an improper segregation. There are several ways in which we have tried at Sussex to throw together the two groups, undergraduates and faculty – not *as* groups (for the confrontation of blocs is fatal), but rather as individuals so that the groups interpenetrate, and so that the dangerous 'us/them' disease shall, despite the hard facts of age and examiners' meetings, be given the least possible opportunity to develop. Just as it is their mutual concern with the same sorts of problem and activity which can bring tutor and pupil together, so too in the university as a whole the sense of community may be emphasized by fostering the sense of mutual involvement. Three aspects of our attempts to encourage that sense may be considered – the Bulletin, Falmer House, and (that old English remedy!) committees.

Good communications are essential in a university to foster a sense of common activity by satisfying the legitimate curiosity of all members of the university (where 'members' of course includes undergraduates) as to what is going on. Not all of what is happening can be known to all. But while even a university knows the principle of division of labour, it is important to remember that one of the undergraduate's problems, if he is seeking an education and not merely skills, is how he can find out what the university is besides an imparter of skills to undergraduates. Of course his tutors and his fellows will be his main source of information – but the latter can nurture the wildest misconceptions, while the former themselves may be, in a large university with a highly centralized structure, ill-informed themselves. There are two attempts being made to counter this. First (and essential, of course, on quite other grounds) there is the attempt to involve as many members of the faculty as possible in administration and policy-making. Secondly, there is the Bulletin.

Appearing three or four times a term, it is (to quote the first editorial foreword) 'a clearing-house for news, some of which will already be known to some but the whole of which would otherwise probably not be known to all its readers. . . . The Bulletin passes information'. Consequently its twelve or fourteen duplicated fools-cap sides are not particularly gay, but the important thing is that it contains not merely 'social' but also 'political' news, stemming mainly from Council and Senate discussions. The editors (one tutor, one undergraduate and one member of the Registry) have free access to the relevant papers, and have imposed upon them a minimal censorship. This Bulletin, furthermore, goes not merely to faculty but to all members of the University. Its influence may perhaps be marginal, but at least it is pushing in the right direction, underlining, not by overt emphasis but merely by its presence and contents, the fact that undergraduates and faculty have certain interests in common, that they are sharing something.

Certainly they share Falmer House, the very first building to come into use (a highly significant decision), and containing common rooms, refectory and dining-rooms, bars and coffee lounges, a debating hall, a music room and so on – with scores of paintings on the walls, thanks to generous loans and donations. If one undergraduate problem is how to 'come across' members of faculty other than in tutorials or in lectures, then Falmer House is one answer, for here is deliberately concentrated the social life of the Park and here care has been taken to avoid offensive segregation. For there is not at Sussex a Union Building and a Senior Common Room entirely separate from it. Rather there is one building used by all members of the University with two areas, in particular, being 'mixing' areas, namely the pullulating coffee lounge/bar and the refectory which adjoins it. Here anyone who wishes to do so can serve himself and eat at one of the small tables in the refectory. Similarly, anyone who wishes to do so (and about sixty people a week, often those with visitors, choose to do this) can pay a higher price and eat the same food served by a waiter in a nearby dining-room. That arrangement was decided by Falmer House Committee – which brings me to the question of committees.

Falmer House belongs neither to the Union nor the SCR. It belongs to the University, and as undergraduates are members of that community it is only proper that they should be involved in making decisions about the way the resources of Falmer House are deployed. Three different committees have developed, dealing with different aspects of the running of Falmer House, and on each of these there is active undergraduate representation. A similar mixture of older and younger members is found in the Joint Committee. Its chairmen are the Senior Tutor and the President of the Union, and it is 'empowered to co-opt, either generally or for specific discussions . . . on any matter [relating to the University] . . . members of faculty, or graduate or undergraduate students'. This informal group has thrown up a variety of problems and suggested solutions, with which the appropriate committee has then dealt, amending existing machinery or creating new pieces of it. In this way the first Accommodation Committee came into being, the undergraduate members of which have been carrying out surveys so that well-founded recommendations may be brought before the appropriate legislative bodies.

Of course, participation in the work of these and other university committees is the lot of relatively few of the student body. But it is nevertheless important that there is thus, on the part of under-graduates generally, a sort of vicarious involvement with the run-ning of those aspects of the University which concern them most closely. Apart from other equally important considerations, this incidentally lessens the danger of that dangerous bifurcation into 'Union' and 'University', the former making formal representations *ex post facto* – which is all it can do if its members are not involved in the process of decision making. And in no one area is it more important to reduce the possibilities of mutual misunderstandings than that of discipline, for it is here in particular that the generations meet and differ.

The undergraduate seeks independence, and the answer to 'how much should he have?' is, I suppose, 'as much as is consonant with the achievement of the University's purposes, which include, among other things, the education as well as the training of its undergradu-ate members'. An essential part of that education is involved with adjustment to the fully adult world and 'treating them as adults that they may become more adult' is at once to lay down as a principle that restrictions should be very few. But – and this is what is so difficult for some young people to grasp – adults themselves operate within a framework of rules and any community must have some sort of regulations, whether traditional and acquired by a sort of osmosis or whether written down. Undergraduates are not at the university to do what they like. But while few of them would seriously object to the university's laying down what they should study, it is probably not immediately apparent to the mass of undergraduates that how they conduct their 'private lives' closely affects their acquisition of skills and, still more, their general education. And similarly it is evidently only too simple for members of older generations to suppose that the same rules imposed now will have the same effect as when they were imposed, say, before the war, and even easier still to suppose that because a particular rule might have been quite proper in one social situation, that it is by definition still justifiable and cannot possibly be an abuse. The continued scrutiny of existing rules is therefore desirable – and those who obey them should be involved in this process, as in their enforcement.

The Statutes entrust the Senate with the power of regulating the discipline of students of the University, and this body, either directly or through its chairman, the Vice-Chancellor, is in the last resort responsible for making and enforcing rules. But the initiative in so doing has been delegated to the Senate Discipline Committee. This Committee acts as a clearing house for all disciplinary matters and as a drafting and consultative committee, its recommendations going forward to the Senate or, where applicable, to the Union. On this Committee sit, under a chairman who is bound to be a member of Senate, the Senior Tutor, another member of faculty, two Proctors, the Assistant Warden of Falmer House, the President or Vice-President of the Union and the four other members of the Union Discipline Committee. The last eight people named are all disciplinary officers of the University, responsible, via the Senate Discipline Committee. There is not the simple division, thus, between 'the Union' regulated by undergraduates, and all the rest, regulated by 'the University'. There are, however, allocated loosely-drawn areas of responsibility within which different officers take first action against offenders. Thus the Student Disciplinary officers are normally responsible, in the first instance, for the Park, Falmer House (excluding the Senior Common Room) and for the guest houses. Outside the Park, in the town, in flats and lodgings the Proctors are responsible. But this demarcation is not intended to be absolute, for it is provided that the Proctors may 'take joint action with the student disciplinary officers in all areas and may also take first or supplemental action in all areas in case of necessity'; and what in fact happens is that the various disciplinary officers see one another frequently and sort out between them how particular breaches of the regulations shall be dealt with. In matters of discipline, as in so many other things in a University, what, of course, is overwhelmingly important is the way in which institutional arrangements are worked, and it would be foolish to hazard any prophecy about how these arrangements will be operating in five or ten years' time. And it would be even more foolish to suppose that this sort of co-operative making and enforcement of rules will necessarily exclude all possibility of conflict between the generations within the University. But at least disputes should be 'in the open'; and there will be less chance of the depressing phenomena of 'us' protesting violently against 'them', and of young men and women refusing to accept that they must discipline themselves, preferring the easy adolescent way of having it done for them, by 'enemy adults'.

What few regulations there are which directly impinge upon undergraduates' lives are meant (to quote the University's 'Notes on Discipline') 'to ensure that all undergraduates enjoy satisfactory conditions in which to live and work. Some of the rules may at first seem to restrict individual freedom unduly; they express, however, the University's obligation to ensure that the way of life of its members is orderly and responsible . . . It is hoped that its members will understand these regulations in that light'. Though there is no midnight curfew, absences for more than twenty-four hours have to be authorized by a tutor. And undergraduates may only live in approved lodgings, flats or guest houses. These are minor limitations. More obtrusive is the rule restricting visitors to the common rooms of guest houses in the morning and requiring them to be out of private rooms and common rooms alike by 11 p.m. This is, of course, *par excellence* the type of regulation over which disputes founded on principle (and settled, one trusts, by compromises with reality) are likely to develop in any vigorous university community – and also *around* any university. For it is tempting for members of the public to reflect adversely on what is often termed 'undue freedom' – where 'undue', presumably, is to be understood as reflecting the norms of English middle class upbringing, and particularly middle class attitudes towards relations between the sexes. This last undoubtedly is a problem facing undergraduates and therefore their universities – a problem, of course, which, like so many others, is not of the universities' making (save insofar as they choose not to exclude women and lock up all their men the moment they leave a patrolled campus). Co-education is still rare in the schools which send pupils on to the university, while in England 'strict homes and obstacles put in the way of early courtship are', as Kerr says, 'prevalent . . . especially among the upper and middle classes' – and it is still from these middle classes that the great majority of undergraduates come. The problems of sexual adjustment facing undergraduates are simply those facing everyone in late adolescence, but it is sometimes the case that they are intensified by there being, for some, a disconcerting contrast between the degrees of external restraint imposed by an unduly restrictive home and by the university. But it is useless to propound as the solution 'let the university be like a strict parent'. Firstly, this is utterly impracticable. Secondly, to attempt this would be quite improper, a violation of the basic principle 'treat them as adult that they may become more adult', and would endanger all the other work of the university which rests on this principle. For while doors with locks (and these exist in certain women's halls in this country) do not guarantee the preservation of virginity, they certainly do guarantee a proper sense of resentment and can damage that sense of mutual trust between pupils and their mentors without which the tutorial system, and the informal education bred of casual contacts between undergraduate and tutor, simply cannot exist.

But even if cross-sex relationships do not lead to tension between groups of undergraduates and the university responsible for their education, tensions bred of these relationships will, of course, exist within the undergraduate community. They simply cannot, given the present state of English society, be avoided. As I wrote above, 'the establishment of intimate cross-sex relationships' is one of the essentials involved in the adjustment of late adolescents to full adulthood – and undergraduates are caught up in a situation which helps exacerbate the difficulties generally attendant upon this adjustment. For example, although in the country at large the average age of marriage has receded to the undergraduate age-level, powerful pressures continue to militate against student marriages – among them an as yet unverified belief that marriage and study are incompatible.

Strains, tensions, adjustment – of course all adjustment involves strains and stresses, and adjustment to a new intellectual and social world inevitably involves most undergraduates in some, and a large number in considerable, psychological difficulties. Such difficulties are, it must be remembered, a part of perfectly normal life and, to quote a consultant psychiatrist who is connected with a university, 'although some people are better equipped to deal with them than others, there is hardly anyone who does not at one time or another reach a point where he needs assistance'. Undergraduates are no exception. But neither are they exceptional in the sense of being a particularly unstable section of the community. Contrary to the popular misconception, high IQs and instability have no particular association. 'It is because student life demands such a continuously high standard of intellectual efficiency, not because students are psychiatric weaklings, that the incidence of those [needing] psychiatric help is so high'. The university must be closely concerned with these difficulties, because they can cause suffering and because if they persist they will damage the undergraduate's effectiveness as a learner of skills and impair his general education. It is, for instance, clear that such difficulties play a large part in the wastage rate which, despite highly selective intakes, is currently about 14% in English universities, 80% of those leaving without degrees doing so for 'academic reasons'. At Oxford and Cambridge, however, the rate is only in the region of 4%. This cannot be explained away by advancing the inadequate proposition that students there are 'brighter'. Nor has it anything to do with the fact that over 40% of undergraduates there come from boarding schools and are thus used to living away from home. (There is, on the contrary, some evidence that the wastage rate is far higher among independent schoolboys than among grammar schoolboys of comparable ability, and indeed that children of professional parents have a higher failure rate and a lower 'good success rate' than those of parents in skilled occupations.) It seems most likely, as the Robbins Report suggests, that the lower wastage rate at Oxford and Cambridge is connected with the support afforded students there by their living arrangements and, pre-eminently, by tutorial teaching – for there are many difficulties through which a tutor can help ease his pupils.

That there is in fact a considerable need both for such elementary guidance and for more skilled treatment is indicated by various statistics available. 'Taking the group [of 509 graduates from one university] as a whole, almost 25% gave an affirmative reply [to the question] 'whether they experienced a definite need for skilled psychological help or even psychiatric counselling since they had become undergraduates".' This may by some be discounted as unduly subjective evidence, but surely even they can hardly ignore the 'tough' and objective report from a Student Health Service that, over 11 years in that university, in addition to the 115 (of a total of 12,722) who experienced severe disablement necessitating specialized care and usually a more or less prolonged stay in hospital, 619 presented moderately severe symptoms which, of course, harmed their academic performance, and another 1,300 or so exhibited mild symptoms which left them 'relatively little disturbed or disabled'. Nor are these figures untypical. The incidence of severe psychiatric disorder in British students generally is between 1% and 2%, while about another 15% seem regularly to require what Malleson terms 'help and guidance [from] sympathetic service'. And such help can, of course, be superbly effective. Thus the 18·2% of all undergraduates who, in one year at one university, came to the Student Health Service Centre to have minor disturbances treated (another 1·8% came because of major disturbances), finished up with a failure rate not significantly different from the failure rate of the entry as a whole. Here, then, is obviously the university's 'last line of defence' against suffering and inefficiency on the part of its undergraduate members. Further forward will be all those other institutional arrangements which facilitate adjustment, including housing which fosters friendship groups and a system whereby the undergraduate is not forced to choose finally his School and major subject until he has been up two terms, a system which should reduce the incidence of 'studied wrong subject' students who bulk large in any 'failed examinations' group. Then, too of paramount importance, there will be a tutorial system, invaluable yet again in the context of those large numbers who are mildly disturbed and vital as an agency which can refer those more seriously upset to skilled practitioners. For even if tutors are sympathetic and understanding – and of course there is no guarantee they all will be – there is bound to be a great variety in the skills they command, and later or sooner they are bound to be faced with pupils with whose problems they simply cannot cope. There is the pupil who 'over-drives' with the consequence that he finds himself, to his horror (which only makes it worse), unable to master the work at hand. There are those whose neuroses were, in the closely supervised atmosphere of the school, 'success-promoting', but who 'decompress' rather unhappily in the less structured atmosphere of the university, getting more alarmed and distressed than is explicable merely by the usual difficulties attendant upon settling in during the first year. And then there is the undergraduate who 'balks' at writing essays – by no means necessarily the result of simple idleness – or, much more frequent, the ones who are terribly worried because they cannot remember a thing from the book they carefully read yesterday, and the ones who panic at the approach of examinations.

Pupils thus often need far more skilled help than even the best lay tutor can provide, and for such pupils there needs to be a Student Health Service. Since October 1962 this has consisted, in our case, of two general practitioners and one specialist in psychiatry, who hold frequent clinics in the Park – where a nursing sister is, furthermore, regularly in attendance. Such a provision was certainly not an 'unnecessary luxury' because we only had 400 undergraduates. The statistics quoted revealing other universities' experience surely demonstrate this – and I would add that the very fact that the University was new intensified the need for such help. The very fact of their university's newness can exacerbate undergraduates' difficulties, difficulties which, once the university is a 'going concern', will find their remedies elsewhere or simply not be so intense. I advance this view with diffidence. Whereas what I have written above is founded upon the careful observations of skilled observers in other universities or else amounts to the stock-in-trade opinion of many tutors, what I write now is based simply upon the brief experience of the first two and a half years at Sussex and depends only upon personal impressions.

The importance of more senior students as guides and interpreters is starkly apparent to the tutor of pupils who are among a university's very first undergraduates. There are no undergraduate norms to conform to or reject, no guide afforded by oral tradition. Yet clearly there are conventions, habits, observances proper to this university world and how they can be discovered is a matter of the most intense curiosity and concern. And of course the problem of adjusting to this new world is made all the worse by the facts that it is uncharted by previous undergraduate explorers and that its geography keeps changing – for of necessity a new university is bound to be busy throwing up new institutions, evolving new syllabuses and, in a word, presenting a thoroughly unsettled aspect to the undergraduate, who naturally needs the more guidance the less stable and ordered the universe into which he has been catapulted. It is eminently desirable that whenever possible the faculty should before the first term opens, have met and arrived at decisions about those major items of scaffolding within which and between which the undergraduate builds his new existence. Syllabuses for first year work should be laid out in even greater detail than is perhaps necessary later on, for the first students cannot go to the library and look up past examination papers. Regulations affecting accommodation should be elaborated and made effective from the very first day. No matter that they will very soon have to be changed in the light of experience. The important thing is that the undergraduates should, in their living and in their learning, come into an environment as settled as is possible in the circumstances. Then there should be, as I implied above, from the very start some sort, no matter how rudimentary, of medical 'safety-net'. And above all there should be an unusually high ratio of dons to undergraduates. In 1961–62 there were at Sussex 52 students and 9 members of faculty. This meant that, despite all their other commitments, the nine were able to spend a great deal of time talking with undergraduates. And this informal, continual exchange was facilitated by the smallness of the university community.

But the smallness of this community was certainly not from the point of view of the undergraduates altogether a good thing. It tended to be claustrophobic – because it was not until the third term, quite naturally, that connections were established which led numbers of them to stop spending too many of their leisure hours in their common room. It was too small to provide for enough friendship and interest groups to guarantee the participation of all those who wanted to be involved, and the undergraduates who were 'good at things' could too easily monopolize the scene. In a larger community there is a chance for the less dominant characters to have their dunghills too. And if they do not there is, apart from tension, the danger that they will leave the field to unchallenged leaders who enjoy, but do not profit by, this easy and too total ascendancy. It was a searching community (in a kibbutz there is little privacy), encouraging undue introspection and a certain timidity, both of principles and action, on the part of those who did not care to reveal their ignorance of the big world or their inadequacy in the face of novel situations. It was, in a word, too small to 'support' anyone not already secure and firmly balanced. A larger undergraduate community would undoubtedly help to reduce the tensions among and problems of the very first entrants to a new university, while it would provide in the second year not only a greater number of 'examples', but also, if the 'dunghill argument' is valid, a proportionately greater number of responsibility-takers. Such examples and such leaders are particularly necessary in a rapidly expanding university.

In the very first year the faculty have to do their inadequate best to substitute for the 'seniors' who normally play so vital a role in 'teaching' new undergraduates. But it is essential that the second set of entrants should find waiting for them not only 'old hands' who can act as examples and (possibly) awful warnings, but also the scaffolding of an undergraduate community already in existence. To some extent even 50 undergraduates can make the necessary formal provision. Thus during the first year a constitution for the Union was elaborated and the first officers appointed. Societies were formed and, to facilitate rapid expansion, some 30 undergraduates agreed to act as provisional secretaries for societies which would come into existence in October 1962. By the end of that month, in fact, over 40 societies had been formed. Thus there was a skeletal framework for social life to which the freshmen could not merely be attached but into which, thanks to judiciously timed resignations and elections, they could penetrate as 'organizers' themselves. But of course this is only the formal framework, and it will be seen at once that so far as 'informal instruction' is concerned, there is another very powerful argument for having, if your second intake consists of 350 undergraduates, far more than a seventh of this number in their second year. The problems attendant upon smallness do not persist, of course, with a community of 400. But there are still the usual problems of adjustment which could be helped by the 'strengthening' all along the line of freshman society by the presence of large numbers of 'the initiated' who, if too thoroughly swamped, will not only be unheard, unseen, but may indeed tend to withdraw from this insufficiently congenial community. If in the very first year you need ideally to have twice the usual ratio of faculty about the university, then in the second year you need to have freshmen outnumber second year students by no more than three to one at the very most – which is not a plea for a slower rate of build-up, but for a larger initial intake than was the case at Sussex.

These, then, are some of the problems undergraduates face and some of the measures taken which ought to minimize their frequency and attenuate the seriousness of their effects. Over the years the problems will change. Those related to the difficulties of late adolescence will change, albeit presumably only slowly, as English society changes. Those related to the question of adjustment to the university world will change as the university evolves new procedures, institutions and even aims in response to pressures which will come only in part from its own undergraduates, pressures which may modify insensibly arrangements consciously made at a time when the context in which they operated was quite different. This is why in addition to the boldness (some would say even brashness) with which a new university must try to formulate its intentions and create institutions which seem to give the best chance of their being realized, it must possess the humility necessary not only to learn from other universities, but also to scrutinize its own institutions and purposes, and evaluate the pressures which are continually modifying them. A new university cannot just 'happen'. It has to be made and adapted. Unlike Bagehot's bureaucrats, the faculty must not conceive 'the elaborate machinery of which they form a part . . . to be a grand and achieved result' but instead 'a working and changeable instrument'. Behind their self-confident proceedings there must be self-examination, an introspection which does not inhibit action but which leads, through self-knowledge, on to decision. And one 'constituent part' of the university which needs continual attention is the undergraduate body with its problems, undergraduates who need, not continual prodding and interference, but the support and opportunity which appropriate institutions can afford them during their critical years at the university.[1]

---

[1] For a list of books and articles quoted or used here, see Appendix B, pp. 261–63.

4. *Drawing a New Map of Learning*

The foundation of a new university provides an unparalleled opportunity to fashion a whole curriculum. It is still possible from old letters to catch the distant excitement of the founders of University College, London, in 1826, with Sir James Mackintosh enthusiastically drawing up 'a kind of prospectus' and Henry Brougham warning a political colleague that, however great the enthusiasm, 'the digesting of a proper plan for the course of instruction must be the work of some time'.[1] More recently the founders of the London School of Economics and the University of Keele have enjoyed the intellectual excitement of arranging studies in new patterns, not because they believed in novelty for novelty's sake, but because they were sure that their pattern was academically preferable to those which already existed.

Not all universities, however, have been able to enjoy a full measure of academic freedom during the early stages of their growth. British university colleges, graduating to full university status, have usually been tied initially by the syllabuses of the University of London. Overseas universities have sometimes found themselves even more tied, their pattern of work being determined from outside as a result of educational and social pressures alien to their own society. From the start Sussex, like Keele, has been thought of as a centre of innovation. If it has followed different lines from Keele, it respects the zeal which has been demonstrated there. In turn, it has benefited greatly in a practical way from the radical approach to the curriculum. The freedom to work along new lines and the power to plan new combinations of subjects and new curricula have proved great attractions in recruiting academics from universities where curricula can be changed only with the greatest difficulty. There has also been far greater flexibility – and co-

---

[1] C. W. New, *The Life of Henry Brougham* (1961), Chapters XIX and XX.

operation – in the deployment of specialist academic skills. Lastly there has been exceptional interest in new countries overseas because Sussex seems to stand for the kind of structural reorganization of studies which overseas universities demand when they are free to take their own initiative.

By the end of its first year of active existence, the University of Sussex had drawn up its second prospectus, a full and comprehensive document of sixty pages, which contrasts significantly with the first prospectus of twenty-six pages published in 1961 before either academics or undergraduates had come into residence. The broad outline remained the same, but what had been tentative, vague and incomplete in 1961 had become bold, precise and far less incomplete in 1962. The third prospectus of 1963 extended and completed rather than modified. The changes, which register the intellectual development of the university, were the result of regular and sustained discussion, the 'digesting', as Brougham called it, of ideas which had first been formulated by the Joint Committee and the Academic Advisory Committee.

These initial ideas were, in themselves, exciting. From the start, the idea of a School of European Studies had loomed large in the minds of the sponsors of a university in Brighton. So too had the idea of breaking free from 'excessive specialization'. Multi-subject honours courses were proposed, with history, languages and philosophy being studied in close association with each other. In the sciences also it was suggested that the curriculum should include a study of the social context and application of science. Specialized knowledge was to be acquired in such a way that the boundaries of subjects were to be explored – and crossed – as well as the central territories. The unit of university organization and planning was not to be the single subject Department but the multi-subject School. A range of Schools was suggested, of which European Studies, English Studies and Social Studies were to be the first three. Each School was to have a curriculum which would combine in different proportions – the proportions varying according to the student's own choice – subjects which would normally, except in general degrees, be kept apart in existing universities. The position in relation to the study of sciences was at first much less certain. Indeed, it was not clearly envisaged in the early discussions, before the arrival of the first academics, that science departments would be abolished and replaced by Schools: the most that was hoped was that there would be fewer departments.

As soon as the first academics were chosen, they were drawn into a searching discussion of this provisional outline of the curriculum of a new university. They had to give it both content and organizational shape. They did not await their formal appointment in October 1961 before seeking to define what they meant by a 'School' or by the 'integration' of studies. Interesting memoranda were prepared by the Deans-elect on the work of their Schools and by the Professor of Philosophy on the role of philosophy as an element in the work of all the Schools. These memoranda were exchanged and discussed by post before two crucial meetings were held in April and June 1961 at which the details of the first curriculum were worked out. It was at these two meetings that the material was agreed upon which subsequently was printed in the first prospectus of 1961. The ideas which had already been in the air before the first academic appointments were made were already considerably clarified. In their new form they were given expression in a number of articles and in a talk by the Vice-Chancellor to a conference of the University Teachers' Group at Oxford in the summer of 1961.[1] They were subsequently approved by the Academic Planning Committee.

It is interesting to note what form the clarification took. First, greater stress was laid on the *linked* nature of the undergraduate curriculum. In each of the Schools undergraduates were to combine study of a specialism in depth with common studies in which all the different specialists within the School would share. The specialism was to be the major subject: the common subjects were designed to set the different specialisms in their intellectual frame and to relate them to each other. In the language of the early discussions the specialism was thought of as the 'core' and the common subjects as the 'context'. Second, the Schools were envisaged not as superdepartments, to which 'subjects' were attached, but as centres of linked studies, some of which would be shared with other Schools. Certain subjects – for example, history – could be studied as major subjects within the different contextual frames of different Schools. Certain contextual papers would be common to more than one School. Third, the work of the first Schools was more clearly

---

[1] See W. R. Niblett (ed.), *The Expanding University*, London (1962).

J. S. Fulton's talk, 'The Shape of Universities', is printed on pp. 46–63.

defined, and a plan for a number of new Schools was agreed upon. The title of the School of English Studies was changed into the School of English and American Studies, and it was decided that the work of the School of European Studies should be complemented by a new School of African and Asian Studies. A School of Educational Studies was also envisaged, although it was agreed that its foundation should follow rather than precede the first two years of undergraduate build-up. The *timing* of academic development was very fully discussed. Indeed, the whole question of priorities assumed great importance from this date onwards. It was recognized realistically that what might be very desirable or even necessary might have to wait until after the first phase of growth.

The basic pattern, however, was clear enough. The familiar antithesis between 'specialized' and 'general' education was rejected: both specialization and general education were seen as essential parts of a balanced university education. An undergraduate would be expected not to study a multitude of unrelated subjects side by side or one after the other, but continuously to relate his specialized study to impinging and overlapping studies. Thereby, it was felt, he would become not only an educated person but potentially, at least, a better specialist. He would know about the bearings of his specialism as well as about its content. The contextual studies which would be common to different specialists in particular Schools would always include a critical evaluation of concepts and procedures, preferably comparatively, an examination of historical perspectives, and an exploration of contemporary issues and problems. In the School of English and American Studies and the School of European Studies emphasis would be placed on the unity of a civilization: in the School of Social Studies emphasis would be placed on the inter-dependence of different social studies in the contemporary world.

It followed from this conception of 'general education' that the degree structure would be the same for all undergraduates. There would be no internal status distinctions. A Sussex graduate, whatever his School, would be given the kind of education in three years which would make it possible for him to compare, to relate and to judge. It would be a broader education than he would have received had he followed a conventional single-subject course or even a combined subjects course. At the same time, those graduates, necessarily a minority, who wished to go forward to research or to academic life would have been well grounded in their specialisms and well prepared to pursue them further. Within the teaching of the major subjects it was agreed that there was to be as little reliance as possible on sweeping survey work and as much as possible on learning 'in depth' how to use the skills of the specialist. It was envisaged from the start that there would have to be fourth-year work, mainly of a specialist kind, for a larger number of students than had been conventional in the past. The development of such fourth-year work would not imply, however, that the three-year curriculum was less 'complete' in itself than any other three-year undergraduate curriculum of a more conventional kind in other universities.

Subsequent discussions in 1961 and 1962 turned on the form and content both of the contextual papers and the core papers. It was decided in the autumn of 1961 that at least four-ninths of the curriculum should be concerned with contextual subjects and that certain of these contextual subjects, for example, Contemporary Britain and the Modern European Mind, should be common to more than one School. It was also decided how much of the major work should be work in depth. In history, for example, it was laid down that two of the final papers in the history major examination in any School should be devoted to the detailed examination of a Special Subject. Coverage was sacrificed to depth, although there was to be plenty of choice of period and problems. It was decided finally that two papers on Contemporary Europe – one concerned with economic, social and political history since 1945 and the other concerned with the economics of integration – could form an option within both the economics major and the politics and sociology major and that the papers could be studied both in the School of Social Studies and in the School of European Studies.[1]

Two other conclusions followed naturally from the lines of argument which were being followed. First, a Sussex B A would not offer any kind of 'soft option'. It would demand good students and test the very best. It was also felt that it would attract the best. The first academics at Brighton believed, with due humility, that they

[1] For the outline of this particular European work, see my articles on 'European Studies in a New University' in *Progress* (1962), and the *Journal of Common Market Studies*, Vol. I (1962), and A. Thorlby, 'Eine Neue Universität in Brighton' in *Neue Sammlung*, July-August 1962.

were not simply feeding the insatiable appetite of Bulge and Trend by organizing one more university. Rather they were creating the best kind of university that they could envisage. In colloquial language, they had no chips on their shoulders, no sense of inferiority to anywhere else. Coming from quite different academic backgrounds – Oxford, Cambridge, London, provincial and overseas universities – they were pooling their experience in searching discussions of a kind and range which seldom take place when universities are 'going concerns'. Second, they recognized that experience was not enough. The new curriculum being planned demanded rethinking at every point, not only about content but about methods of teaching and learning. Even given good students, it would not be enough to leave them to the tender mercy of large anonymous lecture classes. Nor could the university afford the congestion of a lecture time table which would make individual tutorial teaching and, even more important, ample time for individual reading difficult or impossible.

It was decided, therefore, at the meetings of April and June 1961 that lectures in the University of Sussex would be ancillary and voluntary. The first two terms of university life – terms which fix the way of work of the undergraduate – would be used for 'foundation studies' which would establish the central significance within the University of the tutorial system, based on guided individual reading, the writing of weekly essays and regular encounters with a tutor. During the second and third years tutorials and lectures would be augmented by seminars, some of which would be 'interdisciplinary'. As the three years went by, the student would become as 'independent' as he was prepared to be. The tutorial system was in no sense considered as a panacea. It was no more 'copied' from Oxford or Cambridge than the curriculum was copied from any other university. It was recognized that it would have to be augmented, modified, treated experimentally, tested frequently, and supplemented by new kinds of teaching. Its main importance was in relation to the content of the curriculum. Tutorials would guarantee that the undergraduate spent a great deal of his time thinking, arguing and writing. In other words there would be an active and personal element in the acquisition of knowledge. The university was to provide the outline map of learning which the undergraduate would then fill in for himself.

There were both practical and theoretical considerations which supported this approach. On the one hand there were the needs of 'new students'. On the other there was the recognition that a university education involves not merely the acceptance of information or ideas, but a personal quest which, if entered upon with zest, continues far beyond the three years of undergraduate study. Just because the University of Sussex was daring to lay down a pattern of related studies – in an age when talk of the 'unity of knowledge' is greeted with some scepticism – there was a strong argument for leaving scope not only for tutorial argument but for individual deviation and rebellion. As Michael Polanyi has put it, while the traveller equipped with the detailed map of a region across which he plans his itinerary enjoys a striking practical superiority over an explorer who first enters a new region, nonetheless 'the explorer's fumbling progress is a richer achievement than the well-briefed traveller's journey'. 'Even if we admitted that an exact knowledge of the universe is our supreme mental possession it would still follow that man's most distinguished act of thought consists in producing such knowledge: the human mind is at its greatest when it brings hitherto uncharted domains under its control.'[1]

Being explorers ourselves in a new university, explorers with ample maps of other universities but with none of our own, we wanted to make our students into explorers also, to encourage them to find relations between subjects where we did not see them ourselves, and to dispute some of our own conceptions. Given the huge changes which are taking place both in the formulation of new knowledge and in the world of action where the knowledge is being applied, we did not want to be confined to our own original territory even though the boundaries within it were being knocked down. We recognized that we would also have to move into outer space.

The main interest was in planning not for present change but for future change. There are likely to be immense rearrangements in the map of learning during the next fifty years – in the biological sciences, for example, where there is remarkable intellectual vitality, or in such fields of study as Asian history and civilization, which will pass from the domain of a small intellectual *élite* to a far broader section of the academic population. There is also likely to be a revolution in communications which will make the changes in the

[1] M. Polanyi, *The Study of Man*, London (1959), p. 18.

communications system over the last fifty years seem like an unsophisticated prelude. We knew, therefore, that a university curriculum which did not allow for far-reaching future growth and change would be doomed from the start. We also recognized our own limitations as surveyors of the intellectual world. As Graham Wallas once put it in relation to only a part of that world, 'every general survey of our social heritage must start from the vision of a single mind. But no single mind can see more than a thousandth part of the relevant facts of even a section of that heritage'.[1] If only for this reason we were more interested in establishing conditions for growth than in plotting a map of learning for the 1960s.

It is remarkable how many times the geographical metaphor recurs in current discussions of learning, just as it recurred time and time again during and after the age of discovery, particularly in the writings of Francis Bacon. It was Bacon, indeed, who complained, rightly it seems, of how slow universities were to change their curricula, failing to consider frankly and honestly whether old courses might be 'profitably kept up, or whether we should rather abolish them and substitute better'. It was Bacon also who related ways of learning to the content of learning, objecting strongly to 'the manner of the transmission and delivery of knowledge, which is for the most part magistral and peremptory, and not ingenious and faithful; in a sort as may be soonest believed, and not easiest examined.'[2] Bacon was complaining about a traditional curriculum which had behind it the weight of centuries. The specialist honours courses which now dominate most university curricula – at least for the best students – have no such length of tradition behind them. They are Victorian or post-Victorian in origin, and need far more critical study from both intellectual and social historians than they have so far received. A good starting point for such a study would be a paper written by Adolphus Ward, the historian, in 1878. 'Our times too have their New Learning, like the Renascence Age,' Ward remarked, and he gave his paper the very topical title, 'Is it Expedient to Increase the Number of Universities in England?'[3]

[1] G. Wallas, *Our Social Heritage*, London (1921), p. 26.

[2] F. Bacon, *The Advancement of Learning*, London (1861 edn., ed. W. A. Wright), pp. 41–2.

[3] A. W. Ward, *Collected Papers*, Vol. V, London (1921), p. 222. I have traced the outline of this development in relation to history in a lecture delivered at and published by the Australian National University, 'The Map of Learning' (1961).

History, however, was not the starting point for most of the academics who agreed, unanimously and enthusiastically, in 1961 that Sussex should develop a curriculum which would offer the 'benefits' both of specialized and of general education. Coming from different backgrounds, different academics employed converging arguments to support the same conclusions. Some of them have written about the reasons why they came to think as they did. The Vice-Chancellor, for instance, has referred both to Scotland and to Classical Greats and Modern Greats at Oxford: he has also written, in more practical and instrumental terms, of the needs of 'new students' and the demand from outside universities for new kinds of graduates. It was in nineteenth-century Scotland that a defender of traditional Scottish education wrote that 'speciality need not be inconsistent with unity of learning'[1]: it was in twentieth-century Oxford that philosophy, politics and economics were brought together in a curriculum designed to illuminate the modern world. In his address to the University Teachers' Group in the summer of 1961 the Vice-Chancellor explained his own approach. 'Multi-subject courses may be of different kinds. I suppose that a course in say embroidery, horticulture and Albanian language and literature would be a multi-subject course of a certain kind, a kind which deserves criticism. But Classical Greats at Oxford is a multi-subject course also. It is a study of the language and literature, the philosophy and the history of one civilization in the Mediterranean basin within a given span of time; the literature, the philosophy and the history are held together by the unity of the civilization. Modern Greats at Oxford is a multi-subject honours course in which three aspects of civilization – philosophy, politics and economics—are studied together. Here the unity is to be found in their inter-relation and their influence upon one another . . . The Schools we propose at Sussex will have this in common with those older Schools, that the subjects included are intended to have an effect upon one another.'[2]

The Sussex Schools went much further than this, however, as the chapters by Professors Corbett, Daiches and Wight show. Within the 'major' work there were to be papers which would link disciplines under the direction of two tutors from two disciplines. For example, there were to be 'special topics in history and literature',

[1] Quoted in G. E. Davie, *The Democratic Intellect*, London (1961), p. 92.
[2] *The Expanding University*, p. 56.

such as 'The Industrial Revolution and the Romantic Movement' or 'The Late-Victorian revolt'. Some contextual papers also were to be shared – 'The Modern European Mind', for example, by undergraduates in the School of European Studies and the School of English Studies and 'Contemporary Britain' by undergraduates in the School of English Studies and the School of Social Studies. Joint seminars with joint tutors would bring both undergraduates and tutors together in 'natural combinations'.

If the contextual papers were designed to set the major work in a frame, the major work itself was designed to illuminate the context. Specialization was not to be neglected, for as Sir Eric Ashby had put it in relation to technological education, 'the path to culture should be through a man's specialism, not by by-passing it'.[1]

In the light of this approach, 'general education' at Sussex was thought of in quite different terms from those of universities which have a two-tier system of degrees. The arrangement of major work and contextual work in Sussex may be illustrated in detail from the curriculum of the School of Social Studies which was already settled in outline in 1961. Four contextual papers were planned to pull together the work of the School: five papers in each major subject were designed to provide the necessary skills of the specialist. The first major subjects to be introduced were economics, geography, history, philosophy, and politics and sociology, with international relations, psychology and anthropology to follow as soon as was practicable. Since a proportion of five out of nine final papers represented a greater share for the study of particular specialisms than in many existing universities, there was no fear that a Sussex degree in social studies would involve inadequate specialization. Specialist skills, indeed, could be employed also in the study of some of the contextual subjects. Economists, for example, could make a distinctive contribution to the study of Contemporary Britain. So too could sociologists. Geographers could make a distinctive contribution to the study of 'World Population and Resources'.

Deciding what the four contextual papers should be did not involve long discussion. One of the papers had to be philosophical, extending, as Professor Corbett had envisaged, the specialist interest of the undergraduate by making him more critical.[2] The second,

[1] E. Ashby, *Technology and the Academics*, London (1958), p. 84.
[2] P. Corbett, 'Arts Studies at the University of Sussex' in *The Oxford Magazine*, 2 March 1961: 'Teach philosophy naturally as it arises out of other work.'

Contemporary Britain, was given its first rubric in 1962 – 'Contemporary British culture and society; demographic and social change; social problems and social policies; the instruments of communication and their control; social judgments in contemporary thought and writing; British approaches to the outside world.' Not only was this paper planned to link work in the School of English Studies and the School of Social Studies – a somewhat neglected link, except among journalists;[1] it was also to incorporate within the formal university curriculum topics which, although of great interest to many undergraduates, are usually kept out of the curriculum and discussed loosely and informally in clubs and societies. The reference in the rubric to 'British approaches to the outside world' was not simply an oblique glance at the Common Market, but a recognition of the fact that although undergraduates taking degrees in social studies can most easily approach the problems of society through the society to which most of them belong, many of the most interesting and strategic problems in society can only be studied adequately within a world framework.

The third common paper was to be specifically concerned with the outside world. A choice was offered between 'international politics' and 'world population and resources'. The international politics paper was to include, with historical orientation, an examination of current problems of strategy, deterrence and disarmament: the 'world population and resources' paper was to bring together economists and geographers and to prepare the way for future cooperation with biologists and engineers. Broad survey techniques were not thought appropriate for either of these papers. For both papers particular cases were to be studied – a post-War dispute, for example, or the geography, economics and politics of a particular commodity, oil, for instance, or sugar. It was envisaged that as the university took shape faculty seminars would discuss fully the scope and method of teaching these and other contextual papers, and that they would revise the field and add to the choices.

The need for continuous faculty discussion was most apparent in relation to the fourth contextual paper called 'Concepts, Methods and Values in the Social Studies', which was designed to be prepared for in seminars towards the end of the undergraduate's three years. By that time the undergraduates would already be familiar with a set

[1] For a recent plea for this approach, see Richard Hoggart's Inaugural Lecture at Birmingham University. 'Schools of English and Contemporary Society' (1963).

of specialist techniques in one social study and ready to compare them with the techniques of others. It was envisaged that in preparing for this paper also the undergraduate would concern himself with a limited number of social 'problems' or 'cases' involving different techniques of identification and analysis and posing different kinds of practical solution. Infant mortality or juvenile delinquency might be examples of one set of problems; disputes, including industrial disputes, examples of another. Philosophers would contribute to the work of these synoptic seminars, but the seminars would not be primarily 'philosophical'.

To make the seminars effective, clearly there would have to be some additional preparation over the whole three years as well as study in tutorials of the undergraduate's major subject. It was agreed, therefore, that all students in the School of Social Studies would be expected to do at least one term's work on statistics and to become acquainted with the mathematical techniques which in some universities are beginning to command the whole field of the social studies. Operational research, including data processing, would find its place at Sussex not so much as a contextual element in undergraduate education as the equipment of the undergraduate with a set of useful techniques. So too would the practical study of social situations and activities. Undergraduates who wished to pursue social studies with this orientation would have the chance of doing so. At the same time, it was hoped that practical survey work would form a part of every undergraduate's education in the School of Social Studies. By the time that the seminar on 'Concepts, Methods and Values' was held, undergraduates would be in a position not only to exchange theories but to compare experiences.

This last of the four contextual papers was felt to be at once the most difficult and the most challenging, and the arguments for experimenting with it were grounded not only in educational theory but in a critical evaluation of the main lines of development of the social studies over the last sixty years. The separate social studies have developed remarkably, though unequally, largely through a process of increasing differentiation. Yet they form a cluster. Their insights and techniques are complementary, and to an increasing extent certain techniques, including mathematical techniques, are common to them all. A knowledge of their historical development depends upon an understanding of comparisons and contrasts, of how both politics and economics, for example, grew out of 'political economy', of how abstractions, like the idea of 'economic man', served a controversial purpose, or of how nineteenth-century anthropology was related to biological and sociological theories of evolution. Similarly the contemporary use of the social studies demands a knowledge of more than one of them. To debate the Common Market it is necessary to know as much about politics as about economics. To study the tangled problems of economic growth many subjects have to be bestraddled, with history, economics, sociology and psychology prominent among them. No single social study by itself provides a proper educational foundation for an understanding of society or for the intelligent exercise of the ability to act and to judge. Specialist honours degrees in economics or sociology which overlook this hardly produce good economists or sociologists, let alone 'educated graduates'.

An education in social studies must necessarily include training in the use of techniques (in politics and sociology as well as in economics), just as an education in European Studies must necessarily include mastery of a language. Yet it must not solely be concerned with this. It must deal also with the contexts within which techniques are employed, and with perspectives and values. It must allow an important place for psychology, but it can benefit from the co-operation of philosophers as well as of psychologists. Indeed, a School of Social Studies will be most effective if it maintains sustained intellectual co-operation. Professor Tawney once wrote that 'if research requires a division of forces, a humane education requires a synthesis, however provisional, of the result of their labours'.[1] In the case of the social studies, research itself requires a synthesis. The frontiers of the map of learning, drawn by scholars far more recently than is usually believed, are being battered down by individual thinkers or being crossed quietly and without fuss by teams of researchers.

It is unfortunate that university organization does not always reflect such changes. New subjects take their place in the map of learning and become sovereign departments, and the map itself is seldom consciously re-drawn. The biological studies, for example, produce exciting new research which rests on cross-boundary thinking, yet in many universities biology, botany and zoology are controlled by independent potentates. Academic distinctions become confused with status distinctions. When a new subject, like economic

[1] R. H. Tawney, *Social History and Literature*, London (1950), p. 8.

history, comes into prominence, it often seeks to command departmental status, thereby shedding its influence with both historians
and economists. Intellectual development is far too often associated
with the multiplication of frontiers and the division of people. The
Sussex curriculum, based as it is on Schools, which are not superdepartments, was deliberately designed to avoid some at least of
these dangers.

Both from the point of view of teaching and research, organization by Schools offers obvious advantages in a period of growth.
'Departmental organization,' as Sir Alexander Carr-Saunders has
written, 'often reaches a condition of monstrous hypertrophy, falsify-
ing the academic map, and bringing about the herding of teachers
into pens surrounded by fences.'[1] Duplication and dispersal of effort,
lack of planning and co-ordination, rivalry and occasionally friction,
boundary disputes and far from splendid isolation are familiar
features, alas, in the twentieth-century university world. It is usually
only when new universities are being created that re-thinking
assumes the necessary proportions. Once again the geographical
metaphor seems the most appropriate. In the modern map of learning within the universities, students and teachers in science and the
humanities, literature and social studies all too often figure as inhabitants of separate continents. A few boats pass between them, fewer
still on regular service; there are a number of distinguished travellers
and a diminishing number of visitors; and there is little long-
distance migration, either temporary or permanent. Inhabitants
know a little of their adjacent territories, but their ideas of what
happens in more distant regions are usually imprecise, frequently
prejudiced, and often wrong. Occasionally joint voyages of discovery are made by outstanding explorers within the universities
who care little, if at all, for local allegiances.

The Sussex plan of a School of Social Studies was based not only
on the idea of a linking of academic studies but on the hope of
incorporating practical work with the curriculum which is often
thought to have no place in the universities at all. Concern
for a technical or professional speciality becomes genuinely educational when the full bearings of the speciality are critically examined. Within a philosophical, historical and sociological frame, for
example, it seemed to be possible to develop a new approach
to 'social work'. Two out of the five major papers in the

[1] A. Carr-Saunders, *English Universities of Today*, London (1960), p. 8.

undergraduate's major subject could reflect his or her own social choices and provide a lead-in to a more practically orientated fourth year. Within the first three years themselves there could be study of a 'workshop' character.

The crude distinction, all too common among academics, that there is some mysterious difference between all undergraduate and all postgraduate work could also be usefully re-examined in this context. All too often new developments of a promising kind – in management studies, for example, as well as in social work – are held back because of authoritative murmurs that they are 'suitable only for postgraduates'. Obviously most of the work that they entail is best thought of as postgraduate in character, but this does not imply that undergraduate education should necessarily ignore postgraduate interest and commitment. The organization of learning at Sussex pre-supposed a continuity of development from common 'foundation' work in the first two terms to a greater measure of personal choice in the third year and from close tutorial supervision to a greater measure of self-reliance. The optional work within the major subject, provided that it is set in its common frame and associated with basic work in the major subject, can cater for quite different aptitudes and point forward to postgraduate study.

It was of interest in working out this approach to know that within 'practical' social studies, there are interesting parallels to developments within the academic map of learning. Jean Snelling has written, for example, of the breaking down of barriers in social case work. 'Ten years ago we might have discussed boundaries in social work. Today the term boundary does not seem right for anything *within* the case work field. A boundary separates off things which are different by nature and centred apart from one another. Where these irreconcilables come most nearly together, there we can draw a boundary line. Now this is not an appropriate concept for us. We can probably think more readily of case work as a figure of . . . interlocking and overlapping circles, each with only a small segment free from its neighbours. I hope that in the next ten years we shall come to feel increasingly certain of the depth and richness and essential rightness of this figure.'[1]

Although no attempt was made in the early discussions of 1961 and 1962 to consider fully the implications of 'professional' studies, including the training of teachers, it was believed that the general

[1] J. Snelling, *The Boundaries of Case Work*, London (1959), p. 5.

pattern of university organization would make it easier to incorporate new developments, possibly in the School of Social Studies, possibly in a new School. It certainly made it easy from the start to embark immediately and inexpensively on projects which would eventually lead to the creation of new Schools. Historians and economists interested, for example, in African and Asian Studies could be recruited and employed in other Schools before the new School came into formal existence. They could even constitute a kind of 'shadow School'. Outside teams, particularly a team of biologists which was appointed in 1962, could prepare at once for quite distant developments. In the meantime the fact that academics were not appointed to one particular School and could be employed in several Schools after their arrival meant a widening of teaching experience. Not only did a number of academics from different disciplines work together to prepare proper syllabuses for such new papers as 'The Modern European Mind', but some academics were drawn into the teaching of more than one 'subject'. There are, of course, dangers in pushing cross-subject teaching too far, and it was decided in 1962 that no 'subject' would be introduced into the university unless there was a reasonable expectation that within five years it would have at least five academic specialists concerned in the teaching of it.

The study of education, it was agreed, would not be peripheral or separated by departmental barriers from other parts of the University. Academic members of the School would usually be members of another School as well, and university specialists in particular academic disciplines would be brought directly into the education of teachers. The School would also concern itself with the evaluation of some of the experiments in 'higher education' which were being carried out in the University as a whole. Was the University proving successful in linking together major subjects and common subjects? Was the tutorial system producing the results which were expected of it? Such questions would obviously have to be asked from the start and answered as soon as adequate evidence was available. They were felt to be appropriate questions for a School of Educational Studies, particularly when Sussex was the first of seven new universities. Decisions about the shape of the School of Educational Studies, including the possibility of linking teacher training and training for social workers, were deferred in 1961 not because the relevant issues were thought to be unimportant or lacking in urgency, but because they were held to be so important that they needed the most searching examination.

The same consideration influenced early discussions about the relationship between 'arts' and 'sciences'. In the summer of 1961 the Dean of the School of Physical Sciences had not yet been appointed, nor had his colleagues in the various science subjects. The discussions about the shape of the curriculum within the School of Physical Sciences, raising remarkably similar questions to those raised in the arts and social studies discussions, took place a year later. It was felt that the relationship between 'arts' and 'sciences' could only be examined fully when science had taken its proper place in the university, when there were as many scientists in the academic faculty and the undergraduate body as there were specialists in arts and social studies. As a result of the discussions between members of the science faculty, which also brought in a working party of scientists interested in biological studies, the organization of the curriculum in the sciences was given a very similar shape to that in the arts and social studies. This is described in another chapter by Professor Blin-Stoyle.

Against this background the answer to the question of 'the two cultures' – a question which is often formulated in such a way that the role of the social studies is completely ignored – seemed to be to seek for 'natural links' between arts and sciences and to strengthen them. The Keele pattern, interesting though it is, of expecting all scientists to study one arts or social studies subject and *vice versa*, was explicitly rejected. It was hoped that the same links would be forged between the Schools of Physical Sciences, Biological Sciences and Applied Sciences on the one hand and the Schools of English and American, European, African and Asian and Social Studies on the other hand as were already being forged within and between the Arts and Social Studies Schools.

A number of possible links were examined – the intellectual history of the development of the sciences within the map of learning, how they became separated from each other and how they converge in practice; comparative procedures in natural sciences and social sciences, including the use of hypotheses and of experiments and mathematical model building; the organization of science, including such topics as the social background and education of scientists, their numbers and remuneration, and how their research is financed, the use of science – or the failure to use it – by government and business, the time lags in the application of new scientific discovery and how they arise, the formulation of scientific policy and what factors, scientific and non-scientific are taken into account in shaping it; and the moral role of scientists, how they conceive of it themselves in a complex society, and how other people conceive of it. Subjects of this kind represent a direct extension of the existing interests of scientists and are, indeed, a proper part of a scientific education. At the same time they are natural extensions of interest for many arts students also, or perhaps more particularly of students in the social studies. Other subjects, like linguistics or psychology, provide different links, and it was hoped that they might be added later. Both in the early stages of the scheme and later, it was felt that the undergraduate seminars would have to be supplemented by guided reading and the preparation of individual dissertations, and that, despite the collective nature of the undertaking, some specialists would have to be engaged to deal with some of the 'link subjects'.

Discussions about the long-term future in 1961 and 1962 inevitably became concerned with the logistics of planned growth, and a 'table of growth' was prepared which within a five-year-plan allowed for the necessary element of flexibility. Much that is settled by bargaining power in existing universities was settled quickly with genuine consensus. In the short run, however, the immediate teaching problem pivoted on the needs of first-year undergraduates, and it is not surprising that in 1961 and 1962 as much attention was paid to the 'preliminary work' before an undergraduate began his final work in a particular School as to the future work of the Schools themselves. In both Arts and Social Studies and Physical Sciences the same kind of pattern was agreed upon after careful deliberation. It had something in common with that 'broadly philosophical and historical approach to the languages and the sciences through grounding in first principles',[1] which characterized Scottish education at its best. Yet in other ways it represented a quite new pattern, the logical pattern in relation to what was to follow later.

All undergraduates were to take a preliminary examination after two terms' study, and this examination had to be passed before they could proceed to work for the finals examination within a particular School. Honours would not be awarded in this first examination, a 'foundation' examination, and candidates would be adjudged solely to have passed or failed. Three papers were together to constitute

[1] See G. E. Davie, *op. cit.*, especially Chapter I.

the preliminary examination, and in both the Arts preliminary examination and the Science preliminary two of the three papers would be common to all undergraduates. Again the emphasis was being placed on common elements in university education, the subjects which bind and orientate. The third paper was to be chosen according to the interests of the undergraduate, in the case of the Arts preliminary examination, which was the first to be planned, according to the undergraduate's likely choice of School. There was to be a fourth paper in Translation to be taken only by undergraduates proposing to enter the School of European Studies (whatever their major subject within it).

The two common papers in the Arts and Social Studies preliminary examination were to be 'Language and Values' and 'An Introduction to History'. Both these papers would mark a break with school A-level subjects, and both would be taught tutorially in such a way that they would force the undergraduate to criticize, to argue and to judge. The 'Language and Values' paper required 'a thorough study of the nature and justification of value judgements, especially of moral judgements and judgements about society and policy'. Undergraduates were to be asked 'to examine extracts from current controversial writings in the light of these theories as well as to answer direct questions about them'. It was clear that this paper demanded tutorial teaching: the way of teaching it was closely bound up with its content.

The same was true also of the second common paper 'An Introduction to History'. This paper was not to be pinned to the study of a particular period, and it was to be attempted, of course, by many undergraduates who had not studied history to A-level at school. It was designed 'to provide an understanding of the historian's craft and of a number of major historical themes which will be useful in all later work at the university'. In the first prospectus the rubric on this paper began 'Historical sources and materials and how the historian uses them; the nature of historical problems; why historians disagree; past, present and future'. In 1962 the rubric was narrowed to read 'With what problems is the historian concerned and how does he define and investigate them? Why do historians disagree in the answers they give?' The narrowing of the rubric was evidence of the influence of experience – and of further thought – on the development of the curriculum.

It was also decided, as broad survey work seemed less and less important as a constituent element in university education, to consider the leading questions about history and historians in terms of two modern historical works. The books initially chosen were R. H. Tawney's *Religion and the Rise of Capitalism* and P. Geyl's *Napoleon, For and Against*, the first concerned with the interpretation of a society and the second with the interpretation of an individual. Together the two books, it was thought, would encourage a probing of values as well as a discussion of ideas. A close study of them would be as beneficial to the non-historian as to other undergraduates, and tutorial arguments about 'Language and Values' and 'An Introduction to History' would naturally converge.

The combination of two common papers and one 'specialist' paper anticipated the combination within the final work of the Schools, although there was to be a difference of proportions. The 'specialist' paper itself was a 'foundation' paper, however, acquainting the undergraduate with tools of analysis which he would employ later on in his studies. In both the School of English and American Studies and the School of European Studies undergraduates were to spend their two preliminary terms in tutorial work on 'Critical Reading', students in the School of English and American Studies concentrating upon 'European Tragedy and Fiction' (back to Sophocles). The close parallelism in the work of the two Schools was achieved not in 1961 but in 1962 when the second prospectus was being drawn up. Undergraduates intending to join the School of Social Studies were to do a paper on 'The Economic and Social Framework', although it was not finally decided how much of this paper should be devoted to economics and how much to other branches of the social studies. The main emphasis was to be placed on what might be called 'economic reasoning', but the first rubric also mentioned 'economic groups and social groups' and 'the political element in economic decision making'. Full discussion of the content of this paper was to await the very rapid build-up of an economics faculty.

It did not prove difficult to achieve a similar symmetry in the Science preliminary examination. Again there were to be two common papers, one of them, on 'The Structure and Properties of Matter', deviating sharply from A-level work, and the second on 'Mathematics', guaranteeing that all scientists would be adequately grounded in this subject. Interesting discussions took place in 1962 on the possibility of incorporating within the first of these papers the basic biology of the cell as well as the physics of matter, and plans were made to devise an entirely new way of developing this 'lead-in' course. The third science paper was to involve choice, in the first instance between further mathematics and chemistry.

It was one of the features of the curriculum of the preliminary examination that it forced attention on difficult problems which could be reviewed later in the undergraduate's career in the light of finals work. In the School of Social Studies, for example, the probing of value assumptions in the last paper to be studied, 'Concepts, Methods and Values', marked, in some sense, a return in spiral fashion to the problems first posed in two common papers of the preliminary examination. In the Schools of Physical Science and later of Biological Sciences there would be a return at a different level to problems first stated in the preparation for the study of 'The Structure and Properties of Matter'. Although it was realized that only experience would show whether Sussex graduates educated in this fashion would prove particularly qualified to embark upon new branches of research, there was sufficiently widespread interest in the University and its programme for research workers to be attracted to the University both in the School of Physical Sciences and the Schools of Arts and Social Studies.

For all its preoccupation with the education of undergraduates, the University of Sussex recognized from the start that its freedom to grant postgraduate degrees, a freedom which Keele had not enjoyed from the start, was one of its greatest academic assets. A university which is concerned only with the communication of existing knowledge is not really a university at all. The pursuit of new knowledge is a necessary part of its work and a guarantee that it will take its place in the international comity of universities. The first academics at Sussex realized that they would be judged not only by the way in which they planned the work of their undergraduates, but by the work which they themselves produced. They hoped that they were creating an environment in which new learning could flourish, remembering again Francis Bacon's famous judgment that 'the commandment of knowledge is yet higher than the commandment over the will: for it is a commandment over the reason, belief and understanding of man, which is the highest part of the mind, and giveth law to the will itself'.[1]

[1] F. Bacon, *The Advancement of Learning*, p. 42.

DAVID DAICHES

5. The Place of English Studies in the Sussex Scheme

It is still not so very long since English literature became a respectable academic subject, in the teeth of strong opposition from those who maintained that the study of one's own literature at a university would at best simply encourage the production of impressionistic critical chit-chat. The fight to establish the subject as on a par with the Latin and Greek classics has been fought on several fronts. Some maintained that the stern linguistic discipline of Anglo-Saxon and Middle English would guarantee the proper academic toughness. I remember the late Sir Herbert Grierson – who was the first Chalmers Professor of English literature at Aberdeen before succeeding Saintsbury in the Chair of English at Edinburgh – telling me that he insisted on compulsory Anglo-Saxon for honours English students because it kept out the amateurs and the light-weight frothy essayists. One could also make English respectable by making its study involve the acquisition of a large and detailed amount of information, historical, biographical, textual and bibliographical. Or one could take quite a different line and argue that the critical study of major works of English literature not only brought the student into contact with the great sensibilities produced by English civilization, to the vast benefit of the student's own mental and spiritual culture, but also provided a training in critical discrimination which would be of permanent value in later life. Or again one might hold that such a study, by introducing the student to English literature and increasing his knowledge, understanding and appreciation of it, increased his capacity for literary enjoyment and so helped him to make a more fruitful use of his leisure throughout the rest of his life. Not all of these defences are incompatible with each other, and many university teachers of English seemed to hold in the back of their mind a loose amalgam of a number of them. On the other hand, some of these views are quite incompatible with others and in some cases were formulated with deliberate belligerence in order to discredit one position and establish another. Thus the view that the serious critical study of works of literature constitutes a strenuous intellectual and (some would add) also a moral discipline in its own right is in direct opposition to the view that a stiffening of Anglo-Saxon is required to prevent literary study being 'merely' critical. Or again, I have heard university teachers of literature protesting against the notion that a university English Department should train literary critics, arguing instead that they should train scholars, providing a body of knowledge rather than opinion.

I began my own formal study of English literature with the traditional four-year honours English degree at Edinburgh University. There we had to do a one-year course in British history and another language (I did Latin), and I also had a year of philosophy, each of these three subjects being taught in separate departments in a wholly self-contained way and with no cross-reference to any of the others. But the main study was four years of English literature. The first year course was for the most part a vast survey of English literature from the Anglo-Saxon period to as far into the nineteenth century as the professor managed to get in his third term's lectures. While a few set books were read, the essence of the course was the provision of information about the course of English literature over the centuries – the main facts about the writers and their works, something of the intellectual and social background, something about the development of different *genres*, and so on. Essentially, what one got was *information about* English literature. Students who attended and listened to the lectures (and every student was expected to attend the lectures) could write a knowledgeable answer on, say, the development of verse satire in England before Dryden, talking about Marston, Hall and others, whom he had never read and was not expected to have read. Or he could write a comparison between Richardson and Fielding, or explain in what sense Blake was a 'romantic' poet, or discuss the importance of Addison and Steele, or give an account of Chaucer's 'French', 'Italian' and 'English' periods – again, without having read the relevant literary works, or perhaps having dipped into one or two of them only. In addition to this, the student would be able to produce some biographical information about the major English writers and would be quite knowledgeable about movements, tendencies, intellectual currents, and so on. He would be able to tell you about Spenser's neo-Platonism and bring in the names of Bruno and Ficino in this connection. The honours student would then go on to a more intensive study of a particular century (conducted on the same lines) and a term's intensive study of Shakespeare and another of Chaucer. The term on Shakespeare, when I was at Edinburgh, never got beyond the middle comedies, and barely to them. We spent two weeks discussing the textual and bibliographical problems of the *Henry VI* plays. We did however do special work on *Hamlet*, which was a set book, and actually had to *memorize* the variant readings of the two quartos and the folio (I can still recite some of them). What I remember from the term on Chaucer is mostly long arguments about the order of composition of the two versions of the Prologue to the *Legend of Good Women*, discussion of the character of Criseyde, and 'background knowledge' relevant to the Canterbury Tales.

There was more, of course. I recall some brilliant lectures on seventeenth-century poetry and on the Romantics by the professor – lectures which moved freely between the history of ideas, biography and critical appreciation. Here literature was set illuminatingly in its intellectual and social context and presented as a human product of its time rather than as a group of independently existing timeless works of art. We learned the history of literary criticism from Aristotle's *Poetics* to Matthew Arnold's *On the Study of Poetry*, with all the information laid out in lectures, to be supplemented (by a particularly keen student) by reading in Saintsbury's anthology of criticism, *Loci Critici*. When we finally graduated with an honours degree in English, we felt *professionally* qualified: we knew all about English literature, we knew what the major critics had said, we knew what the main scholarly problems were and in general how they were tackled. Few remembered any of the Anglo-Saxon and Middle English they had worked so hard at in their second and third years. (Indeed, the question on dialectical criteria in Middle English, which came up every year, was always answered by knowing students the moment they came into the examination hall, having been studiously mugged up early that morning. The knowledge had evaporated by the time the examination was over.)

It is easy to point to the shortcomings of such a study of English literature. It had certain advantages (apart altogether from the advantage from coming into contact with the mind of a particularly interesting and widely ranging professor or lecturer – Professor

Grierson, for example). The student who had been through this four years' course knew the map of English literature and of English intellectual history pretty well. He had a sense of the past, a sense of the special flavour of each period and century, an awareness of the place on the map of any given author. Such knowledge is more useful than is often allowed: even to know who comes before whom is a help, as anyone can testify who has taught American students who could do highly sophisticated analyses of particular works without having the foggiest idea whether George Herbert came before or after Coventry Patmore. Further, his study of Anglo-Saxon, even if he had forgotten nearly all of it by the time he graduated, would have made him aware of certain native strengths in the English language and enabled him to recognize (to put it no more highly) the different strains in English and the characteristic effects of each.

When I went from Edinburgh to Oxford, I was struck by the comparative amateurishness of undergraduate English studies at Oxford, and this in spite of Oxford's emphasis on scholarship and insistence on Anglo-Saxon. It is true that I did not read for the BA in English at Oxford, but from what I saw of those who did, I got the strong impression that, apart from some specific linguistic and academic skills, what they obtained, or sought most to obtain, was an elegant and witty way of discussing those literary works that they had read. The professional element in the degree seemed less than at Edinburgh, and the course of study seemed to provide a somewhat uneasy combination of scholarship and urbanity. Edinburgh had taught one all about English literature; Oxford seemed to teach one how to *talk* about it, with a stiffening of dogged scholarship to make everything academically respectable. (I should, however, emphasize that my impressions of Oxford English in the 1930s are fragmentary and far from fresh.)

From Oxford I went to the University of Chicago, arriving at the very moment when R. S. Crane was leading the attack of the so-called 'neo-Aristotelians' on conventional ways of presenting litera-ture at universities – the 'survey' course, in which the lecturer recited the facts of literary history; the mélange of bibliography, biography and history of ideas offered as 'criticism'; impressionist remarks about a writer's greatness or classic stature, offered as 'appreciation'. Instead of this, Professor Crane and his associates offered a rigorous analytic account of the individual literary work;

Crane actually went so far (he has changed his mind on this as on several other points since) as to remark to me that literary history was a contradiction in terms, since literature consisted of unique individual works about groups of which no meaningful historical generalizations could be made. This was part of a wider revolt in America against the survey course in literature, a movement which insisted on the prime importance of the student's careful reading of the individual literary text and objected violently to their receiving information about works they were not expected to read – sometimes even to their receiving any historical or biographical information at all in connection with their critical study of literary texts. This is all bound up with the somewhat unreal fight between criticism and history that has now pretty well played itself out among American literary academics, and I do not wish to go into this here. I wish to point out only that during my years of teaching at American universities I came into close contact with the so-called New Criticism and saw how in varying ways literary criticism was being developed in America as a stringent intellectual discipline of its own, unrelated to philological, historical or biographical scholarship.

After my American experience I went to Cambridge, and ten years of teaching English there (both as university lecturer and as college supervisor) gave me an intimate knowledge of both the advantages and disadvantages of the Cambridge English School. Differing traditions were operating simultaneously, and they were not always compatible. The 'literature, life and thought' approach to the study of a given period was still preserved in some papers but not in others. Anglo-Saxon, as a result of earlier accidents of personality, belonged to Archaeology and Anthropology, not to English, and was taken as an optional subject by a very small number of those undergraduates who were reading English. Dr Leavis's ardent belief in the central educational importance of the careful critical study of major literary works was an important force in the university, yet it was by no means shared by all of his colleagues. Some thought of English studies as bound up with intellectual history and the study of the main traditions of moral thought in the Western world – hence the Moralists paper in Part II of the English Tripos. Others thought that the objective of an English school was to provide undergraduates with a diversified experience of reading in a variety of periods, with an appropriate background of knowledge and of critical awareness, so that they would lay a foundation for intelligent and appreciative reading in later life. Hence the very wide choice of questions in examinations, which enabled the undergraduates to decide in advance which writers they would 'get up', and be fairly certain of finding a question on them when the time came. I have heard this practice both attacked and defended in Cambridge.

The most interesting aspect of the Cambridge English School I consider to be Part II of the English Tripos, where the undergraduate is given a chance to broaden his interests to other literatures than English and to other disciplines than criticism. The compulsory paper on Tragedy includes European as well as English tragedy, and everybody must know something of Greek tragedy and of French neo-classic tragedy as well as more recent European playwrights such as Ibsen. This involves the problem of translation, for few undergraduates reading English can read all these plays in the original; but a careful study of a good translation, with critical help from the appropriate scholars, is better than ignoring these important European works altogether. There is also a paper in French and Italian, which requires a reading knowledge of these languages and a study of certain set classical texts in them. And Part II of the English Tripos, like Part I, maintains the Cambridge tradition of close practical criticism with a paper in which candidates are asked to compare and assess anonymous passages of poetry or prose and to date selected anonymous passages by paying attention to the language, the tone, the literary convention, the kind of thought and feeling, and so on. This sort of dating exercise, by the way, while it can descend to being a mere trick, can be a profoundly civilizing discipline, encouraging students to cultivate a sensitive awareness to the different ways in which language is used, to shifts in attitude and convention, to the 'feel' of a period and to movements of taste and sensibility. The skills it requires cannot be acquired without much and varied reading. In Edinburgh, we had been *told* about these attitudes and movements by our lecturers, and we knew about them as objective historical facts; at Cambridge the student was encouraged to find out and test this sort of knowledge for himself. The good Edinburgh student could have written with complete confidence an account of Augustan taste or the main verse forms used by the Romantic poets, and in a sense he would have known much more about all this than the Cambridge student now does; yet it would probably have been *information* rather than *experience*. But of course the Cambridge student often got up a few 'gimmicks' to help him with his dating question, and for the rest picked out a few authors that he knew were bound to appear in the various period papers, so that in addition to the confusion of objectives to be found in the Cambridge English School there was also likely to be a large gap between the objective and what was actually attained by a given student.

I have given this autobiographical account of my various experiences of the academic study of English before I came to Sussex in order to show where I started from when I responded to the exciting challenge of helping to build up a new university by presiding over its School of English Studies. At Edinburgh, I had received a professional English degree, qualifying me to talk knowledgeably about English literature from Beowulf to the late nineteenth century. In America I had seen the development of critical analysis of the isolated literary work as an academic discipline in its own right. At Oxford and at Cambridge, in different ways and degrees, I had seen English studies as (putting it at its narrowest) education for gentlemen and (putting it at its widest) education for life. Where did I now stand?

In one sense my position was defined in advance by the declared policy of the new university, which was to resist the tight compartmentalization of subjects in independent departments and to encourage fruitful cross-fertilization of subjects by refusing to have departments at all and organizing the university in flexible Schools of Study. If I had not felt that such an organization held immense promise for English studies, I would not have come to Sussex. I have always believed – and this is what led me to English studies in the first place – that literature is a subject of central interest and importance because it is an illumination of life; that this illumination is achieved by the work of literary art uniquely, in a way that no other form of discourse can achieve, but that at the same time the work of literary art, being produced by men in a given time and place in response to given personal and social forces, both can and should be seen also in relation to its intellectual and social context. I had learned from Edinburgh the importance of having a sense of literary history, a sense of the past in its shifting movements to which I could relate individual works; I had learned from America the dangers of confusing critical description and evaluation with historical and biographical information and the need to respect the uniqueness of the individual work; I had learned from Cambridge ways in which evaluative criticism can be related to a sense of time and place and the possibility of widening the literary context to look beyond England to the Western tradition as a whole. I had of course also learned many negative lessons. From Edinburgh, for example, I had learned to distrust the vast information-giving lecture course and the view that a student could pass all his examinations from lecture notes without having read the literary works he was discussing; from America I had learned the fatuity of developing sophisticated techniques of critical analysis without the sensitivity to language and tone and feeling which only wide reading and some historical awareness can provide; from Cambridge I had learned how easily a curriculum that was wide and deep in theory could in practice degenerate into a simple 'wine-tasting' course for casual readers with a few bright ideas.

It is best, I believe, to give up altogether the notion of a 'professional' first degree in English literature, that is, the idea that in a three-year BA course the student can learn 'all about' English literature from the Anglo-Saxons to the present day. This is in any case an unsatisfactory concept of what is meant by 'professional' or 'expert'. 'You have an honours degree in English; you must, then, know all about Giles and Phineas Fletcher; you must be able to tell about George Wither's pastorals and the poetry of the Della Cruscans and Anglo-Saxon riddles and the novels of Charles Maturin.' This is surely an impossible – and a *wrong* – expectation to form of anybody with an English degree, though I am not sure that this expectation did not exist of Edinburgh graduates in English in my time there. It is a kind of dictionary knowledge, bound to be largely second-hand and to involve a great waste of time spent reading about second-rate literature in secondary sources. Nor do I think that the other kind of professional English degree, which teaches the student how to edit a text, compile a bibliography, and translate Anglo-Saxon, is very much better, considered as a liberal arts degree rather than as a special kind of technical training. On the other hand, it is utopian to believe in the civilizing power of a few great books, to expect that by training students to appreciate *Measure for Measure*, the *Dunciad*, *Middlemarch* and *The Rainbow* one is solving the baffling problems of culture in our time and equipping the students with the ability to regenerate civilization. (It may be somewhat unfair to ascribe this view to Dr Leavis, but it is not an overwhelming over-simplification of his position.) Nevertheless, it is in this direction, rather than in the professional direction, that we must move if we want to provide a first degree in English which really makes educational sense, though we shall have to move in some other directions as well.

An English School must train its students to read with discrimination and appreciation. In an age when the 'mass media' are threatening standards on all sides, when the battle between highbrow, middlebrow and lowbrow rages continually and 'popular' as applied to art is often taken to be synonymous with 'bad', a prime responsibility rests on the university to teach *critical appreciation* (both words in this phrase being equally important). Here, with Matthew Arnold and Dr Leavis, we look to 'the best', great works of literature that ought to be known by educated people, works which are stimulating and profitable and exciting to read, which enrich and develop the personality, which provide means of developing critical techniques and insights, which provide standards and help to form taste, which give some idea of the stature of the English literary achievement. This is one major objective. At the same time, we do not want to prescribe an orthodox reading list of 'great books' beyond which the student must not stray. Quite apart from the fact that there are some important differences of opinion concerning which books are the greatest, the range of fascinating minor works in English literature is enormous, and students should be encouraged to find their own favourites off the beaten track, to discover something of the *richness* of our literature as well as of the greatness of its classic works. How can we achieve this in the brief three years at our disposal?

We can achieve this by uniting this aim with another important aim, an aim recognized by all the Schools at the University of Sussex. This is the relating of the study of literary works to the study of other relevant subjects – subjects which illuminate and are illuminated by the study of works of literature. If on the one hand we ask our students to read with careful critical attention a selection of the greatest works of our literature, on the other we also ask them (at a later stage in their academic career) to study carefully the relation between certain social and intellectual movements in history and the literary works which arise from them (if the phrase 'arise from them' seems to beg the question as to how literary works are produced, and the whole question of the relation of individual genius to external forces, we could substitute the phrase 'of the same period'). This does not mean simply adding some historical knowledge on to some literary knowledge learned in quite a different context. It means actually studying the literature and its context in one and the same course, under the joint direction of a historian and a man of letters. Now, when we are studying the texture of a culture in this way, we are as interested in the minor writers as in the major. Indeed, the minor writers are often more helpful, being more typical of their time and reflecting more accurately the tastes and preconceptions of their generation. So if our students are required to work on a historico-literary topic (e.g., 'The French Revolution and the Romantic Movement', 'The Industrial Revolution and the English Literary Imagination'), they will in this special work on a given period be encouraged to look beyond the major writers of the time and to look closely at minor writers of considerable historical interest and at the same time well worth reading in their own right. This will extend their reading and encourage the development of individual preferences.

A work of art is both timeless and rooted in its temporal context. In drawing attention to the timeless aspect, to the sense in which every work of literature is contemporary and anonymous, modern American critics have redeemed the study of literature from the accretions of history; yet, in ignoring that language itself is a phenomenon that exists in time and draws its meaning from temporal and local reference, these critics have sometimes reduced literary criticism to an ingenious pattern-game. The basic premise of all literary study is, or should be, the fact that literature is a *human* study; literature shows us man illuminating his own condition. The circumstances of that condition are continually changing, and the ways in which those changes affect the conventions of art, the ways in which men employ art to throw light on experience, the aspects of experience which they consider to be most in need of illumination, the attitudes and preconceptions which lie behind their ways of presenting in art their responses to life – a knowledge of all this both helps us to read the literary text more accurately and gives us a richer understanding of the whole human situation in which it is involved. So that by associating literary study with study of the context of the literary work we learn more about what work really *is* in terms of the human experience that produced it. A better understanding of the particular helps us to see through it to the universal.

In the study of English literature, as of other subjects, we at Sussex are concerned to combine study in depth of a specialist subject with a study of 'contextual' subjects which are not simply extra bits of culture thrown in but which are so presented that they really illuminate and are really illuminated by the literary works which form the major subject of concentration. If the student cannot build bridges between the various subjects he studies then, we feel, he is not studying them properly. We do not therefore simply add historical study to the student's study of literature; we try to find ways of enabling him to relate his literary study to his historical study with mutual profit. We train him in critical awareness, and at the same time we try to enable him to see at least some of the works he is discussing critically in their historical, social and intellectual context. With works of our own time, we feel that it is important for the student to be enabled to see them in relation to the whole picture presented by our contemporary culture. That is why we have in the final examination for students in the School of English Studies a paper in 'Contemporary Britain' which he takes alongside students in the School of Social Studies. Here he will study British culture and society of our own time, and will investigate questions of demographic and social change, instruments of communication and their control, and many other of the elements which constitute the framework within which and in relation to which modern literature is produced. It is relevant in this connection to remark that many of the problems referred to so astringently by Dr Leavis in his literary criticism can be only fully understood – not to say solved – with reference to sociologico-cultural investigation. Do we object to middlebrow literature? Is there a literary establishment? Are we dubious of the role of the 'quality' weeklies? Do we wonder who controls the artistic policies of radio and television? Is political debate conducted in terms of meaningless clichés and bogus rhetoric? The literary critic comes up against all these questions and more. Neither worry nor indignation provides the right answers, but a dispassionate sociologico-cultural study of contemporary Britain might.

Critical study of individual literary works; investigation of their social and intellectual context and of other, perhaps minor, literary works flourishing in the same context – these are two of the three main sorts of activity which go on in our School of English Studies.

The third is an attempt to see English literature as part of the larger unit of European literature. This cannot, of course, be done for more than a particular cross-section of literature. We have chosen to investigate the response of the literary imagination to the world of modern industrial democracy, from the mid-nineteenth century to the present. We call this study, more for convenience than wholly accurately, 'The Modern European Mind'. We have chosen this because of the enormous historical importance of this response and also because so many of the student's own preconceptions about art and its relation to life will have been conditioned by it, without his being aware of it. Many of what the student will consider the simplest truths about the relation of the artist to his environment are in fact the product of this special modern situation. The sense of the artist as different, as not bound by the normal laws that govern respectable middle-class life; the concept of the artist as alienated, as an outsider, or as a bohemian; the quarrel between the artist and the Philistine; the view of the artist as maladjusted or neurotic or in some other way at odds with society – this is reflected in a hundred different ways in modern Europe and America, from Matthew Arnold's fight against the Philistines to Joyce's view of the artist as exile; from Thomas Mann's investigation of the relation between art and disease to recent discussions of art and censorship; from the idiosyncrasies and personal excesses of the French Symbolist poets to the exhibitionist nonconformity of certain young American writers. Underlying all this is a view that springs from the artist's confrontation of modern industrial democratic civilization, a view essentially different (though there may be some superficial parallels) from any view of the relation of the artist to society that prevailed in other ages and other cultures. This view, and the special qualities of important modern literary works that result from it, is surely worth careful examination, if only in order that the student should beware of confusing a particular historical phenomenon with something essential to the very nature of art. But of course the more important reason is that he should understand the age in which he lives and the literature which it has produced, while at the same time seeing English literature in the wider perspective of European literature as a whole.

Our conception of a School of English Studies is therefore built round three centres: the careful critical reading of some major works of English literature; the exploration of the relation between literature and its social and intellectual context within a given period; and the study of a cross-section of European literature within a given period. We also bring in European literature with our compulsory paper on Tragedy in the final examination which, like the Cambridge Tragedy paper, includes a study of Greek, Elizabethan, French neo-classic and modern European tragedy. Undergraduates are plunged into their critical reading as soon as they come up. The preliminary examination for all those working in the School of English Studies, whether they will be majoring in English or History or Philosophy, includes a paper on set books (Chaucer's *Troilus and Criseyde* and one of *The Canterbury Tales*; five Shakespeare plays; novels by Jane Austen, George Eliot, Henry James and Conrad; substantial selections of the poetry of Milton, Pope, Wordsworth and Yeats – but this list is not sacrosanct). Their other two preliminary papers are common to all undergraduates in Arts and Social Studies, 'Language and Values' and 'An Introduction to History'. In the third term of their first year those who are majoring in English begin working on European Tragedy. In their second year they prepare themselves for the other three 'core' papers in the final examination – Shakespeare, The English Novel, and Practical Criticism. The third of these is not prepared for in any special tutorials in how to write criticism, but we arrange (over and above tutorials in specific topics) seminars and discussion groups in which undergraduates try their hand at 'dating' and other exercises in practical criticism and apply what they have learned from their reading and thinking to the critical analysis of unseen works. At the same time they are preparing themselves for the 'contextual' part of the final examination, which includes a paper in English history and in philosophy as well as papers in Contemporary Britain, The Modern European Mind, and the historico-literary topic already discussed.

In the School of English Studies it is possible to major in History or in Philosophy instead of English. The preliminary examination is the same and so are the contextual papers of the final examination; the difference lies in the core papers of the final examination, which are relevant to the major subject. It will be seen that historians will do two terms intensive critical work on English literature when they come up, for we believe that literature is important to the historian as history is to the literary student. Of course, a historian can major instead in the School of Social Studies, in which case his contextual subjects will be more sociological and political; and he can major in the School of European Studies and surround his work with a European context. It should be emphasized also that a student at Sussex can major in English in the School of European Studies, thus seeing English literature as a European literature set in a European context more explicitly than is done by those who major in the School of English Studies.

The full title of the School is the School of English and American Studies, and it is possible to major in American studies. The preliminary work will be the same as for all other members of the School; the difference will be that in work for the final examination the undergraduate majoring in American studies will choose an American historico-literary topic (e.g. 'The Gilded Age in American Literature and Society'), will study Contemporary America instead of Contemporary Britain (but on exactly the same lines), and will study largely American topics for their four 'core' papers. If they are primarily historians, three of the four topics will be historical; otherwise they will include one historical, one literary, one historical or literary topic – all American – and the paper on Tragedy. We thus apply exactly the same principles to the study of American literature as we do to the study of English literature. We do not isolate it, but study it both in connection with American history and sociology and in relation with English and European literature. While we wish to encourage American studies, we should never want to produce a graduate who knew Whitman and Mark Twain and Henry James thoroughly and had never done any careful reading of Shakespeare or Pope or Wordsworth or Jane Austen. We do not have a Department of American Studies for the same reason that we do not have a Department of English.

It seems to me that the Sussex 'core and context' principle is especially relevant to English studies and seems designed to resolve the conflict between literary criticism and literary history which has been raging, especially in America, for many years now. We want our students trained *both* in evaluative techniques and in historical understanding. While we will not offer them masses of information about books they cannot be expected to read (and if there are advantages in doing this they are demonstrably outweighed by the disadvantages, chief of which is encouraging wrong habits of mind about literature) we will provide them with the opportunity of investigating in detail the literature and life of a single significant period. They will have no course in literary history as such, but they will (we hope) learn what literary history is by this close investigation of a chronologically related group of literary works and their background. At the same time we shall try to teach them the proper use of literary histories and other secondary sources, so that they employ them not as substitutes for reading the original texts but as aids to seeing the texts they read in relation to each other, to placing them in their context and to learning relevant facts about them.

What previous preparation will we require of those who want to come and study in our School of English Studies? The answer we give is the same as that given by all the Schools of Studies in Arts and Social Studies: except for the study of a foreign language we do not insist on A level GCE performance in the subject to be studied at the university. What we look for in our potential students is the right kind of intellectual curiosity and imaginative capacity, and if we can establish the existence of these qualities by interview and detailed testimonials we are prepared to accept an applicant into the School of English Studies provided that he has the minimum formal qualifications for general entrance. Of course, an undergraduate who starts with very little reading in English literature and no training at all in critical reading, will have to read a great deal and work very hard. But the fact is that even those who come to English studies with good Advanced level performance in English are often faced with something very different from the literary work they did at school, and it is not uncommon to find a student relying on the work he did in his Sixth Form, with disastrous results.

There are in fact two different kinds of Sixth Form preparation for English studies. One is the premature university work taught by some of the more sophisticated schoolmasters, and the other, much more common, is the sound Advanced level teaching which will enable pupils to get a high grade in the GCE examination. We have reservations about the former largely because it takes up time that ought to be spent on other subjects, and partly because it is sometimes rather bogus anyway, a mere learning of fashionable attitudes and jargon. As to the latter, while we do not doubt that Advanced level English is a useful and helpful study, we do not consider that it is invariably more helpful to the future university student of English than to the future university student of anything else. While it is true that any pupil who is capable of doing good university work in English ought to find no difficulty in obtaining a high grade in Advanced level English if he sets his mind to it, it is most certainly not true that every pupil who gets a high Advanced level grade in English is capable of doing university work in that subject. For a large number of candidates, Advanced level English represents the highest point of which they are capable; with reasonable intelligence, sound teaching, conscientious work and a good memory they can get a grade 1, but after they have come to the university they may be wholly at a loss when they discover what is involved in the way of careful original critical response to a literary work and the kind of essays they are expected to write. Some of these can be brought on, by means of intensive individual tuition, to the stage of critical understanding of literature appropriate to university study, and this is one of the many arguments for the tutorial system. Others will remain bewildered that by memorizing what has been written by authorities and taking down what their tutor says they are still unable to produce satisfactory work.

All this might be accepted, yet we might still be pressed to require some minimum work in subjects other than English for those who wish to read English with us. How can anybody really read Milton without knowing any Latin? One might go further and ask how anybody can appreciate whole areas of English literature or understand adequately the variety of resources possessed by the English language who has learned no Latin at all. I confess to being old-fashioned enough to have considerable sympathy with the position implied in these questions. A sense of what the Latin tongue is and has achieved is so built in to earlier phases of our literature and literary language that a reader wholly innocent of Latin inevitably misses a great deal. Ideally, of course, I should like our students of English to be well versed also in British and European history, classical mythology, and the Italian and French languages. But all this is utopian. There is a point in history at which we must declare a language to be self-contained, to have all its riches and resources available for inspection and appreciation without any digging back into where it all came from. Otherwise the process of digging back would be endless. English is now the language of a great national and a great international literature and is an international medium of communication extended far beyond the bounds of countries linked to classical culture. It is, in fact, in the position that Latin was in during the Roman Empire and the Middle Ages. Linguistically, it is as self-sufficient as Latin was in the late Empire and in the Middle

Ages. We are entitled to expect a study of English and English literature that does not refer back to earlier linguistic facts but which contents itself with explaining the English phenomena *as they are.* We do ask our students to familiarize themselves in some degree with the thought and literature of the ancient world: they read Homer and Virgil in translation, as well as Aeschylus, Sophocles and Euripides. But in general they regard English as a modern Western language, and their serious interest in it and in its literature (apart from some work on Chaucer) is from the Renaissance onwards. In a sense, this is the price we have to pay for providing our core studies with adequate contexts and bringing history and philosophy into close association with literature. One cannot do everything in three years. In spite of recent pronouncements about the non-existence of the Renaissance and C. S. Lewis's view that the real break with the past came in the nineteenth century, we believe – I certainly believe and would be prepared to argue the point at length – that European culture from the Renaissance *does* constitute a unity, although of course it does flow back into the Middle Ages for all history is continuous. As for Professor Lewis's great gap between 'Old Western Man' and the modern variety, that is precisely what we study in our Modern European Mind course.

Naturally we want our students to know something about the classical world and the classical heritage of our culture – Professor Wight talks about this in his essay. But as history moves on and subjects proliferate and cultural patterns change it becomes necessary to re-define the area of main educational concentration if our students are to have a sense of dealing with a genuinely *relevant* culture. It is perhaps better to have read Virgil in translation than to know the *Aeneid* solely as a repository of torturing unseens. The fact is that the kind of classical knowledge our schools have been equipping their pupils with has become increasingly mechanical and meaningless. To insist on Latin today (and I repeat that I really would prefer our students to know Latin) means insisting on our students' coming up with half-baked recollections of conjugations and grammatical rules and no awareness at all of classical literature as literature or the classical world as a potent source of Western culture. Similarly, while there is a case for the study of Anglo-Saxon by those who are really committed to the study of English literature, and I myself never regret having studied it and feel that my understanding of the nature of the English language has been deepened by my having done so, the additional insight which it will give to the modern student is marginal, and cannot be compared with the gains afforded by the contextual subjects we provide instead. Three years is not a long time – it is indeed ridiculous that England remains one of the few countries in the world to give an honours degree in such a short period – and if the education received in those three years by the undergraduate is to be genuinely illuminating and enriching, if the subjects studied are to throw light on each other, if the undergraduate is to be able to put together all that he learns into some real pattern and acquire some sense of the unity of knowledge, then the courses of study must be carefully selected and related to a world of cultural understanding that is *real* for him.

For the modern university does not exist to provide facilities for the lone scholar devoted to a life of the pursuit of knowledge for its own sake. It caters for these, but the majority of its students are different: they come in order to learn how to come to terms with their own culture and with their own past, how to clarify their minds, refine their sensibilities and equip themselves to confront the bewildering phenomena of modern civilization. To the pure scholar no knowledge comes amiss; to most of the young men and women taking first degrees at a university today the knowledge that we offer must not only be meaningful and relevant but must be seen to be so. Some may deplore this, and wish that university entrance were restricted to dedicated seekers after truth with infinite leisure. Such a wish is perhaps immoral; it is certainly unrealistic.

At the research level, of course, none of these considerations apply. The student who stays on for research is committed to the pursuit of knowledge for its own sake, and here we do not differ in any significant respect from the more traditional university. The question of how far to organize research studies on the American model is one which we have not yet had the opportunity at Sussex of considering in any detail; but it is a real question, and has a special application to English studies.

One final point: while we try to train our students in the careful critical reading of literary texts, we also insist that they should read much more widely than can be tested in formal examinations. Training in critical reading is not a device for enabling our students to talk with professional arrogance about works of literature or for restricting them to the so many 'great books' besides which all others are to be scorned. Remarkably few people know how to read a great literary work with full attention, with full imaginative awareness, and lacking this knowledge they lack both adequate appreciation and enjoyment of the work and a proper sense of the difference between the good and the rubbishy. But training in proper reading of a few great works must go side by side with wide reading over a great variety of works if the student's sense of literature is to be kept lively and flexible and his capacity for literary understanding and enjoyment is to be enlarged. We therefore continually urge our students to read more widely than any set list of books might suggest or than any given tutorials can test. The test, in so far as there is a test, comes in the final examination, where the essay paper and the paper in practical criticism give them an opportunity to draw on the wider reading they have done. We have no formal course in the history of English poetry, but a practical criticism paper requiring the students to date and assess a considerable variety of anonymous poems can only be tackled by someone who has read widely and sensitively in English poetry. To be able to detect the tone of an example of early eighteenth century *vers de société* (say by Prior) or a characteristic piece of mid-eighteenth century Miltonizing, or distinguish the grace and movement of an Elizabethan lyric from the movement of a Restoration one, or spot the characteristically mid-Victorian elegiac note in something from Tennyson or Arnold, or hear at once the flexible and sophisticated movement of Jacobean dramatic blank verse – to be able to do this is to have a deeper inward understanding of English poetry than memorizing all the volumes of Courthope's *History of English Poetry* could ever give. The nature of this part of the final examination thus defines the kind of reading we expect our students to do. Only experience can show whether we are expecting too much.

I began this essay by listing a number of different justifications that have been brought forward at different times for the academic study of English literature. I have not said explicitly which of these justifications is accepted by the University of Sussex. Our conception of English studies cannot be easily reduced to a formula, but perhaps it is not altogether too absurd an over-simplification to say that our aim is to enable our students to achieve the fullest possible awareness of the human relevance of works of literature. 'The poet,' said Wordsworth, 'is a man speaking to men.' We try not to forget that.

6. European Studies

I

While Europe dominated the rest of the world, Europeans knew no sphere of knowledge called 'European Studies'. They imagined Europe to be synonymous with civilization, and all studies were European. 'The classics' meant the classical languages of Europe, not Sanskrit or classical Arabic or Chinese; and history was European history, except when in remote antiquity it ran back into the Near East. At the same time, there was traditionally little academic study of contemporary affairs, apart from the field of law. The extension of university studies in the nineteenth century was, first, a recognition of other cultures than Europe (at Oxford and Cambridge honours degrees in Oriental Languages came earlier than in Modern Languages or in English); and secondly, a recognition of the contemporary world with the establishment of the social sciences. But the social sciences seemed to assume, once again, a unitary civilization identical with the West. Economics and political science regarded Europe and North America as the norms and hardly considered the exceptions; sociology was the study of civilized, viz. Western society, anthropology the study of 'native peoples'. Between the World Wars there began, in the United States more than in Britain, a development of regional or area studies. A culture or region, the Middle East or Latin America or Eastern Asia, was made the framework of study, and within it various disciplines, linguistic, historical and sociological, could be combined. But it was not until after the Second World War that Europe, now deposed from world primacy by her American and Russian descendants, could become academically self-aware as one among the several civilizations of the world. University curricula reflect their historical circumstances. The end of European hegemony made the concept of 'European Studies' possible.

If the University of Sussex is the first in Britain to establish

European Studies, it was not the first to think of it. In 1947 Oxford considered a proposal for instituting an Honour School of European Studies, which should combine historical and literary disciplines. In the dozen years that elapsed between the defeat of this proposal and the foundation of the new universities, the case for European Studies was strengthened by the progress of the European Economic Community and the possibility that Britain herself might join. A School of European Studies was among the earliest projects of the founders of the University of Sussex.

It will be remembered that, in the organization of work at Sussex, half the work done for the final examination is given to the major subject, which is likely to bring together undergraduates from several Schools of Study; the other half is devoted to the general background defined by the chosen School of Studies, which is certain to bring together students doing different major subjects. (Some undergraduates choose the School of Studies they want to belong to before the major subject they want to specialize in; others are sure of their major subject but undecided at first about the best School in which to pursue it.) European Studies is one of the four Schools into which Arts subjects are grouped, along with Social Studies, English and American Studies, and (from 1964) African and Asian Studies. Of the four Schools, that of European Studies is quite the most complicated. It is the only School in which undergraduates can major in French, German and Russian, and it is one of several Schools in which they can major in history, philosophy, English, politics and sociology, economics, geography and international relations. At present the School of English and American Studies comprises four major subjects; of Social Studies, six; of European Studies, ten.

The seminal idea of the School was of a European Greats, in which European civilization might be studied through the combined disciplines of history, philosophy and literature, in the same way as Oxford Greats studies the civilization of antiquity. The idea is embodied in the preliminary examination, consisting of papers in history and philosophy which are common to all the Arts Schools, together with a paper in European literature and a fourth paper in translation from a modern European language, for students intending to take European Studies. Such a notion does not of course exhaust the possibilities of European Studies. Europe is not a dead civilization; it can be studied empirically. It is a natural unit for a regional study employing the methods of the social sciences. But the wider the variety of approaches, the more diverse the major subjects that can be pursued within the School, the more the School needs to have a principle of coherence. And this cannot be provided by assuming that European Studies have the same kind of place in a scheme of higher education as Middle Eastern or Latin American Studies.

In the first place, regional or area studies are a vocational or specialist education. They are likely to restrict the field of choice for a career, and undergraduates who choose them will probably have a particular kind of career in view. European Studies have intrinsically a different aspect and a wider range. They are bound to include the traditional liberal arts, which attempt a general view of human experience and human achievement. Here would belong classical studies and medieval studies, and perhaps the history of art, though none of these is yet in sight at Sussex. The largest group of undergraduates in a School of European Studies will probably for many years to come be modern linguists; and modern languages, like English, but unlike Oriental languages, are not primarily a vocational training. This is not to overlook the importance of producing modern language graduates who will go into teaching. But there does not appear to be evidence that a larger proportion of modern linguists than of historians become teachers, nor even a larger proportion of German specialists than of French specialists. On the other hand there are increasing signs that modern linguists with a broader cultural background make more useful and desirable sixth-form teachers. And the range of occupations opened up by a degree in European Studies is likely to be greater than that opened by a degree in another kind of regional studies.

Moreover, regional studies necessarily change their character in proportion to the significance of the literature and philosophy of the region. The great civilizations demand a different academic treatment from regions of derivative or primitive culture. The intellectual and spiritual content of the cultures concerned makes an almost generic difference between West African or South-East Asian Studies and Arabic or Persian. The more important the literature, the more it demands to be taken into account. 'To go into this storehouse of dazzling riches and select from among the resplendent vessels of massive gold one small brass ash-tray made in Birmingham – this would be to show a want of imagination, a lack of love, that would unfit us for university teaching of any kind.'[1] This was said of Chinese studies; it is equally if not more true of European. And the more the intellectual and imaginative culture demands to be taken into account, the more literary studies and modern or social studies are likely to present themselves as alternatives between which a choice has to be made. It is not so much that a first degree normally takes only three years, and undergraduates cannot learn everything. It is rather that some will have a natural inclination towards the one, some towards the other. It is worth adding that literary students generally show a greater eagerness to acquire a foothold in modern studies than social students show to acquire a foothold in literary studies. A School of European Studies must make room for both kinds of discipline. But they represent different foci of interest, and sometimes even different philosophies of education. Perhaps the difference between them has superseded the distinction Newman took from Aristotle, between knowledge worth possessing for what it is and knowledge worth possessing merely for what it does. On the one side, the attitude to human affairs is critical, qualitative, normative and introspective; on the other side, descriptive, quantitative, progressive and extroverted. When we say that we want to combine the advantages of literary studies with those of social studies, we cannot overlook that here is one of the acutest points of tension in our intellectual and academic life today.

But if Europe is not simply an area for regional study, neither is it simply a great civilization which we can examine with detached curiosity from the outside. Europe is the seat of our own civilization: it is ourselves. The social scientists in a School of European Studies are anxious to join the Common Market; the students of literature, historians and philosophers have never left it. Ideally, perhaps, a School of European Studies might be a School of European and American (including Latin American) Studies, or of Western Studies, to cover not only Europe but all her brawny and obstreperous children as well. But life is short, and degree courses are still shorter, and no academic organization reflects adequately the unity of knowledge. *Antiquam exquirite matrem.* The concern of European Studies is the root and stock of our culture.

The educational task of the present generation, to which the new universities bear witness, can be described in two ways. At the more

---

[1] David Hawkes, *Chinese: Classical, Modern and Humane*, Oxford (1961), p. 23.

superficial level, it is the purely academic business of cutting new paths through the wood – of gaining some vantage-point from which both old intellectual specialisms and the expanding frontiers of knowledge can be seen in a coherent relationship. But we must not mislead ourselves into supposing that to redraw the map of learning can replace principles of choice about the journeys we want to use the map for. At a deeper level, the task is to satisfy the educational needs of students as persons, to enable them to make sense of their lives, and to find a creative order in the knowledge they acquire and in their own experience. One way of encouraging the discovery of such an order is through the critical study of the values of our civilization, of their development and some of the works in which they find protean expression.

The idea of a School of European Studies attracts different people for different reasons. There are copious suggestions about the interests it should serve and the shape it should have. But if it is to deserve its name, and make its proper contribution to the needs of our time, a School of European Studies will not be primarily a school of regional studies, nor of social studies, nor of linguistic training, nor the seat of a school of interpreters, nor a propaedeutic to membership of the European Community. In due measure it will partake of most of these. But it will be primarily a School of Humanities.

II

To treat European civilization as the frame of undergraduate studies presents interesting problems. It is our own civilization, and therefore more difficult in some ways, if more easy in others, to get a total view of. It is a multi-lingual civilization, and not many undergraduates will know more than one foreign language. Its component national cultures are so rich that they can be spoken of as civilizations in their own right, and may seem units of study as valuable as, and more manageable than, European civilization as a whole. Its boundaries are uncertain. Should it for teaching purposes include the nations of the British Isles, in a university where there is a School of English Studies as well as a School of European? The answer has happily been yes. Does it include Russia, which can for some purposes be grouped academically with non-European studies? This was decided affirmatively at the outset, but the syllabus difficulties flowing from the decision have not all been settled. Again, what are its limits in time? Does it naturally include medieval and classical studies? The initial terms of reference of the School were an emphasis on modern Europe; but it was immediately clear that the earlier phases would have in principle to be included, though the consequences are far from having been worked out.

The syllabus of the School of European Studies has been devised on certain fundamental principles, which may be described as follows:

1. Every undergraduate in the School, whatever his major subject, must have a sound knowledge of one modern European language other than English. He is examined in this language both in the preliminary and final examinations, and it controls his choice of papers in literature, of certain papers in history, and of the European country in which the social scientist will specialize.

2. Europe as a whole is taken as the unit of study where possible, rather than any of its national constituents, in order to transcend so far as possible the necessary limitations of a unilingual approach to a multi-lingual civilization. An attempt is made to place the various national literatures in a comparative setting of European literature, and the compulsory periods of history are not national but European history.

3. Study of the past is combined with study of the present, an emphasis on contemporary Europe with a background of historical range. If a half of a liberal education in the twentieth century is to gain an understanding of the world we live in, the other half consists in breaking its influence, and finding deliverance from the tyranny of the immediate, the novel and the transitory. No undergraduate in the School, whatever his major discipline and however he makes his options, can escape some study of the culture of the past, including classical antiquity, and some study of the culture of the twentieth century.

4. The various disciplines, literary, historical, philosophical and social, are so far as possible combined, and the connections between them are emphasized. Every undergraduate has to offer at least one straight paper in history and one in philosophy. Most undergraduates have to offer a straight paper in literature. Every undergraduate has to offer two papers, one on the Modern European Mind and one on the European Tradition, of which the first combines the literary and philosophical, and the second the literary, philosophical, and historical approaches. If one is to look, in the School of European Studies, for a common thread, a centre of gravity, it might be found

in intellectual history, the region where literature, philosophy, history and social studies meet and cross-fertilize.

To illustrate these principles in the working out of the syllabus, it will be convenient to consider, first the linguistic qualification, secondly the major subjects, and lastly the background or contextual papers which are common to the School.

1. *The linguistic qualification*

The School of European Studies is likely to remain the chief, if not the only, School in which Sussex undergraduates will learn foreign languages;[1] it is the only School that has a linguistic qualification for admission. The languages it offers are at present French, German and Russian. Its undergraduate members may be divided into the modern linguists, i.e. those who are majoring in a foreign language (they are likely to be the largest single group for some time to come), and those who are majoring in something else. The latter, English specialists, historians, geographers, etc., offer a modern European language, in which they are examined, and which governs their choice of certain papers in history and literature of the country in whose economy, politics or geography they wish to specialize. Thus it is not only necessary for prospective modern linguists, but also desirable for all students entering the School of European Studies, that they should have an A level in the language they will offer. (There will always be exceptional cases in which this requirement may be waived, and it is possible that Russian, whose teaching in schools is less well developed, will provide such cases especially.)

Language work is an integral part of the degree course in European Studies. The preliminary examination includes, beside the two papers on history and philosophy common to all Arts Schools, a third paper on European literature and a fourth in translation. In the final examination there is a single translation paper, including prose translation both from and into the language for modern linguists. Of those majoring in other subjects only a reading knowledge of the language is required, and for them the paper consists of two longer passages of prose for translation from the language. Modern linguists will also submit a dissertation in their language, to be written during the year they are required to spend abroad; and will as well undergo an oral examination. In preparation for this, all students in

[1] The School of African and Asian Studies will probably not teach languages in its early years.

the School do a language 'collection' at the beginning of every term and there are language classes in addition to tutorials. Those who are not modern linguists read for these classes a book carefully chosen for its relation to the other work they are doing in the same term. For example, historians studying the seventeenth and eighteenth centuries may read selections from the Memoirs of Saint-Simon or *Le Siècle de Louis Quatorze*; someone majoring in English and working for the paper on Tragedy, whose foreign language is German, may read Nietzsche's *Die Geburt der Tragödie*.

It is not easy to teach languages, at the undergraduate level, simply as a tool for modern studies. The subjects conventionally known as 'modern languages' are primarily a literary discipline, however indispensable a part linguistic training plays in them. Teachers of modern languages commonly hold that language is best taught by means of literature, which means books intrinsically worth reading; and they do not welcome the task of providing a purely linguistic coaching for economists and scientists. Nor is the need supplied by audio-visual teaching mechanisms, whose value is limited to developing full competence in spoken language.[1] The linguistic aim of the School of European Studies, for those who are not modern language specialists, is to develop reading ability, to stimulate the imagination as well as to teach the language, and to produce historians and social scientists whose total cultural experience includes as much literature as possible.

It is now generally accepted by Education Authorities that a degree in modern languages is a four-year course, one year being spent abroad in a country of the language that is being studied. Among the purposes of the year abroad is that undergraduates should gain a sound and flexible command of the contemporary idiomatic language. The difficulties in the case of Russian may perhaps be overcome by entering into a special relationship with a particular Russian university. But a degree in European Studies requires in principle a year abroad for all who take it, whatever their major subject. It is hoped that historians, economists and geographers, no less than specialists in French or German, may in due course have the opportunity to live and study in the country whose affairs they are concerned with.

---

[1] The University has planned from the outset to have a language laboratory, which will be part of the Arts Building under construction. Its most immediate value is likely to be promoting adequate oral Russian.

2. *The major subjects*

The various major subjects are intended to afford mastery of a single discipline, and produce specialists as competent as those who have been through a conventional single subject honours course. The background or contextual papers are meant to enhance the value of the major subjects by setting them in a wider framework of related studies. To make room for the contextual papers, certain papers that are usually part of a single subject honours degree have been abandoned. Modern linguists have been relieved of the philology, the history of the language, and its medieval origins. Historians have sacrificed the continuous history of any political unit, the separate study of English history, and such separate aspects as economic history and the history of political ideas. Economists, political scientists and geographers have lost some of their spread into subsidiary disciplines and special subjects. What they may have gained instead may appear shortly.

The major subjects in the three modern studies, economics, politics and sociology, and geography, belong to Social Studies as well as European Studies; and it seems likely that the majority of students taking them will be in the Social Studies School. The three have a similar pattern. Of the five papers in each, two are common to the subject in both Social and European Studies: Economic Theory and The Economics of Developed Countries; Comparative Government and 'Social Structure and Social Change'; and the Physical Basis of Geography and Human Geography. The other three papers, when the subjects are taken in European Studies, are regional. Economists and political scientists together do the Economic and Political History of Europe since 1945, and 'European Institutions and the Economics of Integration'. More concentrated study is afforded by a fifth paper on either the economy, or the politics and society, of a single European country. Geographers have a range of choice for these papers. If these three kinds of specialist are able to spend a year abroad, they will be required either to write a dissertation on the country where they spend their year, or to pursue a geographical project there. These modern subjects within the European School provide an intensive study of Europe since the Second World War, with a special emphasis on developments under the Treaty of Rome. With the broad background of the contextual papers, and the associated literary and linguistic training, they may appeal to students with flexible minds who are not only attracted by

European affairs, but want to understand them in some cultural and historical perspective.

The major subject in philosophy has a common shape in the three Arts Schools, and is more flexible than any other major. It may consist of five, four, or three papers. The core of the subject lies in the two papers 'Logic and Theory of Meaning' and 'Descartes to Kant', which have to be included if four or more papers are offered. If less than five are offered, the remainder are chosen from additional papers in literature or history. This elastic major subject has been developed to meet the needs of students with philosophical interests but without the desire to become professional philosophers, and it may provide a precedent for other subjects to be treated similarly.

The major subjects in history and modern languages have been planned in close relationship; several papers are common to each, and it is impossible to describe one without diverging into the other. A history syllabus has to combine general span with local depth, a knowledge of the wider horizons of historical change with detailed study of selected periods or problems. The major subject in history consists of two papers on a chosen special subject, one paper on a chosen 'general subject', and a paper on each of two chosen periods of European history. The special subject is the familiar mode of detailed study and training in historical method. It consists in the scrutiny of a confined period or problem with prescribed original sources. All the special subjects are chosen with a view to authorities in a language other than English, and candidates have to choose their special subject in accordance with the language they are offering. An exception occurs in the case of the Italian Renaissance. This has been put on the list because of its intrinsic merits as a subject of study, despite Italian not being taught in the University; and it is clear that there are students who will willingly acquire Italian in vacation courses or visits to Italy, in order to be able to do it.

The 'general subject'[1] is a new kind of paper invented to supply

---

[1] The attentive reader will perhaps wish to call to mind the differences between the major subject, which is a discipline that forms the core of the degree and controls half the work for the final examination; the special subject, which is so to speak the core of the historian's major subject, being his area of most detailed study; and the general subject. These last two concern only historians. By an inconvenient usage, the word 'specialist' is appropriated to the undergraduate in his relation to his major (not his special) subject.

the need for the study of a continuous span of historical development. Ideally, the need would be met by a broad sweep of general European history, but this runs the risk of becoming so thin and patchy that it fails in its purpose. An alternative would be a selection of papers on national histories, but this was rejected because it is desired in European Studies to escape wherever possible the organization of knowledge according to national limits. Instead of national evolutions, other longitudinal themes have been selected in European history: the relations of church and state; the balance of power, or the development of the diplomatic community; aristocracies and bourgeoisies, or transformations of the European social structure; enterprise and industry; labour movements; science, technology and society; the universities. Two more of these subjects may serve the purpose of links between European Studies and other Schools: Britain in Europe, as a bridge to the School of English Studies, and Europe and the World, as a bridge perhaps to the School of African and Asian Studies. Each of these is a theme or aspect of European history as a whole, unconfined to any single nation. Each is capable of being studied in relation to a wide range of European countries, including the British Isles. Each exemplifies the coherence of European civilization, the common responses and the mutual interaction of its various peoples. Moreover, each is capable of being traced through modern history down to the present day. Each may be considered either as a historical development with contemporary relevance, or as a contemporary problem seen in historical perspective. Each becomes problem-type rather than period-type history. It is intended, therefore, that the general subjects will both illustrate the unity of European history, and combine historical with contemporary interest.

It is convenient at this juncture to explain some alternatives to the general subject, since the syllabus now loses its disciplined symmetry and offers the historian in European Studies a choice between different kinds of paper. Time will probably do some stream-lining here. There are two substitutes for the general paper. One is the 'topic in history and literature'. This is a paper with the quite different aim of showing an inter-disciplinary approach to a subject of small scale where literary and historical interests meet. It is a kind of paper which will bring historians and modern linguists to work together, probably in a seminar. The historians choose their topic in accordance with the language they are offering, for the sources will as far as possible be in the original. Examples of topics in French history and literature are 'Politics and Religion in the Age of Pascal' and 'Vichy: Occupation and Resistance, 1940–44'. Examples in German or Russian history and literature are 'Naturalism and the Industrialization of Germany' and 'Writers and Revolution, 1905–30'. Another kind of topic is being considered, on Contemporary France and Contemporary Germany. These would be comparable to the compulsory paper in English Studies on Contemporary Britain or Contemporary America. It might later seem desirable to prescribe these topics for specialists in economics, politics and geography.

In both French and German, as well as in the School of English Studies, there are also topics concerned with Romanticism and its social and political context. An attempt to fuse them into a single common topic with some such title as 'The French Revolution and the Romantic Movement', has led instead to the notion of a future paper in comparative literature on European Romanticism. Perhaps this illustrates a danger that when history and literature are studied in conjunction, one may submerge the other. Literature may be made subservient as merely illustrative of social history, or history may be reduced to noting the impact of events on literary opinion. How to avoid the danger in each particular case still has to be worked out.

The second alternative to the general subject is a paper in regional history. Russian history is a point where the principle of emphasizing the unity of European civilization breaks down. It has been so eccentric to the general development of Europe that it provides an exceptional case for a paper in a national history. For convenience Russian history has been divided into three stretches, divided at the reign of Peter the Great and at the liberation of the serfs. A Russian specialist may choose one of these instead of a topic in history and literature. There is also, in the School of English and American Studies a paper on American History since 1783, and in the School of Social Studies a paper on Asian History since 1800. A historian in European Studies may choose one of these papers in a regional history in place of a general subject. Here is a postern, however inadequate, opening on the world history which is one of the most desirable and difficult things to fit into a history syllabus.

Lastly we come to the periods of European history, which are the staple of history in the School of European Studies. Two must be chosen by history specialists; one must be chosen as a contextual paper by every undergraduate majoring in another subject; and they form also part of the diet of historians in the other Schools. They are overlapping periods of about a century each, to be studied as integral history, cultural and intellectual as well as social and political. Moreover they are defined as comprising the history of the British Isles to the same extent as that of other European nations. The choice in framing historical periods is between span and depth, and a tutorial term of eight essays on so restricted a period as a century can lay a foundation of detailed understanding which makes a more satisfying historical education than scantier knowledge of a wider field.

Most of the periods are of modern European history, since 1500; the most recent is from 1871 to the present day. But two have been added, one of Greek and one of Roman history, and have answered a distinct demand from undergraduates. In due course medieval history will have its place. Appreciating the differences as well as the likenesses between epochs and cultures is an essential part of historical education, to counteract provincialism in time. To study a period of medieval history, so different in intellectual cast and economic structure from the modern world, and recognize beneath the contrasts the same social processes at work; or to study a period of classical history, the fall of the Athenian Empire or the decline of the Roman Republic, intriguingly similar to the present in its international dissensions or class conflicts, and find beneath the parallels an alien and even outlandish thought-world, are paths to historical understanding.

One further paper needs mention here, devised for historians and philosophers and extended to English specialists in European Studies. As they have to take one paper in philosophy, so they must also take one paper in a foreign literature in accordance with the language they offer. (Unfortunately no room has been found for it in the syllabus of those majoring in modern studies.) It is a paper both broader and simpler than those taken by modern linguists. The French Imagination is based on selected readings from Pascal and Voltaire, and from a choice of Racine, Balzac, Hugo and Proust. The German Tradition studies the characteristic preoccupations of the German literary imagination as these appear in Goethe, Hölderlin, Nietzsche, Rilke and Mann. The Russian Tradition studies selected works of the great nineteenth century novelists and of the poets from Derzhavin to Pasternak. The aim of this paper, in its three forms, is to analyse a particular mode of literary experience, and to give the undergraduate one hopes some lasting imaginative stimulus.

The principles underlying the major subjects in French, German and Russian are suggested by the literature paper in the preliminary examination, 'Critical Reading: European Tragedy and Fiction'. This is taken by all undergraduates meaning to enter the School of European Studies. It provides, for modern linguists, a foundation to their major subject, and for the rest, a general introduction to European literary culture. It seeks to harness the freshman's initial enthusiasm and curiosity, by setting chosen masterpieces of literature within a European tradition, and giving an introduction to the concepts, idiom and problems of literary criticism. As examples of tragedy, the common texts are *Oedipus Rex*, *King Lear* and *Hedda Gabler*; as examples of the novel, the *Odyssey*, selections from the *Decameron*, *Emma* and *Madame Bovary*. All undergraduates study these, as well as further texts in the language of their choice. Here, and in the major subjects in the modern languages, the aim is to discourage students from regarding the study of literature as a listless accumulation of background facts, and to expose them to the full impact of great literary works. The goal is to produce not scholars, in the technical sense, but scrupulous and humane readers, open to a variety of moral and aesthetic experience, and capable of arriving at true judgment.

Perhaps the single most difficult task in the European Studies syllabus has been to cram a sound major subject in French language and literature within the limits of five papers; for French is a richer literature than German or Russian, though not richer than English. For all these languages, including English, the papers are arranged not by periods but by genres. This saves the literature from being pickled in the alcohol of literary history, and allows a greater concentration on purely literary categories of form and expression. Obviously it has its own dangers against which the student must be warned; a literary genre is not a literary essence, and it occupies a different place in the total culture of the country at different times. Each language has a single paper each on Poetry, Fiction and Drama. (In the case of Russian, instead of a paper on the drama there is one on Twentieth Century Russian Literature.) A fourth paper deals with one of the summits of each literature – Shakespeare, Goethe, Pushkin; and for French, the analogue has been found in the tradition of moral discourse exemplified by Montaigne, Pascal and

Rousseau. The fifth paper is the topic in history and literature, the paper in Russian history as an alternative for Russian specialists. It is worth recalling here that modern linguists also have their translation paper, an oral examination, and the dissertation written during the year abroad.

The most important negative conclusion in the first year of the School of European Studies was that the Sussex system does not permit of specializing in two languages. In this respect therefore Sussex cannot offer as much as a conventional department of modern languages. The reason lies in the nature of the Sussex degree, with its division of work for the final examination equally between the major subject and the general background, the core and the context. This division rests on the principle that anything less than half an undergraduate's work is insufficient to qualify him for an honours degree in his major subject.[1] A degree in two languages would require either that the background papers should be forfeited, to find room for the second language, or a reduction in their number, which would in effect replace the dual with a triple pattern. It was reluctantly decided that a modern linguist in a single language who has had the historical and philosophical background is more valuable than a modern linguist with two languages who has not. A partial remedy is to make the background papers as rich as possible in comparative literature, and in practice every encouragement is given to an undergraduate who wishes to keep up a reading knowledge of a second language by attending classes in it. But the question of accommodating two languages within the Sussex syllabus is likely to require further consideration, and will obtrude itself again if or when classical studies are introduced.

A compensating discovery, also arrived at after the University had started teaching, was that English is a European language; or rather, that the major subject in English literature, which most of those who take it will take within the School of English and American Studies, could fit no less well against the background papers of European Studies. These students, like any others in the School, need the linguistic qualification and have to offer one European language other than English. But there is evidence that this is going to be an increasingly popular way of reading English.

---

[1] A modification of this principle has already been described in the case of philosophy.

3. *The contextual papers*

The unity of the School is found in the background or contextual papers. These are intended, not as disparate and disconnected morsels of learning, but to enrich each major subject and make an integral part of the degree. It will have been noticed that there is no absolute division between contextual papers and papers belonging to the major subjects. The period of European history and the philosophy option are specialist papers for some and background papers for others. With this qualification, there are five common papers, taken by every undergraduate whatever his major subject. Translation, philosophy, and the period of history are three of them.

The remaining two contextual papers are *sui generis*, and perhaps represent the aims of the School better than any others. One of them is the Modern European Mind. This originated in the School of English Studies, but at once fell into place in the European scheme. The planning of this course, the defining of the field, the selection of the set texts, has been perhaps the most arduous and complicated collective enterprise relating to the syllabus that the University has known. It has involved many interests – literature, philosophy, the history of ideas, psychology, theology; discussions between more than a third of the Arts faculty; the elaboration of a lecture 'circus' throughout the year with eleven participants, not including visiting lecturers; and a tutorial scheme embracing some nine tutors from different branches of the faculty. And the weekly lectures on the Modern European Mind at noon on Wednesdays and Thursdays, the audience of undergraduates and faculty packed on the steps of an inadequate lecture-theatre in the unfinished Physics Building, the excited straggle in argument to the refectory afterwards for lunch, and the reverberations of the discussion in unexpected places all the week, are the most remarkable evidence of intellectual vitality that the University can yet show.

There has been a slight difference of focus between the two Schools which combine to teach for the paper. For English Studies, it is primarily an inquiry into the position of the artist and the intellectual in modern industrial democratic society. For European Studies, it is governed by the rather wider idea of the alienation of man himself in the modern world. The English Studies view of the subject led to an original definition in terms of 'the main currents of European thought and sensibility since about 1880'. The European Studies view was inclined to push back the *terminus a quo* to the 1840s, when the reaction against Hegel began which is illustrated in different ways by the younger Marx and by Kierkegaard. There is not a clash of conceptions here: they are concentric circles. The fruit of the debate is a highly selective reading list which extends from Marx's *Economic and Philosophical Manuscripts of 1844*, and Kierkegaard's *Fear and Trembling*, to Rilke, Sartre, Camus and *Dr Zhivago*. The undergraduate café talk when Mr Betjeman was at Oxford in the twenties has been distilled into a syllabus:

> 'Coffee and Ulysses, Tennyson, Joyce,
> Alpha-minded and other-dimensional,
> Freud or Calvary, take your choice.'

The second paper, the European Tradition, might be sub-titled 'The Classical and Medieval European Mind'. In the Modern European Mind, undergraduates can wrestle with the dark angel of the Zeitgeist; in this other paper, they can throw off the stranglehold of the present, and become familiar with different orbits of thought. Moreover, a syllabus with an emphasis on the history and literature of Europe since the Renaissance, posed the need for a paper to show that the Renaissance was not the beginning of European civilization. It would be a foreshortened education that failed to suggest that to start one's study of Europe with Leonardo, the Humanists or Montaigne is to break in on a debate that has been going on a long time. A background paper was needed to illustrate the foundations of European culture. What form should it take? It might have been a paper in social history; a study of the evolution of Europe as a distinct social unit. It might have explored some strand in the European tradition which is of particular contemporary interest, such as the development of scientific inquiry and theories of the universe. But a tradition has been chosen which, throughout most of Europe's history, has been held central to its civilization: the tradition of moral thought. Three set texts have been chosen: Plato's *Apology* and *Phaedo*, the *Aeneid*, and the *Divine Comedy*. These have a triple purpose. They serve as historical texts: as introductions to the understanding of Greece, Rome and medieval Christendom. They illustrate the dominant tradition of European thought before the seventeenth century, and at the same time throw light upon one another. Above all, they afford the student a contact with three of the great formative minds of Europe, and reflect a conviction that a syllabus which neglects such opportunities is immeasurably impoverished. For undergraduates whose interests are in social rather than literary studies, an alternative set of texts has been added: the *Republic*, selections from the political writings of Aquinas, and Machiavelli's *Prince*. These have been chosen to illustrate the dual political tradition of Europe in which modern social and international doctrines take their place.

Here, once again, the eccentricity of Russia in European civilization has to be recognized. She has other foundations than Western Europe. A different paper has therefore been devised for Russian specialists, the Russian Foundations, which examines the culture of pre-Petrine Russia and its Byzantine derivations. Among the works to be studied in whole or in part are the *De administrando imperii* of Constantine Porphyrogenitus, *Digenis Akritas*, the *Slovo o polku igoreve*, the *Russian Primary Chronicle* and the *Life of the Archpriest Avvakum*. The culture of Old Russia was iconic rather than literary, and due account is taken of its art and religion as well as of its literature and political theory.

The European Foundations and the Modern European Mind, like the paper in literature for the preliminary examination, accept the necessity of teaching comparative literature mainly in translation. In the Modern European Mind, members of the School of European Studies will be encouraged to read texts in the original when these are in the language of their choice, but this is not required, and in the nature of the case will concern only a few of the texts set. In the paper on the European Tradition, all the texts are to be studied in translation; though the Dent's Temple Classics edition of Dante, with text and translation facing, has made it possible to prescribe that candidates will be expected to recognize quotations in the original, and has encouraged some of them to launch upon Italian. Indeed, an unexpected discovery in teaching this paper has been the amount of A level Latin that is brought to the university, usually to atrophy from lack of any stimulus to keeping it up, but here gladly recovered to assist a more extensive and philosophical study of Virgil than is common in working for the GCE.

It has been difficult to arrange for the teaching of these two papers. Each has an unusual spread – the European Tradition in spanning however selectively the whole of classical and medieval thought; the Modern European Mind in embracing four national literatures and more intellectual disciplines. Each however is an experiment in demonstrating the unity of knowledge. Its educational value lies largely in the undergraduate submitting himself to the experience of the set texts under the guidance of the same tutor, who can point the contrasts and draw the parallels, and show what unity may or may not be discoverable in them. It would be unfortunate for the teaching of these papers to be fragmented among specialists. To go from one expert to another, who did not themselves need each to be interested in more than a single department of learning, would suggest to the undergraduate that when his teachers individually are unable to comprehend such a diversity of material, he himself cannot be expected to make sense of it either. A syllabus that breaks down some of the compartments of specialization, in a word, presupposes teachers who are something more than specialists. It requires teachers who will not hold themselves bound by the austere and perhaps old-fashioned doctrine that a man is not entitled to teach a subject in which he has not got a degree, and who will respond to the excitement of extending their interests a certain way beyond their covenanted academic frontiers. This is the only way that new 'subjects' can be created in a new university with a small faculty.

III

What has been described is the pattern of a complicated syllabus which tries to give proper scope to different interests. The BA in European Studies is far from complete. It ought to include Italian and Spanish, classical studies and medieval studies, the history of art and possibly Soviet studies. Nor is the syllabus complete within its present limits. It embodies some unanswered questions, and some alternative answers between which experience may in due course suggest a choice. It is a flexible and provisional instrument that expects growth and change. A new university can probably experiment and keep its syllabus under more constant review than an older institution.

Even something so humdrum, utilitarian and committee-saddled as a university syllabus can do with a vision, which may be expressed in an epigraph.

> Drum, da gehaüft sind rings
> Die Gipfel der Zeit,
> Und die Liebsten nahe wohnen, ermattend auf
> Getrenntesten Bergen,
> So gieb unschuldig Wasser,
> O Fittige gieb uns treuesten Sinns
> Hinüberzugehn und wiederzukehren.

Therefore, since round about
Are heaped the summits of Time
And the most loved live near, growing faint
On mountains most separate,
Give us innocent water,
O pinions give us, with minds most faithful
To cross over and to return.[1]

This is all very well, say the stern voices of democratic opinion, Treasury control and national need. What kind of graduate do you hope to produce? To attempt any description nowadays of the cultivated or educated man is to launch upon waters that are perpetually agitated by controversy and ridicule, by social change and clashes of belief. Sometimes the risk may seem worth taking. It is prompted here by some wise sentences in Professor Levenson's biography of the Chinese historian Liang Ch'i-Ch'ao. 'Every man,' he observes, 'has an emotional commitment to history and an intellectual commitment to value, and he tries to make these commitments coincide. A stable society is one whose members would choose, on universal principles, the particular culture which they inherit.'[2] In the unstable society of the twentieth century, let us say, a graduate in European Studies from a British university should be a man or woman who, by way of a sound training in a certain discipline, has learned to explore the particular culture he inherits and to subject it to the sympathetic criticism of universal principles.

---

[1] From Hölderlin's poem *Patmos*, translated by Michael Hamburger; to be published in 1965 in the definitive edition of his *Hölderlin: Poems* by Routledge and Kegan Paul Ltd.

[2] Joseph R. Levenson, *Liang Ch'i-Ch'ao and the Mind of Modern China* (Cambridge, Mass., 1953), p. 1.

ROGER BLIN-STOYLE

7. *The School of Physical Sciences*

To be able to participate in the academic planning for a new university is a rare privilege and a considerable challenge. The opportunity is there to make sweeping innovations at all levels unencumbered by an existing scheme of things and uninfluenced by any local tradition. In some cases these innovations may be widely recognized as urgent reforms and may already be taking place, albeit slowly, within long established universities. In others there may exist quite conflicting opinions as to their merit, so that their introduction then becomes experimental backed primarily by the personal beliefs of those concerned with sponsoring them. Only experience can judge their effectiveness, and in writing about the School of Physical Sciences it should be stressed that this experience has spread over a year only and that changes, although not major ones, are already under way.

At this stage in the development of the University changes can be effected easily – the University is still small and flexible, and every advantage must be taken of this in order to iron out inconsistencies and to rectify mistakes. For, unfortunately, this state of affairs will not last and in a few years' time when rapid expansion has ceased, the machinery for change will be much more unwieldy, a scheme of things will already be well-established and even minor changes will be difficult to accomplish. It is, therefore, essential to preserve a state of flux in the early years, so that the final crystallization is to a satisfactory and worthwhile form.

Our major concern in the School of Physical Sciences in its year of planning and year of actual existence, has been threefold. The foremost problem has been the design of the various courses and, in particular, the vexed question of the amount of specialization to be allowed in a particular science. Next, and currently of topical importance through the activities of the Hale Committee, has been the issue of the way in which teaching should be carried out. Finally, there has been the planning for research and postgraduate instruction. It is with these three aspects of the School of Physical Sciences that this article is primarily concerned.

The basic idea embraced by all the planning which has taken place for teaching and research, is that physical scientists and mathematicians educated within the University shall be 'complete' in the fullest sense of the word. That is to say they will really understand the fundamentals of their subject, have acquired an intuitive feeling for it, have a well-developed intellectual curiosity about it, and see its relevance not only to other scientific fields but also to the general problems of twentieth century life. It is *certainly not* the intention to produce graduates who only have a nodding acquaintance with science in the broad and little understanding. The courses are far removed from those of a general degree, and take the study of an undergraduate's major subject to at least specialist degree standard. Courses patterned in this way are, to some extent, vocational and this surely is what they should be. It is a rare occasion to find someone who reads a scientific subject at university, but intends to make no practical use of his knowledge afterwards. The use he makes of it may be minimal – he may become an administrator or a Civil Servant and so make little direct use of his knowledge. But his full understanding of scientific method, scientific concepts and, incidentally, of scientists, will pay enormous dividends in carrying out his job.

How then is a 'complete' scientist to be educated, and how in particular is the School of Physical Sciences setting about this task? *Understanding* is the key word in the foregoing description. What is meant by this can, perhaps, be explained most easily by looking at the way in which scientific knowledge progresses and is built up. Basically it is as follows. Experimental data become available, sometimes as naturally occurring phenomena but more usually because of the efforts of an experimenter. An attempt is then made to correlate these data by means of a theory which will be based on a number of postulates. Newton's Law of gravitational attraction together with Classical Mechanics provides the theory in terms of which experimental observations on the motion of planetary bodies can be correlated and predicted. An atomic nucleus surrounded by a cloud of electrons moving according to quantum mechanics is the theory according to which a great many physical and chemical processes can be described. Many other simple examples could be quoted, but the essential point to be noted is that the success of a theory is measured by the extent to which it can account for known experimental results and predict the outcome of future experiments. Should it not be successful in either of these respects, then it has to be modified or maybe radically changed. More experiments are carried out to test its predictions and so on, the pendulum swinging continuously backwards and forwards between theory and experiment as scientific knowledge evolves.

Some theories are very simple in content, although extremely powerful. The atomic concept, for example, allows a very satisfactory description of chemical reactions to be given; it enables some understanding of these processes to be achieved. The description of the atomic nucleus in terms of a collection of neutrons and protons bound together by powerful nuclear forces paves the way to understanding most nuclear properties. On a somewhat larger scale, there is the recent work in the field of Biology, which enables us to understand the nature of the genetic material responsible for evolutionary processes in terms of the properties of highly complex organic molecules.

It is *understanding* of this kind in which phenomena at one level are interpreted and described in terms of processes and structures at a more fundamental level, which needs to be developed in the scientist. Such an understanding is one which not only takes him from one division of his subject to another more fundamental one, but also ultimately takes him beyond its conventional bounds. For example, the biologist in his attempts to understand the nature of living organisms, their structure, their varied manifestations and the fundamental mechanism of heredity, has been forced to seek the aid of the chemist and physicist – indeed many eminent biologists are chemists or physicists by training – because he has found that real understanding can only be achieved in terms of the physical and chemical properties of complicated molecular structures. In the last few years, it is in the borderline fields of biochemistry and biophysics that some of the most exciting developments in science have taken place. To prosecute research in these fields, however, requires competence in contemporary physics and chemistry, a sound knowledge of mathematics and a broad grasp of general biological principles. Unfortunately to acquire such a spectrum of knowledge is virtually impossible within the current framework of university education, where even the strictly biological sciences are frequently quite dissociated from one another. Similarly, the chemist at the fundamental level, has perforce to resort to and fully understand the standard concepts of physics in order to interpret basic chemical mechanisms and phenomena. The physicist, on pursuing some aspects of his subject into more complex and borderline regions, may well find that he is involved in what others call chemistry. The borderlines between the different sciences are diffuse, and science cannot advance or full understanding be achieved without work in and across these regions.

To ensure that an undergraduate acquires understanding of this kind and to leave it at that is, however, to achieve only partial success. Further to this must be encouraged a motivation towards wanting to understand. He (or she) must be imbued with a spirit of inquiry – a spirit sadly lacking in the raw schoolboy and school-girl material which makes its way into our universities. The scarcity of university places and the resulting fierce competition – judged primarily on the basis of a boy or girl's performance in the Advanced and Scholarship levels of the General Certificate of Education – place a premium on distinguished performance in this examination. Little time for inquiry and for the pursuit of interesting side-trails is left for the potential undergraduate. Close attention to the dogmatic utterances of school master and textbook is the norm, for this, on the whole, brings highest A-level achievement. Inquiry, judging by entrance interviews, not, incidentally, only in this university, is rarely encouraged at all and is frequently stifled. So long as this state of affairs prevails, it is one of the primary tasks of science courses at a university to stimulate – even shock – its undergraduates into a militantly questioning, doubting and inquiring frame of mind.

A course built around these two basic pillars of understanding and inquiry cannot but succeed in producing technically good scientists, provided that the undergraduate material is of a sufficiently high quality and that the scientific spectrum studied is suitably chosen. It is with this latter point that opinions differ rather widely. On the one hand are those who believe that the only worthwhile university education is that based on an extreme specialist degree in which study is confined virtually to one subject only. On the other hand are those who support the general degree course in its various mani-festations. In this latter case at least two subjects, and frequently more, are studied throughout the entirety of the university course. No more time is allowed for this, however, and so the depth of study of the various subjects is rather shallow but, it is argued, the breadth of knowledge acquired compensates to some extent for this inadequacy.

Faced with these two basic alternatives, what choice does an undergraduate make? The answer, and its implications, are well known, but frequently the latter are not publicly admitted. Almost invariably the able student will opt (and undoubtedly be encouraged) to take a specialist degree, and it is the less able who are guided to the general degree course or who are relegated into it from the specialist course. Attempts are frequently made to make the general degree respectable, but so long as it remains the dumping ground for lapsed specialists they are unlikely to succeed. The effect of all this is that virtually all professional scientists in this country are recruited from specialist degree courses.

But, in the light of the earlier discussion, it is not at all obvious that such a course is by any means ideal for this purpose – its outlook is in many respects too narrow. On the other hand, the conventional general degree course is far too superficial. So, in the School of Physical Sciences, an attempt has been made to shape the courses so as to incorporate the best features of both specialist and general degree course.

The approach adopted can be summarized briefly as follows. In the BSC degree course, an undergraduate 'majors' in one or other of the subjects physics, chemistry or mathematics, where by majoring is meant that he spends around two-thirds of his time working at his chosen subject. His remaining time is divided between three activities. Firstly, he must equip himself with sufficient mathematical knowledge to understand his major subject. Secondly, he is required to look at the borderlines of his major field of study to see its relationship with another science. Finally, he is encouraged to look further afield and to see the role his specialism plays within the whole structure of scientific knowledge, to achieve some understanding of the interaction of science in general with the world at large, on the human, political, industrial or sociological front and, in a small way, to indulge in some non-scientific work.

Before settling down to the main part of his course, an undergraduate spends two terms of preliminary study, in which stress is laid upon the two unifying aspects of all science – its language and its substance. The language of science is mathematics – all its theories are ultimately formulated in mathematical terms – and every scientist, whether he be physicist, chemist, engineer or biologist, must have a certain minimum mathematical knowledge. This roughly comprises basic calculus, the theory of functions and elementary mechanics. As for the substance of science, this is the material of the world around us; it is matter in all its forms and aggregations, both animate and inanimate. The approach to this study of matter is from the atomic viewpoint, and makes a distinct break for the erstwhile schoolboy or schoolgirl with the present unexciting A-level treatment of science. Throughout the course the accent is on *understanding* the properties and structure of matter in terms of fundamental atomic concepts. The macroscopic world is interpreted in terms of the microscopic. Ideas are introduced, which in more conventional courses may not be encountered until perhaps the final year. Even so, every effort is made to put them on to at least a semi-quantitative footing. The course is unquestionably exciting for the undergraduate, and it is planned to virtually shock him into an inquiring frame of mind. It gives him his first real glimpse of the frontiers of scientific research, and he realizes the vast complexities ahead, and that there are many unanswered questions.

He does not readily accept the ideas presented; many of them are foreign to the way of thinking and approach to science that he has been used to. It is only after contact over a considerable period of time that he is ready to accept them as part of the established pattern of knowledge. For this reason alone, it is advantageous to introduce them at such an early stage in his scientific education. The period of non-acceptance can be a difficult one for the undergraduate, and care has to be taken that he is continually reassured that his bewilderment and confusion are natural and that all will be resolved in time. It is, perhaps, relevant to remark that only with a tutorial system can assurance of this kind be given effectively.

The study of mathematics and matter represents two-thirds of this preliminary course. For the rest, the undergraduate is free to study either advanced mathematics or chemistry, the choice being determined by the combination of subjects he intends to study in the remainder of his university career. At the end of his preliminary course, which comprises in full two terms and two vacations, is an examination, which determines whether he shall be allowed to go on to the main part of his course. He is also, in general, required to decide at that time which shall be his major subject.

The treatment of the major subject is, on the whole, conventional except, perhaps, that there is more accent on fundamentals than is usual. A deep understanding of basic principles of the science being studied, rather than a detailed knowledge of techniques and applications, is the main aim. For example, an undergraduate majoring in chemistry is not required to commit to memory the details of a multiplicity of natural products; an undergraduate majoring in physics is not expected to acquire a vast knowledge of innumerable ways of measuring the surface tension of a small quantity of liquid, or of measuring the thermal conductivity of a bad conductor and so forth. But great stress is laid on his ability to understand the nature of surface tension and the way in which heat is conducted in a solid. This is not to say that an undergraduate is to make no contact with experimental method. On the contrary, he will learn about and use modern experimental techniques and apparatus, but the syllabus is free from details of what can only be called 'old-fashioned techno-nology' – those experimental methods and techniques that give no insight into basic scientific understanding and which bear no relation to present day scientific experimentation. It is surprising to what a large extent in university degree courses the study and understanding of basic ideas and concepts is still neglected in favour of superficial, unrewarding and out-dated technology of this kind. The reason is, of course, that it is much more difficult to prune an existing syllabus than to set up a new one. This is where the new universities have a great advantage over their well-established fellow institutions.

The course in the major subject is also planned to instil into the undergraduate an intuitive sense of the science he is studying so that he can make, for example, a sensible 'guess' about the outcome of an experiment or calculation before it is completed. Such a sense can only be developed by continual contact with a subject, and constant exposure to its fundamental relationships and ideas. In the more quantitative sciences a ready knowledge of sizes is required, and an ability to make order of magnitude estimates – a facility only acquired by familiarizing the student with realistic numerical work. In the field of physics, for example, there is far too much accent in this country at the undergraduate level on abstract and elegant analytical work to the exclusion of approximate, but absolutely invaluable calculations about real – as distinct from artificial – physical problems.

The study of the additional scientific subjects is one to which a great deal of importance is attached. These subjects are not regarded as 'subsidiary' in the conventional sense, and their study continues for the full three-years of the BSc degree course, rather than being abandoned, as is more usual, at the end of the first or second year. This then breeds a right attitude towards this border-line work, and it is accepted by the undergraduate as an important and integral part of the course, rather than a hurdle to be surmounted and then forgotten. Apart from this, the continual contact with the subject throughout the degree course leads to a far deeper understanding and its relevance to the major subject – particularly to advanced concepts – becomes much more apparent. In detail the situation is that the chemist studies atomic structure, quantum mechanics and statistical mechanics to the same level and in the same courses as the physicist. Similarly, those physicists not concentrating on advanced mathematics follow courses in chemical spectroscopy and the chemistry of solids, and the mathematicians in general make a thorough study of a branch of physics (except for a few who are allowed to study economics) to the exclusion of the more useless, artificial and uninteresting branches of conventional applied mathematics.

If we turn to the wider aspects of the degree course, the prime factor here is that most science undergraduates will be concerned in their subsequent careers with more than purely scientific work. Some, indeed, will certainly find themselves in administrative positions in industry or in governmental establishments. It follows that all of them should be aware of the role of science and scientists in the life of the twentieth century. So, of course, should the non-scientist – they cannot escape the fact that they are living in a scientific and technological age. So, as a unifying influence between the Arts and the Sciences, every undergraduate in the University will follow a course of lectures, seminars and discussions contributed to by both the Science and Arts Faculties and dealing with such subjects as 'Science and Industry', 'Science and Government', 'The Moral Responsibility of the Scientist', 'The Impact of Science on Contemporary Thought' and so on. (Professor Briggs's chapter gives further information about the Arts-Science programme.)

This, then, is the basic BSc degree course in the School of Physical Sciences. Besides being a sound preparation for advanced specialist work, it is also, with its accent on fundamental scientific principles, on the interaction between different scientific fields and on the role of science in the world today, an education extremely appropriate for the undergraduate who will become an administrator, a civil servant or even a politician! There is a great dearth today of people with this kind of education – people who have, in addition to a knowledge of and sympathy for scientific method in one restricted field, also the ability to communicate with and understand the interests and motivation of scientists in different fields and of non-scientists. The courses being provided in the School of Physical Sciences can, we hope, remedy this deficiency.

It is quite clear, however, that in any university institution there must be provision for extreme specialist study. Such study is necessary for anyone who intends to take up a career as a professional scientist, and for such individuals, bearing in mind the rapid rate at which science is advancing and the tremendous amount of knowledge which has to be absorbed before any research can be embarked upon, a three-year course at university is just not enough. For this reason the University of Sussex has instituted a fourth year of extreme specialist study leading to the degree of MSc. It is expected that 30%–50% of our undergraduates in the School of Physical Sciences will take part in this course, which will carry them well beyond the level of the more conventional specialist degree course, and will provide the necessary advanced training for anyone intending to embark on a career as a research scientist.

A number of practical advantages over and above the purely intellectual benefits result from the arrangement of degree courses that has been described. There has always been a considerable tendency within universities and the outside worlds to regard a course smacking of non-specialization, even in a small way, as inferior to one which specializes in one of the standard divisions of scientific knowledge. As was remarked earlier, this has unfortunately been justified in so far as a good specialist honours degree of the latter kind has in the past been accepted as the passport to a career as a professional scientist, and has been, therefore, automatically the choice of the cleverer undergraduate, to the detriment of the general tone and reputation of the non-specialist course. But given the situation that all undergraduates follow the same type of course, then, even though it is not specialist in the conventional sense, no stigma is attached to it and it can be maintained at a high standard. Considerable advantage also stems from the arrangements for the preliminary course, because it is so devised that the choice of subject which is to

Falmer House courtyard: main entrance

Junior coffee lounge

Falmer House courtyard

Falmer House courtyard

Corner of the Junior Common Room

Falmer House

Falmer House courtyard: the refectory

Falmer House: top floor

be the undergraduate's major concern need not be made on entrance to the University, but can be delayed until he has had experience of this subject to some depth. The choice is then made with confidence, and is influenced by the right factors and not, as is frequently the case, by the tradition of the school at which he received his education, the enthusiasm or ability of one of his schoolteachers, or any of those other fortuitous and irrelevant factors which so often play a large part in determining the specialization to which an undergraduate precipitously commits himself. Finally, greater scope is given for the 'late developer', and for the undergraduate who has never experienced the inspiration and stimulation of good teaching at school. This is not a trivial problem at all, for there are many cases of the student who, nourished by a university environment, suddenly blossoms out in his second or third years. The type of course being provided in the sciences at Sussex will have a greater stimulating effect on the student and, at the same time, give him increased freedom of choice as to the direction in which he develops.

In summary then, the courses in the School of Physical Sciences are designed to make for maximum flexibility and freedom. An undergraduate is able to indulge his interests and enthusiasms in one particular field of science, but does not thereby cut himself off from the rich stimulation and illumination of neighbouring fields, which are conventionally regarded as belonging to a different specialization. He is not committed from the outset of his undergraduate career to one area of study only, but has some freedom to change the emphasis from one field to another as his ideas develop. At the end of the course he should have a deep understanding of the fundamentals of his major subject, a knowledge of its relation to other scientific fields and an awareness of his role as a scientist and of science in general in the world today.

Such an ambitious programme of learning cannot be brought into being without extremely effective teaching arrangements, and much thought has been given to this problem. Two extreme situations present themselves in the long-established universities of this country. On the one hand there is the intimacy of the Oxbridge tutorial system, with its associated rather cavalier treatment of lectures and on the other, the extreme Redbrick situation in which little attention is given to the individual and teaching is accomplished almost entirely through compulsory lectures and classes. The tutorial system is one which allows proper personal attention to be given to the undergraduate, and individual variations and capabilities to be catered for. It can provide a most intellectually stimulating relationship between tutor and student, and gives to the student a firm sense of 'oneness' with intellectual thought within the University. Against the system can be held that it is extremely expensive on the tutor's time – particularly in the sciences where laboratory teaching has also to be carried out. Further, in the sciences, most undergraduates have essentially the same problems and difficulties in comprehension, and the tutorial can frequently degenerate into a collection of 'repeat performances', where the same problems are discussed with one undergraduate after another.

An impersonal system of lectures and classes is, of course, the most economical approach to university teaching (as far as time is concerned). In this connection one has only to compare the number of teaching hours of an Oxford don with those of a lecturer at most provincial universities. But the consequent loss of contact between undergraduates and Members of Faculty is so regrettable as to be inexcusable. Surely one of the major features of a university education should be the continual exchange of ideas between the young and the established, and this can only happen effectively within the informality of a tutorial. The formal lecture and the class have their place within any university teaching arrangement, but in themselves they are not settings where strong intellectual links can be forged.

With these ideas in mind, teaching in the School of Physical Sciences has been so arranged as to incorporate the best features of these two approaches. The central theme of the various courses is set by a restricted number of good lectures. These by no means exhaust the ground to be covered, but serve to present a cohesive description of the central topics of a course of study. The main teaching effort, however, and the detailed direction of an undergraduate's learning is concentrated into the tutorial. Here his problems and difficulties are sorted out, work (related to that being currently covered in lectures) is set, discussed and criticized, and, in addition, individual reading and investigation is encouraged and guided. However, instead of the conventional Oxbridge tutorial, in which an undergraduate meets his tutor for an hour each week either singly or in pairs, we have an informal weekly, or twice weekly, gathering of four or five undergraduates and a Member of Faculty. In this way the repetitive feature of the tutorial system is considerably reduced, and more efficient use is made of the time of the Member of Faculty. Apart from this practical feature, there seems to be little doubt that the resulting group discussions and arguments can frequently be more invigorating than the duet of a conventional tutorial. Undergraduates are encouraged to answer one another's questions, and learn a great deal in so doing, for one of the finest ways of sorting out one's own ideas is to explain them to someone else. The tutorial groups, must, however, be kept small so that they do not degenerate into classes. Discussion is then not inhibited, and an intimacy of contact between teacher and student is assured.

Of course it is inevitable, in view of the specialist knowledge frequently required in the teaching of science, that an undergraduate is tutored by several different Members of Faculty. Therefore, to ensure that a continuity of the relationship between a Member of Faculty and an undergraduate is maintained, all undergraduates in the School of Physical Sciences have a 'personal tutor' whose subject is the same as the undergraduate's major subject. As far as possible his teaching in this subject is then carried out by his personal tutor. This surmounts the artificiality and impracticability of the more usual arrangement of a personal or moral tutor who meets the undergraduate perhaps once a term to discuss non-academic problems. A scheme of this sort rarely works, because such discussions are generally forced – they do not arise in the natural way provided for by the regular week-by-week contact of a tutorial.

The tutorial, then, is the dominant feature of the teaching system within the School of Physical Sciences, but lectures also play an important role, and provide the overall theme for the various courses. In addition, use is also made of small classes (e.g. for the teaching of mathematical analysis) and seminars or colloquia addressed both by undergraduates themselves or by visiting speakers. These latter are used for introducing the undergraduates to the wider aspects of their subject, and also for the treatment of topics which do not naturally fall into the central pattern of the science and mathematics courses. A certain amount of time is devoted to practical work in the candidate's major subject, but not so much as is usual in most degree courses. The experimental projects are, however, selected and planned most carefully so that maximum benefit is derived from them. The accent throughout is on 'finding out' rather than 'verifying'. Overall the intention is that experimental work shall illuminate an undergraduate's understanding, develop his critical faculty, practise him in the design of scientific experiment and familiarize him with modern techniques. Associated with the experimental work is the requirement that he shall be able to handle a mass of numerical data, and facilities are provided in the form of up-to-date computing machinery, including simple hand-machines, electric desk calculators and sometimes an electronic computer. Science has progressed to such an advanced state that it is frequently impossible for simple analytical mathematical methods to be used in any real practical problem with which he might be faced later on in his career, and it is considered essential that the familiarity with computational methods and machinery is achieved by all science undergraduates.

With teaching arranged in the way described, sufficient time is left for the faculty to prosecute effective research and this is considered to be of paramount importance. However, there is a body of opinion which argues that, for economic and other reasons, there is a case for creating institutes of higher education, possibly even universities, which would be concerned with teaching only. It has further been argued that research ability on the part of university teachers is of minor importance. While such opinions abound, it is essential to explore the situation a little more deeply. In brief, we at Sussex are among those who believe that science cannot be taught so as to develop an imaginative, scientific spirit and critical attitude of mind in undergraduates unless the teachers themselves are engaged to some extent in research work. Here are some of the arguments for this belief.

Our knowledge and understanding of science evolves sometimes continuously and sometimes in abrupt steps which dramatically overthrow previously held ideas, and an active scientist is bound up in and excited by this evolution. However, to make original contribution or observations on a scientific subject and, therefore, to take part even in a small way in this evolution, it is necessary, because of the extreme technicality of most present-day science and in particular the physical sciences, to make a quite considerable effort. An experiment actually has to be performed or a detailed calculation carried out. The extent to which the results of such effort fit in with current scientific theories or indicate the need for, possibly the nature of a change in the theories, is a measure of scientific advance. Thus, whilst in some subjects a lively interest and original approach can be maintained, as it were from the armchair and with comparative ease, in the physical sciences actual research has to be undertaken in order to preserve an equivalent critical interest in the development of the subject.

Now, it is absolutely essential that the excitement and sense of change associated with this progress of science should be communicated to the undergraduate. This is not to say that he must be kept abreast of all the recent developments in the branches of science with which he is dealing – this is impossible. The important point is that he should be studying in conjunction with teachers who *are* involved in scientific research and who appreciate, and therefore communicate in an exciting fashion, the importance and potentiality of the groundwork which is the undergraduate's immediate concern. It is not the direct impact of research on an undergraduate's work that makes it so important, but rather the questing attitude of mind and enthusiasm which it fosters in the teacher and which is thereby acquired by the student.

This does not mean that university faculty positions should be filled only by really first-class research workers – this would be an extreme situation and impossible to accomplish – but few, if any, positions should be held by people with no research interest at all. At the same time, research ability alone is not sufficient, and a dedication to the students and an ability to establish contact with them through lectures and tutorials are also essential. But the idea of staffing an institute of higher education with 'scientific onlookers', however sincerely dedicated, is one which would have a profoundly adverse effect on the education of young scientists. It should be avoided at all costs.

A thriving research programme, therefore, is regarded as a major feature of the School of Physical Sciences, because we believe that only in this way can an exciting atmosphere of intellectual inquiry be provided for the young undergraduate and a high calibre faculty be attracted to the university. Every effort has been made from the very outset to initiate research programmes and to establish a body of graduate students. In this, considerable success has already been achieved and in the School of Physical Sciences there is one graduate student for every six or seven undergraduates.

Proper postgraduate instruction, one of the most noteworthy accomplishments of American universities, is also a feature of the School of Physical Sciences, and one-year Diploma Courses in both Theoretical Physics and Experimental Physics have already been instituted. These courses are also followed by all graduate students working for advanced degrees, and for them the papers taken at the end of the course are treated collectively as a qualifying examination on the traditional American pattern.

To establish extensive research facilities is, of course, expensive. But those concerned with financing new universities must realize that extensive investment in research equipment from the outset is essential if a viable science faculty is to be established. Doubts as to the rate of growth of a new university, about the calibre of research projects, the abilities of research students and staff alike may be legitimate on the part of the University Grants Committee and The Department of Scientific and Industrial Research, but some guarantee should be provided that funds will be available commensurate with planned expansion and development provided they come to satisfactory fruition. Only in this way can the founder members of a Science Faculty proceed with confidence in setting up laboratories and planning for the future.

An ambitious research programme brings with it the further requirement that there should be a sufficient number of graduate students and staff to ensure its success, and hence, through the allowed staff/student ratio, it determines the minimum number of undergraduates to be accepted to study a given science each year. If a balanced treatment of the main branches of the physical sciences is to be given, and experts in those branches are surely necessary in order to do this, then it can be simply argued that this number must be at least fifty. This means that the year by year growth of the School of Physical Sciences will be enormous by conventional standards, and in a few years' time the numbers of undergraduates majoring in Physics, Chemistry or Mathematics will be larger than those in many long-established provincial universities. Naturally difficulties will be encountered during this unprecedented expansion, but there is no doubt in our minds that only in this way is it possible to provide an adequately stimulating and intellectual environment for both undergraduates and faculty alike in the School of Physical Sciences.

8. *School of Education and Social Work*

The attitude towards education in English universities makes an intriguing and also an odd story, whose history might be well worth studying in detail as a sociological phenomenon. This is not the place for the history of the matter, but it is relevant to note, at the outset, that the ice is cracking – indeed, since the Second World War, there has been a considerable thaw. The McNair Report of 1944, which proposed the establishment of Schools of Education and the acceptance by universities of a major responsibility for the training of teachers, marked a big advance – even if one has to add that the universities failed to implement the full scheme and contented themselves with adopting the modified responsibility represented by institutes of education (the University of Cambridge has to this day refused to incorporate the Institute of Education in the University). To accept the idea of training teachers, however, is a fairly easy way out: to offer certificates, even diplomas of education, is not to admit education to any very important degree of academic respectability. Virtually all universities, with the exception of Keele, have continued to exclude education from undergraduate courses, arguing that education is not really a subject, and even if it is that it is not a discipline.

As a result, the assertion has in most instances become the fact. Departments of Education, with their responsibility for providing a one-year postgraduate course for the training of teachers, have not looked much like 'genuine' university departments. They have pursued very little research, most of it in psychology, and virtually none of it in sociology; they have carried a staff many of whom seemed by university standards, non-academic; they have usually been housed 'down the road'; and they have generally suffered from an inferiority complex. If there is some truth in the assertion that historically training colleges were committed, as a matter of policy, to mediocrity, it is also true that university departments of education have been committed, as a result of university policy, to much the same lack of distinction. And thus it is hardly surprising that many undergraduates have preferred to go straight into schools without attending a department of education or acquiring a certificate in education.

However, life changes gradually. Today there is a very considerable interest, among individual members of university faculties, in education and schooling generally. There is a considerable sympathy for the concept of the Teaching University. There is a considerable concern about the state of sixth-form studies. Perhaps it is part of this change of atmosphere during recent years that has seen the growing prestige of the institutes of education and the growing recognition of a university responsibility towards the state of education at large. This change culminated in the Robbins Report, which proposed a return to the full gospel of McNair, only more so. That the Robbins Committee should make these proposals was not wholly unexpected, for quite apart from the volume of evidence which was submitted by all those concerned with the training of teachers, both inside universities and out, the Committee included among its members one of the more influential members of the McNair Committee and also the Director of the largest university institute and department of education in the country. What has perhaps been a good deal more surprising is the quick response which the universities as a whole have made to the Robbins proposals for the establishment of Schools of Education; a few years ago, even one or two years ago, such a response would have been unthinkable. (There seems some evidence, if one must be truly honest, that many of the universities do not seem fully to appreciate the implications of what they are at present agreeing to!)

The changed climate of opinion has, of course, been particularly evident in the new universities. Inevitably a new university is bound to be very much concerned about what to teach and how to teach it, and it is thus likely to have a fairly open mind about the place of education, broadly conceived, within the university. This has certainly been true of the University of Sussex which, from the first, has attached particular importance to the teaching-relationship between members of faculty and individual students and thus, by extension, to the idea of the university as an *educational* as well as an academic and research institution. For these reasons, there was apparently never any doubt in the minds of the founding fathers of the University (and it seems relevant and interesting to note that the author of this chapter, though responsible for the School of Education within the University, arrived on the scene at a comparatively late stage) that Education should be central to its life and not peripheral or subsidiary. The main question which had to be solved, however, was how to incorporate education within the academic life of the University without putting it at a disadvantage compared with other studies and without having to recruit a different kind and calibre of staff.

In other universities it is hard to provide a satisfactory answer to this kind of question (even if it is ever posed). Education is not, in the ordinary sense, a subject so much as a field of study which draws on different disciplines. In this it is fairly closely analogous to medicine. For the University of Sussex, however, this characteristic made education both more attractive and simpler to bring within the pattern of academic thinking. For if education derives its intellectual strength from drawing on a number of separate disciplines, such as psychology, sociology, history, philosophy, literary studies, and others, then it would seem potentially well suited to providing the nucleus of a school of studies in the Sussex sense (as described in some of the other chapters). For this reason, the first thoughts about the place of education in the University assumed that it would figure, in some fashion, as a subject of undergraduate study, and not simply as a field of professional training.

To put the matter in this way is admittedly somewhat artificial, for the University's obligation towards providing professional studies was never out of sight. But the great deficiency of professional schools, independently conceived, (and often independently housed), is that they run the danger of not resting securely on the autonomous intellectual vitality of the separate disciplines which contribute to their studies: the certificate or diploma course has not been sufficiently seen as one of the professional destinations of a coherent group of academic studies. From an early stage, therefore, it was felt that at Sussex there was an opportunity, indeed an obligation, to treat professional certificate courses for teachers as the second step in a process that must begin by establishing the autonomy of the relevant group of disciplines, together with independent schemes of research. And this seemed clearly to imply grouping these separate disciplines within a separate school of undergraduate as well as post-graduate studies. What, it then remained to ask, is the conceptual framework that holds these studies together?

It may seem, from the foregoing account, as if it was possible, at Sussex, to take ideal and wholly untrammelled decisions about the place and character of educational studies within the University. In fact, of course, this was not so. For by the time they came to be discussed, certain decisions had already been taken about other groups of disciplines, which were bound to influence the pattern of discussions from then on. In particular, the School of Social Studies had already been established, which not only robbed the proposed educational school of its most suitable title, but even raised, more importantly, the question whether there was a place for two separate schools at all. At the University of Essex, for instance, education, in the sense primarily of a comprehensive programme of educational research and programmes of undergraduate teaching, will be located in the School of Social Studies; it will be simply one, if an important one, of a number of areas of social study. Moreover, at Essex it is suggested that the professional training of teachers should be embedded in a Graduate School of Applied Social Science. It might, theoretically, have been possible to have adopted a similar pattern at Sussex, and the protracted discussions about a School of Education revealed quite a strong body of faculty opinion which favoured such a solution.

But, in the end, there seemed to be two good reasons for creating a separate School at Sussex. The first reason, probably, was administrative. To bring education, as a group of undergraduate and post-graduate professional studies, within the existing School of Social Studies, would be to create a disproportionately large School (from the point of view of the size of School that a single Dean can administer in a personal way and still have time to teach). Moreover, since Schools at Sussex have none of the characteristics of Departments elsewhere, no formidable barriers between studies would be set up by creating a second School; above all, the same individual members of faculty would be equally free to teach 'educational studies' wherever they were to be located.

Granted this, there seemed to be a second, academic, reason for creating a separate School, for an independent School would enable the University to do something to rehabilitate the study of education and to give such studies a distinct identity and prestige from the first. In the School of Social Studies, the common or contextual papers have a bias towards social analysis in economic and political terms; and among the major subjects which can be studied in that School are economics, politics and sociology (as distinct from sociology on its own), international relations, as well as history and geography. Thus there appeared to be scope for a second School whose bias would be towards social studies as they bear upon the identity of the developing individual: a group of studies which would be concerned with identity of the individual in his social and cultural environment. One might say that a group of social studies defined in this way might be concerned with the kinds of preoccupation exemplified by Matthew Arnold and D. H. Lawrence on the one hand, and by Freud, Durkheim and Riesman on the other, if this collocation can be allowed to convey a particular flavour of study.

The undergraduate course in such a School would not, like the postgraduate course, provide professional training in education or social work. But emphasis would be placed throughout on the disciplines underlying education and social work and the major subjects would be studied in a context of social commitment. In academic terms, then, the proposal as it took shape was to group together six disciplines: three analytic-descriptive disciplines: sociology, psychology, and social geography; and three evaluative disciplines: literature, history, and philosophy. At the undergraduate level all of these would be offered as major subjects; and all would be involved in some fashion in the group of common or contextual studies. (Roughly speaking, an undergraduate spends five-ninths of his or her time on the major subject, and four-ninths on the common papers.)

Such then, was the proposed pattern of undergraduate studies for the new School. After interminable discussion, it was decided to name it the School of Education and Social Work. It began by being called the School of Educational Studies, but the general connotation of the term 'education' seemed likely to restrict the intended scope of the School. The next name proposed was the School of Education and Community Studies; but the latter half of the title, though enlarging the horizons of the School, was felt to have somewhat specialist meanings in other fields of study and would, therefore, be either vague or misleading. In the end, it was decided to use, quite simply, the terms which indicate the ultimate professional destinations of the studies grouped together in this

School – though there would, of course, be no obligation on undergraduates studying in the School to go on to take the postgraduate
professional courses that would be offered. Apart from this question
of a name, the School took shape when the common papers were
worked out in some detail; the distinctive character of a School of
studies at Sussex is largely the product of the papers taken in
common by all undergraduates in that School, whatever their major
subjects of study. It may, therefore, be interesting to specify these
common papers.

The first of the common papers is the one taken by undergraduates during their first two terms as part of their Preliminary
Examination[1]; and is entitled *Critical Reading: Literature and Social
Analysis*. The idea of this paper is to engage the undergraduate in
the critical and comparative reading of a number of seminal works
of literature and social analysis. The list is made up of (*a*) a group of
major literary texts designed to provide training in literary understanding and discrimination; at the same time, they are texts which
focus on questions of moral decision and social conduct, or which
deal overtly with the relations between the individual and society;
and (*b*) a group of central texts in the history of educational ideas
and social amelioration in the past two centuries. The following is
the list of titles proposed initially:

a Shakespeare   *Measure for Measure*
   Pope   Selection from *Epistles* and *Moral Essays*
   Wordsworth   *The Prelude*
   Dickens   *Our Mutual Friend*
   Mark Twain   *Huckleberry Finn*
   Butler   *The Way of All Flesh*
   D. H. Lawrence *Sons and Lovers*

b Rousseau   *Emile*
   Froebel   *The Education of Man*
   Newman   *The Idea of a University*
   Arnold   *Culture and Anarchy*
   Freud   *Psychopathology of Everyday Life*
   Whitehead   *The Aims of Education*

[1] As described elsewhere, all arts undergraduates, in whatever School, take three
papers in their Preliminary Examination. Two of these are taken by all undergraduates,
a philosophy paper called *Language and Values*, and a history paper called *Introduction
to History*; the third paper is related to the School in which they are enrolled.

Beatrice Webb   *My Apprenticeship*
Durkheim   *Moral Education*
Mannheim   *Diagnosis of Our Time*

After their Preliminary Examination at the end of their second term, undergraduates then begin working for both their common and major papers. The following are the common or contextual papers, designed to introduce undergraduates to the disciplines underlying education and social work; though without in any way introducing questions of professional training:

1. *Personality and Social Groups.* This paper brings together a series of topics related to the process of personality formation, with particular reference to the specific social and cultural context of Great Britain. Some of these topics are: family structure and the socialization of the child; primary groups and the development of personality; theories of group dynamics with reference to education and welfare.

2. Either *Developmental Psychology*, which considers some general theories of human mental development, together with a more detailed study of the main stages in the life of an individual, such as childhood, adolescence, adulthood, old age. Special emphasis is put on the forms of behavioural adjustment problems specific to old age.

or *Social Structure and Social Change.* Social groups and sociological concepts, social institutions; culture and social character; modes of socialization; primary groups and the family; power and influence patterns in associations; social stratification; social mobility; factors, rates and forms of social change; social change in selected contemporary environments.

3. *Education and Society.* This paper is concerned with the scope and structure of the educational system in England and Wales, together with some historical and international comparisons. Topics include educational pressures in an industrial society; individual opportunity and social class; the school as an educational institution; the changing role of the teacher; selection, assessment and examination; continuity and diversity in education; the making of educational policy.

or *Community Studies and Social Work.* This paper is concerned with the study of the modern English community; its social structure and tensions, personal and community relations within it, and the ways of investigating it. There is also an examination of the place within the community of the social services; and attention is paid to their history, development and administration.

4. *Philosophy: Thought and Action.* This paper involves the study of the concepts of intelligence and intelligent action, of imagination, of moral responsibility and punishment, of welfare and happiness, and of social control and individual liberty.

It can be seen at once that this pattern of common papers is distinctively different from that offered by the School of Social Studies. And if consumer demand is any criterion in such matters, the plan seemed to please the undergraduates who had already enrolled in the University in other Schools; for some 25 undergraduates applied to transfer to the new School of Education and Social Work in the middle of their first year, before the School was theoretically ready to start teaching. Three of them were originally enrolled to read science and the largest single group wanted to take psychology as their major subject.

Apart from these common and major papers, it is proposed that during their final terms in the School, undergraduates will attend a series of seminars designed to draw upon their separate specialisms and various contextual subject, by examining a range of human and social problems, perhaps on the following lines:

The Individual Society
>   Human needs and development in contemporary society;
>   Growth in, and emergence out of, the home;
>   The school versus the community;
>   'Teenage culture';
>   Adjustment to social change.

Group and Mass Activities
>   Social and political associations and allegiances;
>   The welfare services;
>   Pattern of work;
>   Leisure (including the arts and the mass media) and the audience.

Individual difficulties and deviations
>   Neurosis and maladjustment;
>   Impoverishment and loneliness;
>   Delinquency and crime;
>   Law and treatment.

Through discussions in these seminars the distinctive character and purpose of the School will, it is hoped, be defined. At the same time, it is hoped to set up as a major undertaking within the School a research project into adolescence and creativity.

It is out of this group of undergraduate studies that the post-graduate professional courses emerge. Seen in these terms, the professional courses are not, therefore, cut off on their own, in isolation from undergraduate work. And the academic disciplines on which the professional courses inevitably rest have, by this arrangement, the opportunity of developing their own academic lives and associated schemes of research. In this way, it is hoped that the professional courses will be able to draw on a richer intellectual life within the University than would otherwise be the case, and also that the character and content of professional studies can be re-examined and re-fashioned.

As the title of the School indicates, the professional courses proposed are for teachers and social workers, and it was one of the first decisions of the University that teaching and social work should be closely linked in this way. For they have traditionally suffered greatly by being studied apart from each other. Though, for reasons of historical accident, the social services are administered and financed separately, and thus in practice have all too little contact with each other, they are, intellectually conceived, essentially complementary. Their objective is really the same: to enable the individual, whether balanced or unbalanced, to assume a mature and perceptive relationship with his immediate social environment.

This is hardly the place to go into the details of these professional courses, which anyway have yet to be worked out. But one or two broad general principles have been agreed, which derive partly from the changing social expectation of education and social work, coupled with the changing social composition of people going into these professions. Among these considerations is the fact that young people are increasingly likely to conceive of teaching in social rather than pedagogic terms; indeed, many of them may wish to defer until quite a late stage a decision as to whether they want to be teachers or social workers. Moreover, the facts of statistical life seem to reinforce this changed mood. For it is now clear that the number of potential teachers emerging from the universities will before long be sufficient to meet the needs of *all* kinds of secondary school and not only the needs of selective schools. Indeed, the situation may soon arise when the majority of graduates go into non-selective secondary schools, or at any rate find themselves teaching less academic children. This suggests that many, if not all, graduates will need a considerably broader education than used to be thought necessary for graduates hoping to become sixth-form teachers. But, even more important than this, they will need to develop a different social outlook towards the business of teaching: they will need a sense of the human and also the intellectual potentialities of less academic children; they will need to have some understanding of the world of technology, etc.; and especially they will need to have a grasp of the social complexities of the age, of which 'teenage culture' is so important a feature.

A second, related consideration is that an increasing proportion of university students will be first-generation students and very many of these will be the first members of their families intending to enter the professions. This suggests two separate considerations. Because they will be new to the assumptions both of universities and of the professions, it becomes particularly important to enable them to defer as long as possible their choice of a particular job. But, at the same time, it also becomes important to help them make this social and professional transition, and this suggests that some part of their university course should be devoted to the disciplines underlying professional careers.

Moreover, an increasing number of professions are likely to demand graduate qualifications in their entrants and also to press for an increase of professional studies at universities. It is this consideration which reinforces the proposal, already made, that an interesting possibility for a new university would be to re-examine the intellectual needs of the social professions and, above all, to explore the relations between academic and professional studies.

One or two of the consequences which one draws from these considerations are, for instance, that a large part of the social-psychological studies within these professional courses should be undertaken in common by prospective teachers and social workers; and, as an extension of this, that there should be an integrated course (rather than separate courses) preparing undergraduates for social work – though this integrated course would need to be followed by periods of field-work and case-work for the separate social service professions. Then it seems sensible to bring in, as far as possible, neighbouring institutions of higher education when planning these professional courses. Thus, in the case of courses for teachers, the social-psychological studies will be taught mainly by the faculty of the University, but the 'method' courses will be taught in association with the staff of the nearby teachers' training colleges.

Further, when teacher-students go out on practice, their studies should involve exploring the school community and its environment, as well as learning how to teach their subjects in the class room. Thus these students will probably work in pairs, and they will be mostly centred on non-selective secondary schools (apart from any other consideration, they will be very familiar with the grammar school or the direct grant school, in which they will have spent long years of their education); it is also hoped that selected staff from these schools will participate in these studies, and in this way they might eventually be regarded as 'teacher tutors' working in collaboration with the staffs of the University and also of the training colleges.

A further proposal, which is relevant at this point, is that the School is proposing to offer, in addition to the undergraduate and postgraduate professional courses already described, a four-year integrated course designed for undergraduates who are certain from the outset that they wish to enter education or social work. The course, which will probably include two terms of field study, will lead to the joint award of BA or BSC and Certificate in Education or Diploma in Social Work. It will be very interesting to see what proportion of undergraduates entering the School decide to take this integrated course, rather than to follow the more normal three years plus one year pattern.

At the postgraduate level it is planned to establish some major research projects linked to the professional courses. On the educational side, the two main fields of research seem likely to be determined by the educational needs of the University itself. First in importance among these, in a new university, is the question of testing teaching methods in relation to the curriculum, and the question of selection, assessment and examination. These questions have naturally been discussed, formally and informally, a great deal since the University was first projected; formally they are the preoccupation of a body called the Socio-Educational Research Committee, whose main function, in the early years, has been to identify the problems which need research and to consider some of the ways of setting up such research projects. It became clear, at a fairly early stage, however, that the right way to study these aspects of the University's own academic and social life is not to set up an independent research unit, at any rate in the first instance, but to encourage the maximum participation by members of faculty in discussions about these matters. Clearly the appropriate arena for these discussions is the School of Education, which would thus become something of an educational forum and laboratory for the University as a whole. (This would have the incidental advantage of associating many members of faculty with the work of the School and so ensuring in yet another way that it did not become detached from the main life of the University.) In practice, what this will probably mean is that when new members of faculty are recruited to teach subjects like sociology and psychology, they will be selected partly in relation to their ability to undertake collaborative research work on these major educational problems. In addition, however, it may be necessary ultimately to recruit a certain number of full-time research fellows or assistants, in order to carry out parts of these investigations; but essentially they will do so with the lines of policy determined by the general faculty discussions.

Apart from these functional research projects, as they might be called – projects designed to help the University understand and improve its own educational processes – it is hoped that serious research will be pursued in the fields of the psychology and sociology of education and social work at large. The sociology of education particularly is a territory largely unexplored in this country; and in the absence of such studies, the discipline itself has as yet only a modest contribution to make to the study of education as a whole.

It is plain from the foregoing account that the plans for studies in education and social work at the University of Sussex are more comprehensive than is common at other universities and, relatedly, that these plans presuppose a School which is on a par with the other Schools in the University. It remains to be seen, of course, how many undergraduates entering the University choose to enter this School, though there seems to be a good deal of preliminary evidence that the School's various courses, with their immediate and ultimate professional horizons, will make a strong appeal to many of the young people entering universities generally today. Indeed, it will be important to keep a close watch over the character of this professional appeal which, in some circumstances, could weaken the intrinsic discipline of the academic studies, just as, properly understood and integrated, it could strengthen them. All of this, at any rate, represents a large and ambitious undertaking. But it is in fact only one part of the University's concern with education in the broadest sense, and the School will also be responsible both for extra-mural work, and for what may be broadly described as the 'Robbins responsibilities' of a university.

As was suggested at the beginning of this chapter, the universities as a whole have given an unexpectedly ready welcome to those proposals of the Robbins Committee which are concerned with the training of teachers. These proposals, it will be remembered, are that the training colleges, renamed Colleges of Education, should cease to be LEA colleges and should, together with the universities' departments and institutes of education, be formed into schools of education. This means that the universities, through their transformed institutes of education, would have to assume fairly large administrative and financial responsibilities for their adjacent training colleges; and not only that, for it is proposed that the training colleges themselves should be enlarged so that eventually those with less than 750 students would be the exception rather than the rule. The day-to-day load on the universities would not be quite so formidable as this account might make it appear, for it is also proposed that the colleges should become independent and virtually autonomous institutions of higher education, with independent governing bodies, and financed by ear-marked grants made by the Grants Commission (at present the UGC) through the universities to the schools of education.

Finally, the Robbins Committee proposed that the universities should introduce a four-year course leading to a BEd degree for undergraduates capable of working at this level (which might amount to some 5%–10% of their number).

The Government has not, at the time of writing, announced its policy with regard to these proposals. But, at the invitation of the UGC, the universities have now adopted their own provisional policies and the great majority of universities appear to have welcomed the main features of the Robbins policy and seem to be prepared to set up schools of education and to make it possible for a proportion of training college students to take a BEd degree. Anyone familiar with Senate and Council procedure in universities will appreciate how large an advance this provisional acceptance of the

Robbins proposals amounts to, especially when one couples it with the universities' traditional reluctance to take on extra-mural educational responsibilities. A new university, establishing itself at much the same time as the Robbins Committee made its proposals, is obviously in a much easier position to establish a school of education and to plan BEd degrees, for in such a university there will be few administrative mountains of long standing to move and far fewer academic preconceptions to overcome. Thus, at the University of Sussex it was always proposed to establish a School of Education on very much the same lines as those set out in the Robbins Report. Moreover, since it was known that the Report was in the offing, the University had, in the meantime, carefully done nothing in regard to the training of teachers which might make it harder to accept this policy. Thus the University has never used terms like 'department' or 'institute' of education in formulating its own plans, but has from the first thought in terms of a comprehensive School, which would be responsible for all aspects of the University's educational work and responsibility.

What this means in practice is that the University wishes to establish close academic links with a number of training colleges in East and West Sussex (colleges at present associated with the Universities of London, Reading and Southampton). It so happens that these six or seven colleges make up an unusually coherent and well-varied group, for they include mixed colleges as well as colleges for women only, specialist colleges of physical education and house-craft, an independent Church of England college and also a college of arts and crafts. The University accepts the Robbins Committee's contention that if the training colleges are to have the opportunity of raising their academic and intellectual sights, enabling a proportion of their students to work for university degrees, then they must be given their academic independence within the framework of the university system. This presumably means negotiating a new relationship between the University, the colleges and their respective local authorities, for it is important to add that this scheme does not appear to the University to mean severing the colleges' links with the LEAs, or turning them into pale copies of university institutions.

These negotiations for the transfer of the colleges from their present universities to Sussex, and for their establishment as independent institutions, are going forward. There is no inclination on the University's side to hurry this process of transfer – indeed, there may well be a period of transition lasting for a few years.

These are the administrative details of the plan. What seems far more important is to bring the University and the colleges into a close working and intellectual relationship with each other, partly because, as has been already described, it is hoped that some of the staff of the colleges will help teach on the postgraduate course for the Certificate in Education. The link between a university and the neighbouring training colleges has too often been conceived, since the institutes of education were set up after the war, in terms of devising syllabuses and examinations. It is probably true that the staffs of the colleges and the faculty of the University are likely to derive rather different benefits out of their association within the Boards of Studies which are to be established in each main academic subject. For the training college staffs, the importance of meeting their colleagues in universities is so that they can keep abreast, academically, with research and the movement of ideas in their common disciplines. It is all too easy for academic studies in professional and vocational institutions like training colleges to become eccentric or fanciful, with the growth of an odd-looking subject like 'Training College English' (which perhaps gives over most of the syllabus to intensive study of novels like *Room at the Top* and contemporary kitchen-sink drama), or 'Training College Mathematics' (which may be conceived almost entirely in such speciously attractive terms as 'surveying' or 'navigation'). Since students in training colleges spend about one-third of their time studying subjects in their own right, and not only as subjects to be taught in school, it is particularly important that these subjects should draw some of their stimulus and vitality from corresponding work going on in the universities.

For the faculty members of the university, on the other hand, the great value of links with other institutions of higher education is that it enlarges their conception of the scope and application of what they are teaching. It reminds them that the disciplines with which they are concerned exist quite legitimately in many contexts and at a variety of levels, without this necessarily entailing any essential loss of standards. It brings them into touch with the problems of the sixth form. And finally, perhaps, it widens their conception of the variety of teaching methods. For these reasons, if it is important to establish the autonomy of the university and the training colleges, it is equally important to work for their mutual inter-dependence academically: for there is presumably a higher autonomy, which is the autonomy of the subject itself.

It is within this context that one comes to the problem of creating the degree of BEd for a proportion of training college students. The different universities are evidently setting about this in fairly different ways. In some instances the students will be brought into the university for their fourth year; in some, the degree-students will be selected at quite an early stage of their training college course and will then work on a largely different syllabus from the non-degree students in the college; and in some cases, individual members of the training college staffs will be chosen and designated as 'teacher tutors' within the college; and so forth. It is assumed that the BEd is to be a three-subject degree at pass level, though honours, or a corresponding distinction, would be awarded to exceptional students. At Sussex the detailed arrangements for this proposed degree have not yet been considered, but it seems clear, from the University's standpoint, that a Sussex BEd must reflect a similar intellectual and academic logic to the Sussex BA and BSc. This suggests that the colleges' courses of study may have to be modified somewhat so as to provide students with linked academic studies (comparable to the linking of studies within the University Schools). One way of achieving this would be if the three subjects for the BEd were arranged as follows:

(i) Education I – a broad synthesizing course: years 1–3

(ii) Education II – a study in depth of one of the educational disciplines: educational psychology or sociology, comparative education, or the philosophy of education — years 2 and 3 continued into year 4

(iii) Main academic subject (or two main subjects for first year, one of them being taken for years 2–4) — years 1–3, continued into year 4

A second consideration is that the introduction of a degree into the training colleges must not affect the kind of prestige and work undertaken by the non-degree students. Ideally, the two groups of students would work together for a considerable part of their course, and only in the fourth year would the degree students be taught quite separately, though it seems important that they should remain college-based even though some of their studies might at this stage be under the supervision of members of the University faculty. The training colleges have traditionally been enviably free of intellectual or academic hierarchies, and it would be an enormous pity if the introduction of the BED degree were to introduce into them the bi-partism or even tri-partism so familiar in secondary education. Finally, the introduction of the degree will necessarily involve introducing, for some of the students, more formal and even, perhaps, more externally-designed examinations than are common in training colleges; but it would seem very important that this should not transform or jeopardize the existing system common in most colleges, which takes considerable account of continuous assessment and tends to be based on internal examinations with external moderation, rather than the familiar university examining pattern.

In conclusion, the University is anxious to establish extra-mural courses of all kinds (historically the counties of Sussex have fallen within the realm of the Oxford Extra-Mural Delegacy). The term 'extra-mural' is taken here to include courses ranging from the kind of short lecture courses associated with the WEA to longer residential refresher courses in individual academic subjects, often designed for practising teachers. There are few plans drawn up for this work. Probably the administrative responsibility for co-ordinating such courses will fall upon the School of Education and Social Work, for this School will already have a direct interest in providing refresher courses for teachers, as part of the proposals for teacher-tutors, described earlier – for the one presupposes the other. But in general the proposal is that the separate Schools of the University shall each develop their extra-mural interests and courses, thus extending some of their undergraduate and graduate studies to larger audiences outside the University. If the separate Schools of the University and the members of faculty associated with them come to accept this extra-mural responsibility, the University will have a major achievement to its credit in the field of extra-mural work. For the more usual pattern within universities is that such work is the concern and preoccupation of a devoted minority (historically some of them well-known missionary figures); while the great majority of faculty remain wholly preoccupied with their teaching and research responsibilities *within* the University. The pattern proposed for Sussex is one in which the University and faculty as a whole will accept an outward-looking as well as an inward-looking role in relation to higher academic studies.

Such, then, is the pattern proposed for education and professional courses in social work at the University of Sussex. A part of this exceedingly ambitious programme has in fact already been set in motion, and a large part of the remainder of the programme is in the active planning stage. It is impossible at this stage to tell how far these plans will succeed. But at least it will not be possible to say of the University of Sussex that it was indifferent to its educational responsibilities or that it assumed them as an afterthought.

DENNIS COX

9. *The Library of a New University*

It is impossible to imagine a university without books. Upon them
its work largely depends. They are essential to teaching and research
in every subject. 'The character and efficiency of a university may be
gauged by its treatment of its central organ – the library. We regard
the fullest provision for library maintenance as the primary and
most vital need in the equipment of a university. An adequate
library is not only the basis of all teaching and study; it is the essential
condition of research, without which additions cannot be made to
the sum of human knowledge' – thus wrote the University Grants
Committee in its first Report in 1921. It cannot unfortunately
be said that for a long time much heed was paid to its words.
The ambitions and needs of all learned libraries remain yet unsatis-
fied.

The demands made on university libraries are greater now than
they have ever been. The immense increase in the number of scholarly books and periodicals published has meant that virtually no
scholar can rely on his private library to satisfy his needs. He turns
more and more to public collections. The director of one of
America's leading university presses has recently commented:
'Reports of the long-term sales records of some of the classics in
American history and similar studies of library circulation have
given historians cause for shocked comment and reflection. Books
on which successive generations of teachers and graduate students
had learned to rely were found to have sold only one or two
thousand copies.'[1] The amount of material now published is truly
staggering. It has been estimated, for example, that the output of
chemical literature has doubled in a little over the past eight years.
In 1907, its first year of existence, *Chemical Abstracts* published
abstracts from 465 journals. It now monitors some 10,000 scientific,

[1] Roger W. Shugg, 'The universities and their publishers'. *Daedalus*. Winter 1963,
p. 68.

technical, trade and special serial-type publications. Increases in some other subjects are scarcely less spectacular.

Undergraduates, as well as members of faculty, use libraries more. Perhaps they buy fewer books than their predecessors of a generation ago, although the 'quality' paperback revolution seems to be transforming their habits or, at any rate, enables them to acquire more titles with the money they have to spend.

The greatest European libraries have grown slowly to full stature. The task before the new universities is to develop their libraries rapidly. This development must match their own rapid growth and take place when human knowledge is expanding at an unprecedented rate. Moreover the rarer books and manuscripts will not long be available, except (and praise be to the pioneers of documentary reproduction) in photocopies. There is increasing competition, from all over the world, for those that have not yet passed into the permanent keeping of institutions. Fortunately in book collecting time is transferable. If a new library had the good fortune to acquire a number of important private collections, it would go a long way to achieving maturity at once. The very names of some libraries, the Bodleian at Oxford or the Folger in Washington, are a reminder of the piety that inspired their benefactors.

The university librarian's first duties are to support the teaching and research activities of the institution in which he serves. The task of providing books for undergraduates is a smaller and more manageable one than that of providing material for post-graduates and faculty. It is no less vital, more particularly in the humanities, in a university where the tutorial is the primary method of teaching.

An undergraduate, at any rate on first coming up, usually judges the quality of the university library by a simple test – can he get the book that he has been told to read when he wants it or can he, less preferably, find a substitute? The library will almost certainly possess a copy, but another reader may have borrowed or be using it. It is of little comfort that a library has on its shelves a complete set of the British State Papers if it cannot produce, before the next tutorial for which it must be read, a copy of Sir James Neale's *Elizabethan House of Commons*. Undergraduates must be persuaded to buy some books for themselves – their grants contain an allowance for this – but book-buying is a habit which many, accustomed to having books handed out at school, have to learn. Nor can they be expected to buy all the books that they ought to see.

Before 1939 university librarians, crabbed and confined by limited funds and rightly anxious to build up research collections, almost to a man resolutely refused to purchase duplicate copies. In these days of increasing student numbers this is no longer possible. An undergraduate is wasting his time and somebody's money if books are not available when wanted. The librarian must experimentally solve the problem of many students chasing the same title at the same time. In Sussex one or more copies of titles are bought according to anticipated or experienced demand. One copy of the most used titles is confined to the library for use during its long opening hours, while others may only be borrowed for one or two days (the normal period of loan is a fortnight). Students are persuaded by their tutors, and by the refusal of the library to duplicate some titles, to buy books – those studying literature should, for example, possess the most important poems, novels, and plays. Tutors can partly spread the load by programming their teaching and varying their essay titles.

In the United States the larger numbers of students (more than 20,000 in some universities) and the greater size of library collections have led in some places to the establishment of undergraduate libraries in separate buildings. Those at Harvard and Michigan are especially notable. These libraries provide a service, matched by its cost, tailored to undergraduate needs. They contain the most commonly wanted titles, probably up to 50,000, and there are in addition many duplicates. Their advantage is that an undergraduate is able to find his way in a small collection more quickly than in a large. Their disadvantage – though it must be added that access to the full collections is possible if wished and that this opportunity is taken up by many – is that the student is not daily conscious of the mass of publications and learning that have gone into the writing of the handful of textbooks which form his staple diet. It seems right, until the size of the library or of the student body prevents it, to expose the undergraduate to the full resources of the University Library. When the freshman comes up it is unlikely that he will have used before a library of equal size. A consequence of giving to the undergraduate free access to all the collections is that they must be arranged in a readily comprehensible order and that both formal and informal assistance to readers is available.

The selection of books for an undergraduate collection, whether separately housed or not, presents no alarming difficulties. At this sort of level, once the subjects to be taught are decided, most of the books choose themselves: in literature, the standard editions of authors and the major critical works about them; in history some of the primary sources as well as the secondary; and so on. The needs of third-year undergraduates begin to merge with those of post-graduates and faculty and are best considered under that head. The problems in a new university in providing books for undergraduates are to spend the funds equitably between subjects, to judge the right sort of coverage that the available money permits, to gauge accurately the required amount of duplication, and to find copies of out-of-print books. In book collecting, whatever may be said of some other pursuits, the pleasures of capture exceed those of the chase.

There is one aspect of undergraduate use of libraries which is immensely satisfying and rewarding to those who work in them. The library, with the union, is in most universities the place to which all students come, and come moreover on equal terms. The librarian holds no examinations, does not grade students according to their abilities or even to their courses, imposes no moral sanctions or discipline other than in respect of the errors of not returning books on time, or, less forgivable, of writing in them. He simply says: 'Here is a great treasure house; come and use it as often and as well as you can; the library staff will help you to find and use books if you wish – most of them have themselves undergone the great adventure that you are experiencing and the feast of learning and discovery continues to refresh them.' In the library, moreover, the student can find new intellectual pastures beyond those which his tutors and courses have brought into view. He can hope to discover some point of view, some new fact of knowledge, that has escaped his teachers, whose fallibility is as certain as that of the books themselves. In the library a beginning can best be made of the painful journey away from unquestioning obedience to authorities. Moreover unless students are quite unadventurous they will be attracted to taking an interest outside curricular demands – to reading contemporary literature, the weekly and quarterly general periodicals and magazines, or books on social and political problems. The library is open for long hours – longer than any of the other university services. In planning the library building at Sussex an underlying desire has been to provide a building of quiet attractive comfort which will reflect the above conception of its use by undergraduates. There will be armchairs as well as seats at tables, and the latter will have partitions and individual lights to give privacy. All readers have access to all collections, only subject to request in the case of rare books and manuscripts. Most books may be borrowed.

Undergraduate needs have been the most urgent and were given first priority, but the provision for post-graduate research students and members of faculty is the larger, more difficult task. Already there are post-graduates in Sussex, and their presence has fundamental implications for its library. The largest university library in the world, that at Harvard, has just catalogued its seven millionth book; in the year 1961/62 it added 201,000 volumes to its collections and received 24,000 periodicals. In the United States thirty-two universities possess more than one million and ten more than two million volumes. The state-wide University of California announced in 1961 its programme for the following ten years. The plan for libraries 'is to maintain and further develop major libraries of great size and distinction at Berkeley and Los Angeles and to make available the collections on these two campuses to faculty and graduate students on all campuses. Berkeley's library is expected to reach a size of three million volumes by 1965, the collection at Los Angeles by 1971 [the latter will increase by one and one-half million volumes in ten years]. By 1971, also, collections on the other [seven] campuses will total at least three million volumes.'[1] At the beginning of this great expansion, in the academic year 1960–61, the University of California was spending on books, periodicals, and binding, four-fifths of the expenditure on these items by *all* the British universities.

This is not to suggest that the new universities in Britain should aim at collections of two to three million volumes within a decade or two. Only Cambridge, London and Oxford of the older universities have more than one million books and many have a great deal less. Five in 1961–62, the latest year for which figures are available, had less than 200,000 volumes each. It is merely to emphasize the size of the problem and the magnetic power that a large library has for scholars, on whose original work the justification and reputation of any university chiefly depend. There can be nothing surprising in the continuing migration of scholars to American universities where the materials they need are more lavishly provided. The American figures should stimulate a demand for higher standards.

The British situation is, of course, different from the American. Brighton is only an hour's train ride from one of the world's great

[1] *A university plans its future*, 1962, p. 7.

library centres and from one of the world's greatest libraries, the British Museum. There are, too, long established facilities for inter-library lending among libraries of all types – although the British Museum and the universities of Oxford and Cambridge, the copy-right libraries, are largely outside them. These facilities improve, albeit as the strains imposed on them increase. The recently estab-lished National Lending Library for Science now offers a fine service in lending scientific periodicals. It is in respect of older and foreign books in the humanities that the position is worst, and here there are no grounds for complacency about national coverage. Readers, however, in no university are dependent on its unaided library collections. The more energetic of them also learn to tap private sources and institutions.

Given that no library, not even the largest, can be self-sufficient, a new university must acquire as soon as possible as much as it can of the basic materials in the subjects which have faculty and research students. There must be an immediate base to support research and from which visits to, and borrowings from, other libraries can be planned. There must be some material with which to begin the training of postgraduates. Nor can it be forgotten that travel to other libraries, and borrowing from them, is in man-hours expen-sive, or that continuity of work is inevitably broken. There is no adequate substitute for the university's own possession of a large research library. In its first three years the library acquired 80,000 books. An annual growth of 25,000 to 30,000 volumes must be maintained and improved if possible. Moreover this figure should comprise only truly significant items and be supplemented by new books, current periodicals and by microforms. This is the first, modest, target. It is not possible to say that so many hundred thousand volumes will, or will not, suffice. The function of the scholar is to push forward the frontiers of knowledge, and library collections expand continually. A library that stops growing is dead.

There is an important difference for the library between research in the humanities and research in science. Scientists will be largely content if they have access to the periodicals which record the results of work done, but an historian of the Reformation, for example, may want books published at any time since the invention of print-ing as well as archives and manuscripts. This difference reflects itself in library expenditure. Edwin E. Williams, Counselor to the Director on the Collections at Harvard University Library, has recently written[1]: 'University administrators may be reluctant to recognize facts that call for heavy expenditure by libraries. One of these facts, which has already been mentioned, is that library resources adequate for graduate work in most fields of the humanities and social sciences are of a different order of magnitude from those needed for graduate work in the sciences ... As a single example of what is meant one may cite the fact that the Massachusetts Institute of Technology finds it sufficient to have a library of 745,767 volumes, on which it spent $543,957 during 1960–61, or less than one per cent of its total expenditures. Its near neighbour, Harvard, heavily engaged in the humanities and social sciences, spends nearly seven times as much for library purposes, or approximately 6% of its total expenditure.'

If the selection of titles for an undergraduate collection presents no great problems, that of choosing from an enormous range of background material in every language and of every date does. There is no excess of money with which to afford errors of judgement. A great reservoir of specialized knowledge exists in a community of scholars, and drawing upon this the library staff develops the collections. In a university book collecting divorced from the expressed needs of its present readers is impossible, yet its library will never be adequate if it ties itself slavishly to them. Fundamental research is unpredictable, and that library is best which can answer unforeseen questions and suggest unimagined lines of inquiry. A good library inspires research.

An almost instinctive judgement as to which books ought to be acquired at any stage in the library's history, having regard to the funds available – this is the most necessary quality in a librarian. A university library is an expensive piece of equipment, and its administration demands economy and efficiency, but its senior staff are first concerned with the promotion of scholarship and teaching. Their crucial responsibility is the proper development of the collections. The senior members of the Sussex library staff share this work, concerning themselves with acquisitions in the subjects in which they have graduated or have knowledge. A larger staff will permit a more manageable division. Suggestions are received from readers, bibliographies and the review journals looked at, catalogues of second-hand booksellers searched. The library has acquired many

[1] *Resources of Canadian university libraries for research in the humanities and social sciences*, 1962, p. 18.

collections of books both large and small, but most of its stock has been individually selected and ordered.

It is sometimes suggested that new universities cannot build up adequate research libraries because the necessary material is no longer available for acquisition. Certainly many early printed books are very rare and expensive. A new library, moreover, starts cripplingly late in the competition for other than recent historical and literary manuscripts many of which have passed into the keeping of institutional libraries from which they will not foreseeably be released. Nevertheless given a sufficiency of money there is no reason why a new British library should not have some of the success of the young transatlantic libraries in collecting the books of past centuries. The sands of time are running out. This is the last generation which will see many of these items appearing in the sale rooms. It is, however, with current publications and with books published after 1800 that the library is primarily if not exclusively concerned. Here only shortage of funds can prevent the assembly of collections able to support research. The acquisition of a basic collection of 250,000 books in less than ten years, which has been suggested above as a minimum target, would cost about half a million pounds. The initial capital grants provided by the University Grants Committee, added to recurrent grants and supplemented by private generosity, have enabled the library to start off at a reasonable pace, but further substantial grants will be necessary if the target is to be achieved.

One, among many, of the pleasures of coming to work in a new university, in a new library, is to be immediately aware of the fund of goodwill that exists towards it. Any new library must be greatly dependent on the co-operation of other libraries and on the generosity of donors. Sussex has already been fortunate enough to receive gifts from many individuals and institutions ranging from one to hundreds of volumes, and to all these benefactors an immeasurable debt is due. Many urgently wanted books, no longer in print, have been received in this way. Gifts of collections or working libraries place a responsibility on the university not only to see that a proper and full use is made of them but also, if at all possible, to develop them. It is always sad to see a scholar's private library dispersed at the end of a life, but there is hopefully some compensation in making it not only available to other workers in the field but also in joining with it new books so that the older retain their vitality and relevance.

Among working libraries gathered together by scholars which the

University has received is that of the late Professor William Rose, formerly Professor of German in the University of London. This was presented by his widow and contains three thousand books, mainly the texts of German authors with critical works about them – Goethe, Heine, and Rilke are prominent – with items on German history and culture. The philosophy section has been strengthened by a substantial gift from Emeritus Professor H. F. Hallett, and the classics section by five hundred volumes from the library of the late Stuart E. P. Atherley. Modern language periodicals were presented by Miss E. M. Pool. The present editor of *The Countryman*, Mr John Cripps, arranged for the University to receive as a gift a great part of the library of his predecessor as editor, J. W. Robertson Scott, including many items on journalism. Material relating to British politics in the twentieth century has come from the books of the late Professor Reginald Bassett and on international relations in the same period from those of W. W. Gottlieb. Gabriel Naudé wrote in one of the earliest works of librarianship – 'I should set down without hesitation as the first [way of obtaining books] above all others the promptest, the easiest and the most advantageous, the acquisition of some other entire and undissipated library.'[1] What was true in the seventeenth century retains its validity today.

It is upon donors that the library is likely to depend in its early years for any rare books and manuscripts that it may acquire. A rare book collection has a significant role to play. It provides valuable research material and can give a vitalizing meaning to bibliographical studies so important for the textual critic and others. The first manuscripts that the library has received are, with great propriety, a collection of documents relating to the abortive attempt to found a University College of Sussex just before the 1914–18 war. The library also has possession of the account book relating to the building by Nicholas Dubois of Stanmer House in 1720 to 1727; this is among a collection of manuscripts, mainly nineteenth century, and printed books which have been deposited in its keeping by the Trustees of the Chichester Furniture Settlement. The University Library began in the original library rooms at Stanmer House, the former home of the Earls of Chichester. Among the Chichester books are a copy of Humphrey Repton's *Designs for the Pavilion at*

[1] Naudé, G., *Advice on establishing a library. With an introduction by Archer Taylor*, 1950.

Brighton 1808, and of the first edition of Hobbes' *Leviathan*. First editions of modern literary works have been presented by several individuals, and they include a fine collection of the works of D. H. Lawrence.

With two or three exceptions the research libraries of the United States have been significantly developed since 1900. Not only have rich assemblies of the commoner, recently published materials been mustered in a short time, but also splendid rare book and manuscript collections – almost too splendid looked at from Europe. The export of rare books continues and will only know an end when there are no more to go. Where sufficient copies of not only European but of American *rariora* have been unavailable, microfacsimile has been called in. When projects for their filming are completed, it will be possible to buy from the stocks of commercial agencies a microform copy of most books printed in Great Britain before 1700 and of books printed in the United States before 1800. Other spectacular projects include the microprint edition of British Parliamentary Papers to 1900, the filming by the Library of Congress of the manuscripts of St. Catherine on Mount Sinai and in the monasteries of Mount Athos, and by St Louis University of a large portion of the manuscripts in the Vatican. There are many more.

The first spur to library use of microfacsimile was its ability to provide copies of rare books and of manuscript, and therefore unique, material. The scholar was enabled to consult materials which he would otherwise only have been able to see in another library, possibly thousands of miles away, and was provided with a copy whose accuracy a scribe could not match. Full-size photocopying has also long been available to the library user, but its cost, greater than that of microforms, has been until recently prohibitive except for a small number of pages. The number of documentary reproduction machines, for whose manufacturers the richest market is not libraries but offices and industry, increases annually. The most significant recent library development in this field has been the invention of Xerography. This enables a full-size copy to be printed from a microfilm on a continuous roll of ordinary paper, and, incidentally, makes the film a means to an end rather than an end in itself. The cost is within manageable proportions and the life of the paper is that of an ordinary book. The qualities of miniaturization in saving storage space were in libraries, if not outside them, paradoxically less quickly seized upon. This is no longer so and, in particular, a great number of past volumes of newspapers and periodicals are now available for sale in microform. The amount of space required to house a complete set of the London *Times* in the original is not inconsiderable, but that of housing the smallest selection of the major newspapers of the world beggars the imagination.

Technically, then, there is no reason why a microcopy or full-size copy cannot be made of any printed or written document. The librarian of a new university is thus much better equipped than his predecessors to meet readers' demands. A copy cannot produce a watermark or show the way in which a book has been bound, but such facts are not often significant. Microcopies can save expense in storage space. There are obstacles to the use of photo-copies. Copying of material in which copyright still subsists is not possible without permission except under the limitations of the fair-dealing agreement relating to copying for private study. Publishers and authors are protected against indiscriminate copying. The book is a splendid instrument. It can be read in a library, at home, in a train or bus, or in bed. The microform, cheaper than a full-size copy, can only at present be adequately read if enlarged by a desk machine. For this reason there is some resistance to its use, but scholars prefer a microtext to no text at all. For much used material the book remains supreme.

In the 1962 World's Fair held at Seattle the American Library Association organized an exhibition and gave it the title *Library 21*. Its descriptive brochure explained that it was 'an automated Library of the future designed in co-operation with leading firms in the electronic and publishing industries'. The visitor was invited to 'See National Cash Register's Micro Image Library of the Future where 40,000 books and pamphlets will be fitted into a single volume through the micro image process which reduces materials to one 40,000th of its original size' and then in the RCA video library to 'see how through television communications the unique materials in library centers throughout the world will be made available on call at the press of a button'.

Such developments are indeed in the future, although necessity may hasten their arrival. The problems, for example, of the librarian of a new university in one of the underdeveloped countries separated by long distances from rich library centres make those at Brighton seem trivial. Already microphotography enables a new library, or an old one, to make a significant addition to its resources for research in traditional form. Already full-size copying, apart from meeting individual requests from students who prefer photographic copies to the labour of making them by hand, permits the acquisition in suitable form of often consulted out-of-print books of which second-hand copies cannot be found. Each year more photolithographic editions of books and back runs of periodicals are published to make important material available again. The new library building will be equipped with a photographic reproduction unit and with readers for the various sorts of microfacsimile. It is intended to make the fullest possible use of these new aids to library making, but aids they as yet are, not substitutes for large libraries in traditional form.

The use of modern methods of documentary reproduction is but one example of the way in which inventions of the machine age can help the librarian solve the greater problems that this age has brought for him in the concurrent expansion of knowledge and increase in the number who seek it. The Library at Sussex has also been looking at the ways in which data processing equipment might help its work. Many inquiries have been undertaken in the past few years, and continue, into the use of computers for the storage and retrieval of bibliographical information and of the intellectual content of books and documents. It is clear that these machines at present have no wide application in a general university library. The library, which has access to a computer, is continuing to investigate the possibility of a limited application. It has been possible, however, for Sussex to develop a method of using punched card equipment for the maintenance of its book issue records. This is proving successful and has significantly reduced the time taken on the tedious routines of sorting and filing.

As soon as the first books are received their cataloguing and organization must begin. In order to keep pace with the large intake of the early years a short-title catalogue is first made of items on their arrival so that the books themselves may be available to readers almost at once. Fuller cataloguing of the collections proceeds as quickly as possible. The full library catalogue is on cards and comprises two parts – an author catalogue and a classified catalogue with accompanying subject index. This is a usual arrangement in British university libraries and attempts to provide an answer to inquiries by author or by subject. Special attention is being paid to the subject index, which, it is hoped, will become a valuable tool. Intelligent use of a catalogue, which is more than a means of finding a particular book, is an acquired skill. Like any other tool a catalogue is quickly spurned or cursed if inefficient. Its production demands special skill and a knowledge of the ways in which readers use libraries. The juxtaposition of catalogue cards, whether arranged by author, subject, or date, can reveal new facets and contrasting views.

Alongside the public catalogue when the new building is completed will be shelved a collection of bibliographies and printed catalogues of other libraries. There is a special case in a new library for collecting this sort of material so that a reader may be able to discover what has been published in his field, and, if possible, where a copy is available. The debt owed by scholars to the many anonymous workers whose joint efforts have brought forth such aids to learning as the printed catalogues of the British Museum or the *British union catalogue of periodicals* is great.

Books are being classified by the scheme used in the Library of Congress, the national library of the United States of America. This was judged the most suitable of the published schemes. Books are placed on the shelves in order of the classification, the intention being to enable users to find together items which treat of the same subject. No subject classification can ever be completely satisfying because many books can be allotted to more than one place – does economic history go with economics or history, for example? Some, whose number increases as the traditional barriers between subjects disappear, are virtually unable to be classified by an analytical scheme. In using the Library of Congress classification regard is had to the Sussex map of learning and to new developments in subjects, and modifications are made.

Answers to many of the questions that librarians are asked can only be given from personal knowledge of books. Those members of the library staff who are responsible for the development of various subject groups are also available to assist readers as far as they can. The division of staff duties is by subject rather than by function. All members of the senior staff suggest books for acquisition, catalogue and classify them on arrival, and assist readers. They are not, as in many libraries, divided into three distinct groups – acquirers of books, cataloguers of books, and helpers of readers. Assistance to readers has so far been informally given in response to individual requests. Tutors also give help and advice. There seems, however, a strong case for the provision of more formal instruction in the use of books and libraries, and the opening of the new library building will provide an opportunity for this. The object of such instruction would be to enable the student to find his own way in the literature of his subject, not to spoon-feed him. One of the main problems facing scholars when the growth of publications is exponential is to discover again what has already been found out.

That there should be a catalogue hall of adequate dimensions near the entrance is one of the few essentials on which almost all librarians would agree in planning a library building. Beyond that one further thing may perhaps be said with general consent – that the present generation of librarians has witnessed so many new buildings become inadequate either to provide for accelerated growth or for changes in character and emphasis within two or three decades of their erection that an attempt is now advisably made to plan adaptable buildings capable of expansion. Few librarians are brave enough to accept a building which imposes on their successors the present pattern of book use.

The library of the University of Sussex is now phased in three stages, but great care has been taken to design a building which is complete in itself at any one stage. Modular structure and an open plan will permit the future redisposition of books and reading tables as desirable. The first two stages will be ready for occupation in the summer of 1964. They will house, besides ancillary accommodation, almost 250,000 books and nearly one thousand readers. These, and they will be at least doubled as the university grows, are large numbers. Perhaps the chief problem facing library planners is to reconcile them with the fact that reading is a private occupation. Something of the quiet comfort of the study seems desirable, yet the reconciliation has to be accomplished within budgetary limitations – every student cannot be given a private room in the library – and with freedom of access to all the books. The building contains no vast reading rooms in the old style. Smaller, more intimate spaces will be created by the shelving and by other furniture. There will also be a seminar room and some enclosed studies. Books and reading places are intermingled and circulation will be largely through book stacks to protect readers from the disturbance of movement. Quietness and comfort with virtually complete freedom of access have been the aim in all the internal arrangements.

The building has been designed by Sir Basil Spence and occupies a commanding position to the west of the Great Court of the University. Behind a long, reticulated brick façade of great visual strength it is developed about a series of enclosed glazed courts of various shapes and sizes. The west elevation looks out on to the trees of Stanmer Park. Until the new building is ready the library is housed in temporary accommodation. One special feature of the new library demands mention. It will contain a recorded speech section in which it will be possible to listen individually, in small or in large groups, to recordings of the spoken word. The library proposes first to acquire recordings of literary works, and beyond this to make tapes for itself. Ciné and slide projectors will also be available for use by small groups to display visual material. No longer can the librarian concern himself only with printed books and manuscripts.

The stimulating pleasure of planning a building in co-operation with Sir Basil Spence has been but one of the excitements of being the first librarian of a new university at Brighton. There has been the delight of acquiring the first book, cataloguing the first book, and above all of welcoming the first reader. There has been the chance to experiment. The use made of the library, particularly by its undergraduates, as one would expect under the tutorial system, has been very great. It has also been satisfying to have been able to begin to lend books to other institutions, including some abroad, through the various inter-library lending schemes. Something of the debt that Sussex owes to others can thus be paid. A university library does not serve its own institution alone but the world of scholarship in general. The one disadvantage of youth is that only time brings the chance to acquire large and significant collections, but there is no reason to suppose that this need be any other than a temporary disadvantage. Given adequacy of funds the library will be fully able to support the demands that a vigorous and expanding teaching and research programme will place upon it.

10. Steps Leading to the Foundation of the University

The grant of a Royal Charter to the University of Sussex in 1961 stemmed directly from proposals formulated in the winter of 1955 and approved by Brighton Town Council in March 1956. Consummation would appear to have come sooner than has been usual in the history of university foundations. But had an attempt not been made to establish a university college half a century before, even though it proved abortive, and indeed had been forgotten by the many, the later proposals would not have been framed as they were nor the 1961 foundation have become the first of a new line. To recall the work of the pioneers is more than an act of piety; with lecture and library schemes as tenuous but valid links, the university's descent can be traced unbroken down the years.

The 1911 project was almost the last in a series to establish a network of universities and colleges in the provinces and followed immediately upon a decade of university foundations from Birmingham in 1900 to Bristol in 1909. In these years which saw established a local authority system of grammar schools there developed too a national awareness of the importance of higher education, local initiative and private benefactions being matched by increased Treasury grants. The university was first proposed – at an inauspicious moment – at the mayoral banquet held in the Royal Pavilion on 9th November 1911, at the beginning of the second term of office of Sir Charles Thomas-Stanford. Mr Charles Edward Clayton, an architect, in a vote of thanks 'took the opportunity to put in a powerful and eloquent plea for the founding of a university in Brighton'. The reporter of the *Brighton and Hove Herald* continued: 'It was an admirable speech but the pity of it was that coming at the end of a ponderously long function, with the clock well on the way to midnight, it fell upon tired brains.' Not all the brains were exhausted. On the following Tuesday at a meeting of the Education Committee, the chairman, Alderman (later Sir Herbert) Carden, strongly supported the project, and a month later on the 12th December 'in response to a numerously signed requisition', the Mayor convened a public meeting.

'Rarely if ever has a meeting so representative of the culture of the County shown so much enthusiasm in a common cause. Brighton, Hove, East Sussex and West Sussex contributed Mayors, Churchmen, secretaries of education committees and heads of educational institutions.' (So the *Herald*.) 'In view of the splendid send-off it received yesterday it should only be a matter of time before the College becomes an accomplished fact.' (*Sussex Daily News*.) 'There was a pouring out of a veritable torrent of eloquence.' The Mayor said that it was not altogether unreasonable that Brighton should take the lead as it was the town with the largest population and the highest rateable value and was responsible for the greatest educational progress in the county. Great scientific discoveries meant that leaders of industry must be highly educated men, a point not recognized in England as it was on the Continent and in America, so that we were not making progress commensurate with that of rival nations. A large number of boys were leaving Sussex secondary schools. 'We want to bring the possibility of university education to their own doors; we want to put the coping stone on the excellent education already provided.' Mr Hannah, son of the Dean of Chichester, wanted 'to show the North that we are just as good as they are', while the Reverend Rhondda Williams hoped that the sponsors would not be so concerned with rivalling Germany in the technological field as to neglect art, literature and philosophy.

It was resolved that it was 'in the highest degree desirable that a college of university rank should be established for the county of Sussex with a view to such institution becoming recognized as a college of the University of London, or in combination with other similar institutions on the south coast forming part of a separate university'. The Mayor thought the advantage lay with the first proposal. 'Naturally Brighton looks to London.' The Bishop of Lewes, moving the resolution to set up a committee of leaders in public life, said that a university by increasing local interest would get some belief in education into the homes. Other nations went ahead because the people believed in education, and so many English people did not. The French Consul, an Oxford graduate, was enthusiastic. 'Brighton is the town to which more than any other French people would prefer to send their children for education in England.' He added, 'If we had at Oxford the same climate as you have in Brighton, I think every man would have taken first class honours.' The Mayor of Hove said that a sum of £250,000 had been mentioned as requisite to launch the scheme successfully, but immediately, by using some of the accommodation of the Technical School (then used almost exclusively by evening students) and of the Training College, and with the income from fees probably only a little over £5,000 per annum would be needed from the public to commence with. 'There are ladies and gentlemen in Brighton who could pay such a sum out of their pockets without feeling it.'

The Committee acted promptly and vigorously. It found able secretaries in Mr Hackforth, the Education Officer for Brighton (who on leaving a year later was replaced by Mr Thomas Eggar, a solicitor), Mr Hannah and Mr F. Bentham Stevens, also a solicitor, whose interest in the university is still maintained. More committees were formed including a committee of influential ladies, meetings were held where Mr Clayton and others expounded the project, pamphlets were published and articles were written for the press. Meanwhile the Executive worked out the details. It was agreed to aim for incorporation in London University which meant the extension of the 30-mile limit imposed on the University in 1898, one of the matters under consideration by the Royal Commission then sitting. The document submitted to the Commission, largely the work of Mr Bentham Stevens, was a model of drafting, well-documented, cogently argued, elegantly phrased. A bald summary follows.

Sussex had a population of two-thirds of a million, one-fifth living in Brighton and one half in the coastal belt: only a quarter was engaged in agriculture, yet the sole industrial establishment was the railway works at Brighton. As so many young people had to adopt professional careers, university provision was the more necessary. A relatively high proportion of children entered secondary schools, notably in Brighton, where 900 boys and 400 girls were enrolled, representing 10 per 1,000 of the population. A sample inquiry had shown that in 21 schools with 1,100 leavers, 30 per cent obtained matriculation standard. Only a few, and these mostly from the public schools and not exclusively from Sussex, went to a university, a fractional percentage only from municipal secondary schools.

Opportunities for higher education locally were confined to the teacher training colleges (two in Brighton and one in Chichester), the Brighton Technical College (for engineering), Uckfield (for agriculture) and Chichester (for a few students of theology): in addition the Law Society conducted classes for articled clerks. In 1911 six London degrees had been gained from the Technical College and one by a Law Society pupil. Significant, as heads of schools testified, was the number of pupils who might have benefited from greater opportunities. Local provision was essential: to attend daily at a London college was time-consuming and expensive (and Sussex, more individualized than the other Home Counties, was less bound up in metropolitan affairs), while few could afford to go elsewhere. There was no prospect of an increase of the maximum of six scholarships granted in any one year; local authorities were averse from giving money to be spent outside their area whereas they would take a pride in a local college. 'England is being quickly covered with a network of universities. There is no reason to believe there is less need in the south-east.'

The executive Committee had considered the establishment of (i) an independent university, (ii) a university college, forming in conjunction with other institutions a university for the south coast and (iii) a university college associated with an existing university. The difficulty of obtaining the necessary money as well as experience (all English universities had developed from modest beginnings) suggested the rejection of the first proposal. To link up with other south coast colleges presented difficulties of communication and, in as much as these institutions lacked the prestige of an established university, would prejudice local support. The guidance of a university would help in fixing standards and settling educational policy. The ancient universities would not find it easy to co-operate with new institutions: such aid as they rendered by means of affiliation elsewhere had been ineffective. For a number of compelling reasons, London, 'the first fruit of that new desire for university culture' was the obvious choice, and such developments had taken place since 1898 that it seemed reasonable now to remove the 30 mile limitation so that a college at Brighton could be recognized as a school of the University. Initially the College would have departments of arts, science, engineering and mathematics and later law, medicine, commerce and agriculture (including forestry and colonial science). The form of government would resemble that at other colleges: a supreme Court, consisting of representatives of the local education authorities, of universities and of the college teachers, as well as donors and co-opted members; a Committee to be appointed by the Court; and an academic Council. By arrangement with the Corporation the University College would take over the work – and the income – of the Brighton technical and training colleges and house additional students in the same building. £1,800 (the annual yield of the hoped-for £50,000 endowment fund) plus the income of the colleges would give a total income of £9,000 which would allow for the appointment of five professors (£2,500) and eighteen assistants (£3,400). It was reasonable to expect that there would soon be 250 full-time students (including 120 teachers in training) as well as part-time students.

In April 1913, the Royal Commission recommended that the area for the recognition of Schools of the University of London should include the County of Sussex. Reassured by their first success, the Committee thereupon appealed for funds. In little more than a year the country was at war. A statement made in 1921 reviewed the position. At the outbreak of war, subscriptions amounting to £8,000 had been promised, of which £2,800 had been received. Since the Armistice it had appeared useless to attempt to carry out the original scheme; the necessary money could not be raised while conditions laid down for new university colleges had become more stringent. (That year the University Grants Committee recommended economy and concentration on 'consolidating existing activities'). Possibilities discussed were: the return of the money to subscribers; an attempt to co-operate in founding a university for South West England; the institution of an annual lectureship; and the creation of a scholarship fund. Ultimately a Sussex University College lectureship was founded, the inaugural lecture being given on 6th December 1924, in a crowded Dome, by the Earl of Birkenhead.

In 1925 (whether influenced by the modest start at Leicester in 1922 is doubtful) an attempt was made to take up the university scheme at the point reached in 1914. It was claimed that the need for a local college was greater than before: an increasing number of young people were leaving school at 17 and 18 with advanced qualifications, but few were able to afford residence at a distant university, while the expenditure on providing scholarships was prohibitive. Even with the existing Brighton institutions as a valuable nucleus, an endowment of at least £250,000 appeared necessary to launch a University College worthy of the county and this amount the Committee looked to Sussex to find. In the meantime, while the original lecture scheme continued, it was proposed to institute extra-mural lectureships in the Technical College as well as a scholarship scheme. But the original impetus could not be recaptured, contributions were few and in December 1930 a halt was called. It was agreed that the money collected should be employed in assisting the Technical College and Training College 'which would inevitably form the nucleus of the future university college'. In 1934 the Board of Education made a Scheme under the title of 'The Brighton and Sussex Students' Library and Educational Foundation'. Five Trustees represented each of the local education authorities in the county, while seven were co-optative. The income of a fund, amounting to £4,950, was to be used to form a library for the use of local students or for promoting lectures and research work but in effect was devoted to the first object. The books were housed in the Technical College. At the last meeting of the Trustees in March 1960 when approval was given to the draft scheme transferring funds and books to the University, the Chairman was Mr Bentham Stevens to whom and to Mr Eggar appreciation was recorded for services to the University project since 1911.

From its foundation in 1897 until 1919, Brighton Technical College confined itself mainly to evening work, much of that at a modest level, although an increasing variety of courses was offered. After the war the College was reorganized. Day students enrolled for professional courses or to read for London degrees, and by 1924 when the University project was revived, in addition to customary technical college work, courses were established for pass and honours degrees in science and engineering and to a small extent in arts. Graduate work in pharmacy and commerce developed later. The number of students in any course was never large and not more than twenty graduated each year but the achievement was impressive. At the end of the Second World War numbers were swollen by ex-service students, many of whom opted to read for degrees, while local industry and commerce increasingly demanded the part-time training of young workers. The strain on accommodation and teaching resources would alone have called for a reappraisal of the College's function and future, but these were inevitably seen against the national background. The Percy Report (1945) called for more and better qualified scientists and technologists and recommended that a few technical colleges should be selected for the development of high grade courses comparable but not identical with degree courses. The Barlow Report (1946) developed the theme and suggested the granting of university status to certain technical colleges 'geographically remote from existing universities'. The same year the Parliamentary Scientific Committee specifically suggested Brighton as one of four technical colleges to be granted university status. So, in 1946, the College Governors deliberated whether the College should be developed as a college of technology or as a university. A university was favoured partly from a fear that the College, because not based in an industrialized county, might fail to become one of the 'Percy selections' for national status. It was assumed that if the College became a university college it could still provide technical and commercial training.

Brighton, and subsequently the other Sussex education committees having given their blessing, the Governors decided to explore the matter with the University Grants Committee who on 13th January 1947 met the Principal, the Education Officers of East and West Sussex and myself (who had taken up office as Education Officer for Brighton on 1st January). The College, it was claimed, already in large measure performed the function of a university college, with 461 students enrolled from all parts of Sussex and beyond, of whom 215 were reading for London degrees (although only a third had reached a stage now normally catered for in universities). Over 400 degrees had been gained, 70 with first class honours. The proposed foundation would embody faculties of arts, science, pharmacy, engineering, architecture and building, commerce, education (based on the Training College) and social studies and might incorporate the Sussex Law School. Later a medical School might be added. Part of a large site at Stanmer, earmarked for rebuilding the Technical and Training Colleges, might be made available for the University College. It was necessary to know what financial help might be forthcoming from the State.

The Chairman of the UGC, Sir Walter Moberley, said that the economic use of the additional teachers required for the national task suggested the extension of existing university institutions rather than the creation of new ones. Nevertheless the Sussex Authorities at a later date might submit plans indicating the quantitative scope of the proposed provision, the output from Sussex schools of students with higher school certificates, and the nature of the support, including local education authority financial support, which might be given. A Ministry of Education official said that the Ministry would need to be satisfied that the proposal would not be detrimental to the provision for technical education: they would not favour an arrangement such as existed elsewhere whereby the college would conduct for the local education authorities the technical education for the area. Advice was sought of a distinguished Vice-Chancellor who underlined the view expressed by the UGC. Existing university institutions could not be sympathetic in view of the need to conserve manpower, while the Ministry would fear an adverse effect on technical college work and on teacher training. Any later submission would have to show at least two major faculties (say, arts and engineering) with a substantial number of students in each and with promise of development.

No more could be achieved at the moment, but the Committee accepting the logic of the situation looked ahead. Despite misgiving on the part of some, who felt that Brighton could not sustain two worthwhile Colleges and who preferred the development of an all-embracing College of Further Education, they recommended as an ultimate aim the establishment in Brighton of a university college as well as a regional technical college.

The establishment of a University College to be built adjoining the rehoused Technical College was accordingly proposed in the Brighton Draft Scheme of Further Education prepared in 1947–48. It was suggested that halls of residence, common rooms and possibly even workshops and libraries might be shared, although the exact relationship of the University and Regional College had yet to be worked out. Unresolved controversies on the nature of provision for technological education made it impossible to comply with the Minister's natural wish to see the respective functions of the colleges clearly defined, so eventually the Scheme was approved with the inclusion of a brief statement of the authority's aspirations. The immediate dilemma of the Technical College remained unresolved.

To advise how a University College could be established in Brighton was a congenial duty for one who as student and teacher had spent eight years in three universities, but there was little prospect of its immediate fulfilment. In 1963 it requires an imaginative effort to perceive the viewpoint of the early fifties, so dramatically has the problem of further education changed. Even in the autumn of 1955 it was necessary to convince enlightened members of the public that in the foreseeable future one more University College could be justified. Yet a few years later seven new universities had been approved and there is a general recognition that others must follow. The task was primarily one of determining the data for an exercise in logistics (i.e. number of potential students minus available places) and for ensuring that when the right answer appeared Brighton's claim was well-documented and the first to be submitted. But it also involved consideration of the nature and purpose of universities, particularly in the modern world. In the event it meant living with the idea of the University for eight years before the time seemed ripe to call for an advance, and in the interim so to order other matters that the University when it came would fit easily into the local scene.

The University Grants Committee in annual and quinquennial reports gave detailed information about the number of under-graduates and staff in each university, the spread of subjects and the method of financing current expenditure: their assessment of demand and supply and their commentary, were eagerly awaited. Year books and annual reports of British universities were studied as well as reports of national advisory and other committees and of study groups and conferences. Books about universities from Newman to Moberley and from Flexner and 'Bruce Truscott' to Armytage were read or re-read as well as all obtainable reports and articles dealing with university problems of curricula, government and related matters. There were visits too to Vice-Chancellors, Heads of Houses and dons, all of whom were sympathetic and ready with ideas (Lord Lindsay, when still Master of Balliol, suggested a version of MIT), but left the impression that the enterprise, though of no little academic interest, was destined to abort. Facts spoke for them-selves. During the post-war years returning servicemen caused university numbers to rise steeply and a pre-war population of 39,000 to become 85,000 in 1950. Universities expanded physically particularly on the science side and as numbers slowly dropped, in 1953 to 80,000, some faculties had empty places and there was talk of 'scraping the barrel'. That year the University Grants Committee stated 'it is probably true that, except in certain faculties, few school leavers who desire and are capable of profiting from a university education would now fail to gain admission to some university or college'. In 1954 the Parliamentary and Scientific Committee, noting that the 'Barlow' expansion had been achieved, added 'for the time being there is no need to envisage any further expansion of the university student population'.

So when early in 1954 Councillor Cohen asked Brighton's Development Committee to consider the revival of the university project and the Education Committee in turn were asked (the twin proposals in the Scheme having apparently been forgotten) what steps they were taking to secure the 'eminently desirable' upgrading of the Technical College to university status 'which would add greatly to the prestige of the Borough', the report could only be that the winds were unfavourable and the barometer low. At that time 'upgrading' in the sense envisaged by the Council seemed the least likely development; indeed the pursuit of this ambition was one reason why the problems of the Technical College had become pressing. In 1946 the College authorities had recognized the advantage of singleness of purpose but circumstances dictated that development should take place on several fronts. In 1951, students obtained a peak number of 75 London degrees, yet as university admission became easier and the ablest students fewer, the retention of a range of undergraduate courses alongside a rapidly developing body of diploma and vocational studies was becoming uneconomic, educationally unsound and restrictive of more fruitful development. Until a national lead was given necessary surgery was delayed. At last in December 1954, Lord Salisbury announced government policy. 'There is room for advanced work in selected Technical Colleges . . . but for work complementary to that provided by the universities: advanced courses in close association with industry and in close relation to the less advanced work of the technical college system.' New technological awards were to be established, not identical with degrees, but equivalent in standard. The way was opening for the College, if it acted promptly, to develop as a major college of technology concentrating on high-grade professional studies.

Many concluded that the university college project had been abandoned. This was far from so: indeed the refashioning of the Technical College seemed a necessary preliminary to the eventual planning of a university college based primarily on the humanities and pure science. Nevertheless when, in July 1955 Brighton Council approved a motion of seven members (Councillors Deason, Briggs, Knowles, Tompsett, Mrs Hider, Alderman Robbins and Councillor Deane), calling on the Education Committee to report 'on steps taken and projected to secure' such a college the time seemed hardly ripe to recommend action. But within the next few months there were indications that the tide was about to change and as the latest statistics became available, hope grew. By December I was confident that the Council's long-cherished ambition could be realized. Many factors contributed to optimism but of special significance were statistics of the birth rate and of university admissions. The existing university student population had been born for the most part in the years 1934–37 when the annual birth rate for England and Wales was about 600,000. But for the years 1951–54, after the post-war 'bulge', the rate had remained fairly steady at nearly 680,000. It was reasonably certain that after the anticipated pressure on places in the sixties demand would continue at a high level well into the seventies. And this assumed only that the proportion of the population seeking university admission remained stable, which, in view of the increasing number of A level passes being gained in the GCE and of social and economic trends was unlikely. Furthermore, although only slightly, university enrolments had begun to rise. The conclusion was set out in an introduction to a report here quoted.

> For those who are convinced of the need for a University College of Sussex and who wish to see their dreams become a reality the position today, to my mind, is more favourable than at any time since 1911. Taken at the flood the tide may lead on to fortune. The national picture has changed considerably since I submitted an interim report in October 1954. Until recently it had generally been assumed that apart from the special problem of the nineteen-sixties the doubling of university places since the war would meet the country's needs indefinitely. But the peak number of full-time students (85,421 in 1949–50) swollen by ex-service students has not dropped to the extent generally anticipated. In 1953–54 the number was 80,602, but in 1953 enrolments were higher than those in 1952, and in 1954, a thousand higher than in 1953. Will the same pattern be repeated after the coming bulge years in the 1960's? The multitude of babies born at the end of the war who crowded infant and junior schools and are about to strain the resources of secondary education will in the 1960's create a new

problem for the universities as well indeed as for the colleges of further education. A new focus of educational thought will inevitably develop.

There is no doubt of the need for short-term expansion. More important is long-term policy. After a second peak is reached will numbers stabilize themselves at a higher level than at present? The indications are that they will. For one thing the birth-rate since the war despite a decline after the peak period has remained above the pre-war figure. Moreover two main forces are at work which seem bound to influence this matter. First, there is the widespread and increasing recognition that in the highly competitive world of today the nation is still not making the fullest use of the abilities and skills of all its people and (admittedly less strongly recognized) that in addition to many more scientists, technologists, technicians and craftsmen there is a need for more highly trained men and women in management, administration, teaching and the social services. The second influence is a social one. Constantly and increasingly the many demand for their children the opportunities hitherto restricted to the few. More and more parents recognize that further education is a key not only to knowledge, but to social advancement. These may not in themselves be grounds for increasing university places, yet in a society becoming increasingly democratic the pressure of the double demand is likely to affect the amount of university as well as other further education provision. It may be that both employers and future employees can be persuaded that a university education has something far more valuable to offer than mere technical training for a career, and that the nation may become increasingly educated as well as instructed.

But this was only part of the case. Why another university and why Brighton? It was suggested that Oxford and Cambridge might not wish to expand and that, beyond the extension of Imperial College, further development in London might prove difficult and indeed of doubtful desirability. Extra places would have to be found in the provincial universities but these in no small measure met local requirements. The problem would be eased in the Home Counties were there another foundation. Brighton and Sussex could claim a long history of ambition and endeavour which after the early days had been manifest in the part which Brighton and its neighbours had asked the Technical College to play in providing degree courses not only for residents but for many others from far afield, often at great cost and sometimes to the prejudice of bread and butter needs. The withdrawal of university courses from the College and its new development as a major college of technology made more necessary the provision of a complementary foundation with ample provision for the liberal arts. The south-east was one of the few large and well-populated areas of the kingdom without a university and, apart from lack of provision for undergraduates, was deprived of that close association with a university which could be so beneficial to schools and to civic and social life. And Brighton and Sussex had a great deal to offer: natural and architectural delight, music, theatre, art galleries and a sustaining diversified intellectual life.

It was natural to think of a small university. Enrolments at some of the newer foundations were: Exeter 932, Southampton 863, Hull 715, Leicester 650, North Staffordshire 495. Moreover while provincial universities drew students from all parts, the smallest fraction living within thirty miles (at Exeter) was one fifth. 200 Sussex students a year (of 500 qualified) were being admitted to universities and even when the number increased, as it undoubtedly would, not more than one in three or four could be expected to choose the local college. (There would be no question of any 'direction'.) Then, as it seemed unlikely that residence could be provided for more than say 200, the concept of a small university seemed attractive: accounts of life in many of the larger institutions in industrial cities suggested that many students had little chance of gaining a sense of community. And, as has been noted, in 1955 (in 1956 the position was changing) there was little support for the suggestion of any marked expansion of university places. Finally there was the question of cost and of the amount the local authorities could be expected to contribute. So a college for 800 in the first instance was posited.

It was difficult to be precise about finance. Published tables indicated that 70% of recurrent university income came from Parliamentary grants, 13% from fees and 8% from endowments, donations and local authority grants, but that at Hull this last item formed 12% and at Keele 18% of total income. A college of 800 could look for an income of £200,000 to which the local authorities could be expected to contribute at least £20,000. This represented less than $\frac{1}{2}d$ rate to the five Sussex education authorities and most authorities (admittedly with lower rateable value) contributed a 1*d* rate. Then there was capital expenditure. A College for 800 would cost more than a million pounds to build. The extent of non-recurrent grants had varied of recent years and would need to be investigated, though presumably most of the cost, say up to 90%, would be met by the Treasury, leaving the rest to come from the local authorities or from a public appeal for funds, say £7,000 per annum by way of loan charges.

Observations were offered on organization and curriculum. A foundation such as Keele would be attractive and would allow experiment, particularly into how a student's right to the opportunity to become a 'capable and cultivated human being' was not defeated by the prevailing vocationalism and its attendant specialism. But with the demands being made upon national resources and with work at Keele still experimental and conducted with an expensive staff-student ratio, it seemed that the UGC might favour a more traditional development with work in preparation for London degrees. Even so, to secure from the outset the avoidance of a rigid departmental structure, London University might be persuaded to enter into some kind of 'special relationship' which would allow a measure of autonomy in the College. (None of the senior university officers consulted, however, felt able to express any opinion on this.)

It was recommended that the other Sussex Education Committees should at once be invited to co-operate in the appointment of a joint committee, and that, if such committee favoured the active prosecution of the proposal, steps should be taken as follows: (i) each authority to be asked how much it would contribute; (ii) Brighton to be asked to make available a site at Stanmer and to allow Stanmer House to be used for university purposes; (iii) the U.G.C. to be asked to receive a deputation; (iv) support to be invited from leaders in public life; (v) a subscription list to be opened.

A report to Council was due by November, but other duties pressed and the occasion called for a detailed statement (which ran to over 20,000 words). In February this went to the Education Committee, who were enthusiastic about prospects, and in March to the Council who gave their blessing. Representatives of the five Sussex Education Committees met, under the chairmanship of Alderman Kippin of Brighton, on 24th April. The meeting was exploratory: no one from outside Brighton could commit his committee although some, notably Alderman Caffyn, expressed strong personal support. Nevertheless the matter was urgent. In an informal talk the Chairman and Secretary of the Grants Committee (whose interest and help throughout the following years was of continual encouragement) had recommended that a deputation should call at an early date on the Committee so that the Sussex proposals could be before them at the outset in their consideration of policy to cope with 'the bulge' in the sixties. It was yet to be decided whether expansion of existing universities would suffice but the degree of local enthusiasm and of financial support could be an important consideration: a favourable factor was the availability of student lodgings outside the holiday season. The Joint Committee agreed there was a sufficiently strong *prima facie* case to go to the authorities and that they would meet again in June. In the meantime Brighton felt it must give a lead. On 21st June the Council agreed to make available a large site (about 145 acres) at Stanmer for the University on lease for 999 years at a nominal rent of £1 per annum, and, in the early stages of development to make an annual payment of £12,000 (then nearly a 1*d* rate). In addition rating relief would be given at least to the same extent as was enjoyed by universities elsewhere. It was also agreed to place Stanmer House (then in a dilapidated condition) at the disposal of the university on terms to be negotiated.

Before the deputation went to London and with the 1911 precedent in mind it seemed important to call a public meeting so that the proposal might have a broader basis than local authority support. Councillor Cohen, then Mayor, acted as host in the Royal Pavilion to a representative audience assembled to hear a distinguished Sussex platform. The Lord Lieutenant, the Duke of Norfolk, had consented to take the chair. His approach was cautious. 'Nothing would be worse than that we should start something in Brighton with great excitement and then find that possibly the county or other people would have to come to the rescue financially.' Other speakers gave unqualified support. Lord Hailsham was eloquent. After asserting 'We are very short of universities in this country. Brighton is an ideal place for one' he continued: 'Let no one think that the possession by Brighton or other town of a college of advanced technology is going to meet the needs of a scientific age.' There could be no continued advance in technology without reference to science which was a vocation of universities. Moreover, the demand upon the ordinary citizen in cultural and spiritual resources had never been so high. This theme was reinforced by the Bishop, Dr Bell, (who, hopeful of success, said: 'All Sussex is involved in this and all should play their part'), by Mr Donald Beves of King's College, Cambridge, an old Brightonian, and by the Mayor. The remarks of Mr Dancy, the Headmaster of Lancing, recalled those of the French Consul on an earlier occasion. 'Brighton has a quality of vivacity which Paris has and provides an ideal background to the serious pursuit of the discipline of higher education.' It was left to Mrs Normanton, QC, another old Brightonian, an enthusiastic supporter from the outset, and the first of the University's benefactors, to bid the Chairman in spirited fashion not to be overcautious. 'When your illustrious namesake Lord Howard of Effingham sent out all those boats to meet the Armada, he did not weigh the cost.' 'With a majestic sweep of an elderly hand,' said the *Times Educational Supplement*, 'England's first woman QC dismissed pounds, shillings and pence as contemptible hindrances.' The resolution approving the proposal, which was unanimously carried, was moved by Alderman Caffyn and seconded by Brigadier Thwaytes of West Sussex in terms similar to those used in the same place in 1911.

When the Joint Committee met again in June the representatives could report little more than that discussions were continuing locally. As some members from East Sussex had reservations about Brighton as a university town and as unanimity was desirable, it was agreed to inform the Grants Committee that all authorities favoured university provision in the south-east and that there was 'a general measure of agreement' that the place should be Brighton. On 19th July the deputation was cordially received in Belgrave Square, stated its case (which was already known) and was informed (as it already knew) that no decision could be given until new university provision generally had been surveyed and until the Government had determined the amount of the quinquennial grant. Nevertheless the five chairmen and their officers all felt heartened. The meeting had gone well.

There followed a period of waiting and uncertainty. When a group of people, suddenly, in a matter of three or four months, has been caught up in a common enthusiasm and there is no immediate prospect of advance the temperature tends to drop: and it was desirable to maintain it, for the venture was new and a great deal of backing was needed from the general public, as well as from the Sussex authorities who had still to declare their financial support. Fortunately in this respect the proposal had occasioned wide publicity, most of it highly favourable, which led to constant press inquiries and to requests for articles for a variety of journals, to invitations to broadcast and above all to address scores of meetings, groups of teachers and other bodies of professional and university people, political societies, Rotary clubs, churches and women's organizations. The project was kept before the public eye. Not unnaturally there were doubters and opponents who made their voices heard and captions 'facts and dreams' and 'university cost worry' appeared amongst more frequent encouragement. There was even a canard that building at Stanmer would prejudice Brighton's water supply. In May 1957 a fillip was given by a debate on university provision in the House of Lords inaugurated by Lord Pakenham (now the Earl of Longford). Both he and Dr Bell were well versed in the Brighton case, which was strongly urged. The opportunity was not missed of reminding Lord Hailsham of his eloquent advocacy. He replied: 'I still retain all the sentiments I entertained then. I do not unsay a word or syllable of it but I am advised it would be constitutionally improper for me to endorse a word or syllable as Minister of Education or spokesman for the Treasury.' After outlining the views of the UGC and their difficulties at the time in approving a new institution (when years would have to pass before it was 'economic') he continued, 'yet a new college at Brighton has special attraction for the Committee'. He added, 'At the moment the Committee await a reply to a letter which they have sent to the director of education.'

In a letter, of the 2nd April, the Secretary of the UGC had written to regret the lack of progress. It was not possible to consider the project in isolation and the wider problem of enlarging the capacity of universities raised major issues of government policy: the deciding factor was likely to be one of cost per student place. The Brighton proposal, however, seemed sufficiently promising to warrant further exploration. As the College would need to be planned on the basis that suitable lodgings would be available for students within a reasonable distance of the college and that houses would be available for the staff (say a hundred for the size of college proposed) assurances were sought about available accommodation. Secondly, reference was made to a recent visit which the Chairman and

Secretary had made to Stanmer, and Brighton Corporation were asked if some adjustments could be made to the site, admittedly an attractive one, to provide additional flatter land. A third point related to an inquiry made of the Grants Committee about academic studies since the Ministry had temporarily suspended consideration of plans for the new College of Technology lest engineering (suggested in the original proposals), were to become a faculty in the university. 'While the Committee would not wish to limit the ultimate development of the university college they would envisage it as covering initially a range of pure science and the humanities but not applied science.'

After consultations with hoteliers and boarding house keepers and from knowledge of the situation in respect of local colleges, an assurance could easily be given with regard to student lodgings. Estate agents were confident that suitably-priced houses were available for staff, while Brighton Corporation agreed to erect, if requested, a block of flats for junior dons. The site question caused greater difficulty. After the request for flatter frontage land had been met, in August 1957, when the proposal still awaited approval but when the need for more university places in the future had become widely recognized, the UGC suggested that to make possible any desirable later expansion of the university the site should be enlarged to about 200 acres. This was a subject of consideration by the Joint Committee and more particularly Brighton Corporation for the best part of a year and involved several meetings with the UGC officers. An extension to the south-west was unacceptable to the Corporation since it would impinge on Stanmer Park, which they wished to keep in its natural setting. The alternative extension, to the north-east, meant acquiring land from the Chichester Estate. The Corporation were willing to purchase on behalf of the University but the Trustees were reluctant to sell (the Ministry felt unable to approve a compulsory purchase) while its development would have meant a change in the character of the land adjoining Falmer Village to which East Sussex Planning Committee were opposed. It was not until the spring of 1958 that the Town Clerk reported success in his protracted negotiations for the purchase of land to the north-east including Falmer Village and that East Sussex were persuaded to give permission, if required, to the development of 45 acres of the site for university purposes.

In December 1957, eighteen months after the deputation had

visited Belgrave Square, the Chairman intimated that the UGC were hopeful that the Government would shortly make available capital to start the college and that they were anxious for other matters still outstanding to proceed swiftly so that no time would be lost if and when support was announced. They recognized that the site problem was being tackled but needed to know more about financial support, since only Brighton and recently Eastbourne had committed themselves. As a result East Sussex agreed the following February to grant the equivalent of a halfpenny rate (about £12,000) although West Sussex and Hastings were not able to reach a decision until the summer. In the event a total annual sum of about £38,000 was promised by the authorities which in 1963 has been increased by 50%.

On the 20th February 1958 the Chancellor of the Exchequer announced a programme of £60 million for new university building for the years 1960–63, and added that £1½ million had been provisionally reserved for the early building of the University College of Sussex. The conditions as stated later (in July 1958) by the UGC were the granting of a Royal Charter and a satisfactory outcome of matters which in the meantime had been referred to an Academic Advisory Committee. Recurrent grant would be paid from 1962, the first year of the quinquennium, and it was suggested that any earlier commitments might be met from the income promised by the local authorities. Although approval was still conditional few doubted that the establishment of the University of Sussex was at last assured. But there were still difficulties to be overcome and problems to be solved.

The Joint Committee met eight times from its appointment in April 1956 until October 1958. After the receipt of the official letter from the UGC and the implied assumption of greater responsibilities, it was felt that its constitution should be formalized and the basis of membership enlarged. So it was recommended to the five local education authorities (who concurred) that the Committee should be reconstituted as a provisional College Council with its membership reflecting that of the Council of a provincial university, and comprising three members of Brighton Education Committee, two from both East and West Sussex and one from both Eastbourne and Hastings with the five Education Officers, six members of the Academic Advisory Committee and eight persons of distinction in the County. The Provisional Council had a preliminary meeting in

January 1959 when Alderman Caffyn, who had succeeded Alderman Kippin as Chairman of the Joint Committee, was elected chairman. In a matter of months it was to achieve status as a legal entity. The local authorities had expressed their willingness to make contribution to the university project before 1962, when the UGC were to make their first grants towards current expenditure, but the Minister found it difficult to give the necessary approval in accordance with Section 84 of the Education Act 1944 until the University College was in being. The Minister, however, was most anxious to help and with what might be regarded as benevolent sophistry agreed that if the College Council were incorporated as a company with the name The University College of Sussex, he would consent to financial aid being granted by the local education authorities. Through the good offices of the Town Clerk of Brighton, a Company was registered with the Board of Trade on the 20th May 1959. The original directors of the company were the members of the University College Council. As I had acted from the outset as secretary of the Joint Committee I was appointed secretary (with the registered office of The University College in the Education Office), while the Town Clerk of Brighton accepted appointment as honorary solicitor and the Borough Treasurer as honorary finance officer.

Reference has been made to an Academic Planning or Advisory Committee, and some account is necessary of its conception and functioning. The University Grants Committee were sympathetic with the desire of the Joint Committee to see some new approach to university studies – possibly a breakaway from a rigid departmental organization, from excessive specialization or even from syllabuses which might be overloaded. Changes of any kind would be difficult were students to be prepared for degrees of another university: it is simpler to introduce new ideas in a new institution than to modify existing patterns of work. But if the College were to award its own degrees from the outset other universities and indeed the public at large would have to be assured of the maintenance of satisfactory academic standards. The UGC wished to explore how this might be achieved without the benevolent but manifest sponsorship of other institutions. After informal discussions it was accordingly suggested to the Joint Committee (who in January 1958 agreed) that an advisory committee should be appointed of persons of high academic standing, including an industrialist, together with a local representative. This Academic Planning Committee would advise on ways by which standards could be guaranteed, on the range of studies during the first years and the general character of the undergraduate course and, in consultation with the Joint Committee, would prepare a petition for a Royal Charter for the College and a draft for such a charter, and would nominate the first Principal of the College, and with his advice the first Professors. Sir James Duff, then Vice-Chancellor of Durham, agreed to act as chairman and with him served Professor, later Sir Neville Mott (Cavendish Professor of Physics at Cambridge and later Master of Gonville and Caius College), Dr Wilson (Vice-Chancellor of Leicester), Professor Christopherson of Imperial College, London, Dr, now Sir Ronald, Holroyd (Deputy-Chairman, ICI) and Mr Oakeshott (Rector of Lincoln College, Oxford). I represented the Joint Committee and acted as secretary. The sponsors were deeply indebted to the distinguished academics for the devotion and detailed study given to their task. The outcome has provided a new pattern of university studies which is likely to affect many institutions besides Sussex.

Although a report of the deliberations would provide fascinating reading, only a brief note of one or two issues discussed and of the recommendations which were accepted by the College Council and by the UGC can be given here. Not only did the Committee meet frequently but there were many discussions between individual members as well as consultation with non-members. A number of Vice-Chancellors and others were invited to submit memoranda based on their experience of specific procedures and experiments and a deputation was received from the Association of University Teachers.

The Academic Committee asked at the outset about local intentions. The Promotion Committee had properly regarded this as in the main a matter for the academics (although the education officers were anxious to express certain views and were given the opportunity). There was however general agreement that studies should be 'complementary' to those in the Technical College, that they should range over the arts and social studies (which should be read by half the students) and pure science, and that any engineering course should be of a more general nature than those at the Technical College. There was a feeling too that the single subject honours degree should have no virtual monopoly. Some tentative personal suggestions which had the intention of giving the university a contemporary look and which had been put forward in an article in the *Universities Quarterly* were repeated: a school of politics and administration linked with history and philosophy, economics and psychology (resembling in some respects PPE at Oxford); and a school of European Studies, concerned not only with languages but with other aspects of civilization. (It was suggested that with the developing concept of a united Europe, political and economic thinking needed to be reinforced by cultural studies and that Brighton seemed peculiarly fitted to house a school of this kind.) And, should not universities be more generous in offering a home to the creative arts? Could drama, possibly the visual arts, and certainly music, which flourished in Sussex, and in the schools, play a significant part in the new college?

The following are a few examples of many topics considered by the Committee in the course of wide ranging discussions.

1. The advantage of a four-year course for all students and the difficulty of achieving or indeed justifying this with the increasing demand for university places.

2. The desirability for students who would be entering industry to have some background knowledge of industrial structure, trade unions, etc. Should such study take place concurrently with the study of science or might it be undertaken in a postgraduate year?

3. Within the limits set by a small university, how best to take the opportunity to do something new and to recommend some distinctive approach to studies, recognizing that were studies to be too much out of alignment with those elsewhere, it might be difficult to attract teachers.

4. How courses might be broadened without resulting in too great a fragmentation of studies.

Sir James Duff with the Principal-elect and with the Chairman and Secretary of the Provisional Council made public his Committee's recommendations at a press conference in London in February 1959. At the outset there would be two faculties only: science, and arts and social studies, each with some 400 undergraduates normally pursuing a three-years' course. In science there would be a usual organization of courses in departments except that there would be a single department of physics and mathematics and a single department of engineering science without specialization (a student needing specialist qualifications should be able to obtain these in a technical college, possibly Brighton). There would also be departments of chemistry and biology. The possibility of broadening courses had been explored but, given a three-year course, specialist demands offered little opportunity. A three-year concentrated study of a single subject had proved its educational value and appeared essential to produce professionally qualified people. But the Committee believed that for many of the ablest people such a course was not by itself sufficient and that great profit would be derived from the opportunity of attending some broadening course, perhaps in a fourth year so that scientists might be better able to see their science in perspective and to use it in the context of the society in which they lived and worked. (This pattern of studies has been modified. It was however recognized from the outset by the Academic Committee that planning could be on general lines and provisional only until a Principal was appointed – in January 1959 Mr Fulton accepted appointment and was immediately available to attend meetings – and that many matters of curriculum must for determination await the coming of academic staff.)

In the faculty of arts it was proposed to organize studies in three main honours schools, English studies, European studies and social studies. In the two former schools in addition to language and literature would be included options dealing with different aspects of the history and civilization of the country or countries studied. This specialization would be accompanied by some breadth of approach with the co-operation of the different subject specialists in a common degree course. Social studies would allow alternative study in politics, economics, history and philosophy. A suggestion that there should be some compulsory science studies for arts students and compulsory art studies for science students had been fully explored but rejected, although in the organization of the university college community every opportunity would be taken to allow for 'cross-fertilization' on a voluntary basis. In due course it was proposed that the College should provide a postgraduate course in education and that there should be an Institute of Education to serve the five or six training colleges of the region. (The Director of the University of London Institute of Education had already expressed his personal approval of a new grouping of colleges which would relieve the pressure on London.) The courses of study had regard to a total enrolment of some 800–1,000 students, and there would therefore be inevitable limitations. But when the College increased markedly in size, there were interesting and indeed exciting possibilities for extended fields of work.

In the spring of 1958 as the Advisory Committee were beginning their task, Oxford University through the delegacy for Extra-Mural Studies were good enough to sponsor a course of six lectures in Brighton to throw light on some of the problems the new university might face. These drew large audiences and were not only stimulating but highly encouraging to the sponsors. Dr Alan Bullock, Censor of St. Catherine's, spoke on 'The Purpose and Conditions of a University', Lady Ogilvie, Principal of St. Anne's, on 'The Problems of a Non-Residential University', Sir Douglas Logan, Principal of London University, on 'The Governance of a University', Mr A. D. C. Peterson, of the Oxford Department of Education, on 'The Universities and the Schools', Mr (now Professor) Corbett of Balliol on 'The Content of a University Education', and Mr R. B. McCallum, Master of Pembroke College, Oxford, on 'The Methods of University Education'.

The Joint Committee and the Academic Advisory Committee and later the College Council gave much thought to the form of government. Originally many of us considered the common Court-cum-Council arrangement to be cumbersome and had in mind the institution of a Council only. However, there appeared virtue in inviting a wide and representative section of the County to be associated with the College and so the concept was evolved of a Court lacking the ultimate authority usually vested in it. The Council thus became the supreme governing body, which it was agreed should have a lay majority, partly representatives of the education authorities, partly independent persons, but with a substantial minority of academics. At one time a Congregation was favoured but the proposal was dropped, although it was agreed that on the Senate should serve a fair number of non-professorial staff. It was thought at the time that the first charter would be in respect of University College status, although it was hoped that within a few years a further charter would concede status as a university. As, however, from the outset permission would be sought to award degrees – and not only first degrees – the Academic Advisory Committee recommended that it or a similar body should for a period be 'written into' the Charter, with these functions: the election of two members of the College Council; the right to advise either Council or Senate on any academic matter and to satisfy itself on the arrangements proposed for external examiners; the nomination of a member to serve on appointment committees for senior faculty members; and the power to approve the institution of higher degrees. Provisions on these lines appear in the University Charter.

In 1958, after the go-ahead given by the UGC and the Treasury and following the resolution of site difficulties, it was time to consider the layout of the site, preparatory to the design and erection of buildings. A special committee was authorized to deal with this matter and after consultations, the study of plans, drawings and photographs and after interviews with several eminent architects, Mr (now Sir Basil) Spence was, early in 1959, invited to prepare a layout from a general briefing on the scope of the work and activities to be accommodated, both immediately and subsequently, prepared by the Planning Committee and approved by the Joint Committee. At the Committee's request the Architect agreed to design buildings which would fit naturally into Sussex parkland by avoiding high buildings and using local materials. Both the layout and subsequently the design of the buildings undertaken by Sir Basil have given great satisfaction. In the meantime after considerable negotiations between the College Council and Brighton Corporation, Stanmer House, a small but gracious 18th century mansion once the home of the Pelham family, was rehabilitated and leased to the University for twenty years. It has proved invaluable as a temporary administrative headquarters and as an initial library. It also gives a modern university a valuable link with the past.

In September 1959 Mr Fulton took up his office as Principal. The first phase of the University College project was complete. But the University College remained for only a brief period as a milestone on the way to full University status, and by the time the doors opened to the first students Mr Fulton had become Vice-Chancellor of the University of Sussex.

A word in conclusion. Necessary compression has meant the omission of any reference to many people and to many matters of significance in the history of the proposal. But a special final mention must be made of the members of education committees, finance committees and planning committees as well as of the five local education authorities and of their many officers without whose full co-operation the venture would not have come to fruition. All Sussex played its part, and, as the University's arms bear witness, can claim a share in the foundation.

11. *From the Cage: An Undergraduate View*

Anyone writing from the guinea-pig's viewpoint in an anthology of aspirations must necessarily find himself in difficulties about his subject matter. One could write at considerable length of the trials and stresses of the first year of the Union in Preston Road, of the strange events surrounding the performance of *The Glass Menagerie* by Tennessee Williams, of the abominably smelly cellar below '237' and the dissipated parties that were a frequent occurrence there, of the visit of the BBC View film unit, of bonfire night spent on the beach cooking sausages and exploding cans of baked beans. This is a rich potential for another article in another place. What I wish to do instead, however, is to outline, as frankly as possible, the kinds of thing that became apparent during the first year, the shock of the move to Falmer where we felt suddenly that we were dispensable units in a large impersonal Plan, life there at the time of writing, and what I think life will be like in the long term when the University is complete. Somewhere in this scheme room has to be found to describe, within the terms of my own experience, what it is like to undertake a Sussex course. I hope I may be forgiven for taking this opportunity of expressing certain weaknesses, which could very easily be eradicated, which are generally felt to exist in both the academic and social fields.

The first year left a considerable impression on all those who lived through it. Fifty undergraduates and about ten faculty members inhabited two Victorian houses on the London–Brighton road. Inevitably, at the outset, the atmosphere was that of experimentation; everyone felt that this was a short and passing stage in the University's development. As the year progressed, however, we all became rather fixed and unwilling to believe in any hereafter. Fifty is really rather a small community to live together in harmony, apart from the fact that there were twice as many women as men, and the air was often a little stormy.

The Students Union, under the excellent Presidency of Adrian Mugridge, came into being, and began elementary sparring with the Powers that govern the student's life, over such topics as the wearing of gowns, and the possibility of living in flats as well as lodgings. The fact that the Union decision prevailed in the case, one would have thought the more important case, of the flats, and failed in the case of the gowns, served to show where the real power lay. With tiny funds and a general lack of desire to congregate with people whose personality, background and attitudes we all knew, the Union, and the societies that had some life in the early days, trailed lazily away into the summer term, which was greatly enlivened by the sun and the springing to life of Brighton with the arrival of 'the Season'. Those who had felt themselves forced by the minute society to act up their natural tendencies – the Dedicated Student, the Driver of Old Cars, the Poet, the Rugger Club Type, the Femme Fatale – relaxed in the sun and read in quiet and blissful isolation among the boats on the beach.

All the first students were reading Arts subjects. Despite the fact that a couple of people had taken Science A levels, these being thought of rather as converts and subjected to occasional head-patting, there was much discussion of what it would be like when the Scientists came. There were several visits from guest speakers, on which occasions one felt for an hour that one was really at a university. No one in the town seemed to know or want to believe that the University, that mysterious and sinister building-site on the Lewes road, was actually open. Academically, despite the toughness of a course that means one cannot forget subjects one loathes, and in which some kind of commitment is vital for survival, things went on in a leisurely way, except for those doing Social Studies, who then, as now, had a constant air of doing four times as much work as anyone else. The Sussex concept as outlined in the Prospectus became a reality. On the whole there was less shock attached to this for us than the general publicity might have suggested. One only became aware of the importance of Sussex the more one learned of courses elsewhere. Most people had been studying three subjects at Advanced level, and now were continuing, in a modified way, to do this at degree level, the one being the logical outcome of the other. Most of us haven't appreciated the value of the History-Philosophy-Major Subject set-up until this, the third year, where all the component parts of the course, with one or two extraneous and, one hopes, short-lived exceptions, begin to fit together, giving, in Arts subjects at least, a valuable 'stereoscopic' model of thought, historical conditions, and literature, each governing and developing the other. It becomes impossible to talk about 'backgrounds' any more; one is forced to give adequate attention to all the causalities involved in literature and the arts.

Throughout the first year we were interrogated by the dons on all facets of the course. This could only resolve details. It will take many years to achieve the subtlety of balance and focus necessary to bring out the full benefits of the wider course range. The two main problems at the time of writing seem to be to integrate the components of the course and attain the 'stereo' effect, and more pressingly, to get some kind of exchange between the arts and science students. Seminars have been tried in order to find common ground, but these have not generally been successful for numerous reasons. The possibility of breaking down, in one seminar per week, years of accumulated traditions of separateness that the older universities and particularly the schools have helped to create and sustain is very remote. Since the building is neatly packaged into 'Arts', 'Physics', 'Chemistry', 'Falmer House', one is allowed still to think of separate disciplines. In addition to this, the time table of someone studying physics is so far removed from his guest-house neighbour reading history that all possibility of finding much in common seems remote. What is needed ultimately, and I think it must come, is the establishment of joint projects where scientists and arts students must work together, although doing different and quite precisely defined jobs, in a concrete partnership. It is unrealistic in any venture to stress intellectual exchange and minimize practical work-sharing. The outstanding thing about Sussex is that when needs like this are realized people go out of their way to get things done.

The move to Falmer was quite traumatic. For a year, fifty of us, which meant about twenty-five in effect, since half the students avoided the Common Room like the plague, had been living in a close and limited society. In October 1962 we found ourselves in a strange new building, swamped by 450 new and forceful undergraduates and lecturers, all of them conspiring, it seemed, to create the impression that this was really the first year of the University, In a sense, of course, they were right. The buildings were smart, luxurious, set in parkland that somehow managed to preserve its tranquillity despite the intense building programme, with its vast overhead cranes, concrete slabs, seas of mud, and busy dumper trucks. After the initial shock, which lasted about one week, the now second year settled into the new patterns of life that Falmer created. For a while the old images were preserved, until it was realized that the types of performance that the Preston Road days would have gloomily accepted, where many people seemed to be acting out exaggerated caricatures of themselves, were a bit out of place.

Numerous societies sprang up, this time with organized financial arrangements and a more or less guaranteed membership. Falmer House became the scene of almost perpetual argument about who could use room x or y at any one time, until eventually the anarchic situation was remedied with a booking system. Of course, arguments still continue, but the people who take the trouble to book usually win now. For the first term the Coffee Bar was always full of arguing, philosophizing students, clutching the ubiquitous copies of *Language, Truth and Logic*, and fighting over the meaning or merits of the film at the Continentale or, before it was closed, the Paris. The cinema has always played an important part in Sussex life. In the first year roughly half the undergraduates went to the Paris once a week, and to the Theatre Royal about once a month. With the move to Falmer a film society was formed that has continued since then to show art films every Friday evening. Besides this, the film society has begun to show films on Saturdays which are relevant to some of the principal interschool subsidiary papers; for example, we have had Contemporary Britain and Modern European Mind seasons, in liaison with Deans of Schools, which have helped to create the kind of atmosphere where academic work can genuinely be thought of as something living, and something that has a relationship with the problems of everyday life.

With the expansion and the move to Falmer came the guest house system, whereby a certain number of people would live together in a Brighton guest house during term time. To those of us who had been living in flats for quite some time this concept seemed utterly without attraction. We continued to live in small groups, but watched with astonishment the ease with which the guest houses began to work. Inevitably there was discontent in some places, over conditions, rules, food, bathroom facilities, and a real dislike in some people, myself included, for communal living worked itself out steadily, and those who simply could not stand it went into lodgings. Only the Preston Road pioneers had flats at this stage, and so came in for a very heavy social obligation in providing some sort of home for those who found the guest houses a trifle insecure or didn't get on with their room mate. At least the guest houses did, and do, keep students in Brighton, in a working society. I think it will be tragic if the time ever comes when the entire University is resident at Falmer. Pleasant though the surroundings are, most people, I am quite certain, would much rather, for various reasons, live in the town and travel out to the University when necessary. It is quite true that students spend a lot of their time in Brighton coffee bars, such as the Lorelei or the Cottage, but without a doubt the brasher, older environment is relaxing after the new, slightly inhibiting atmosphere of Falmer. Undergraduates also began to perform in Brighton, in pubs and coffee bars – folk-singers and the modern jazz quartet mainly. Both folk music and jazz have been made part of the life of the Union – folk-song perhaps because it hints at values which are felt and not calculated; jazz, because its improvisatory nature gets close to the *geist* of the University at this time, a strange mixture of the planned and the on-the-spot.

Perhaps the outstanding thing in the second year of the Union was the fight to pass what has perhaps mistakenly been called a political motion. *Winepress*, the sporadic student newspaper, had several busy weeks as all points of view were put. Everyone was studying the constitution of the Union, and for a while Bergman and Antonioni gave way to amateur legal disputes. The motion tabled was a condemnation of South Africa's *apartheid* policies. After a long and very worthwhile debate the motion was carried by a substantial majority. Many people had misgivings about the effect political discussion would have on Union meetings, but by the time the motion had been passed the body of opinion was with those of us who feel that the Union is not only administrative but representative, and becomes more alive through this kind of decision. The over-all debate continues, however, and the current seems to have moved to a roughly equal division of opinion now. Everyone who has anything to do with the Union in Sussex is very aware of it as something being formed, and very anxious that it should be the best possible servant of the student interest.

The second year ended with an Arts Festival. This will almost certainly become an annual event. It is probably a very good idea to have some small cultural target like this towards which people can work. The undergraduates are trying very hard to create something worthwhile in the arts, and it is a pity that extensive facilities for drama and music will not come until the final stage of the building project. Makeshift stages are found in Brighton, but this is expensive and cumbersome. The Union Finance Committee come down quite heavily on expenses, which are boosted by the cost of hiring halls and equipment. Despite this, already Sussex has had a play in the NUS Drama Festival at Aberystwyth, and two bands in the Finals of the Inter-Varsity Jazz Federation's National Competition, one of which came top in one of the sections.

The last two years have shown many things: that the precepts on which the Sussex course is based are very healthy and rewarding; that when the right facilities are available and funds adequate, this could become one the most alive universities in this country; that the links between the town and the University must be strengthened to provide expanding facilities for students at all educational centres in Brighton.

This is perhaps a very cold analysis of the Sussex situation. But it would be impossible to give an average description of a day at Falmer, or in Brighton. The very nature of the set-up leaves so much up to the individual that I would have to resort to describing my own day, which is probably untrue to the way most people live. The site at Falmer continues to grow; one can hardly have a tutorial in the Arts building without watching out of the corner of one's eye the steady procession of trucks, bulldozers and men from one part of the construction to another. The buildings still seem far from permanent, somehow. The colour of the life at Falmer is still struggling to compete with the colour of Falmer House, with its brick walls and bright cushions. One is always very conscious of the buildings, in a way that will be impossible when they get a bit soiled. Almost every afternoon the gravelled court-yard echoes the sound of leisurely jazz from the Common Room, and when the sun shines the numerous open areas of Falmer House take on a distinctly sea-side appearance, with an aura of laziness and drowsy reading. Bit by bit facilities come to Falmer; television, table-tennis, enough people to form an orchestra, records, home-made entertainment of all varieties, beer at the coffee bar, better food, better guest speakers, more actors, more administrators, inevitably more bureaucrats, smart people looking for the gay life, academics, students from abroad. It is very strange, having experienced the little world of the first year, to watch the scope and interest of the University expanding so quickly and so richly. The growing pains are still very much with us; all the new universities will unavoidably have this air of wearying self-examination that has been called the Sussex Blues. The authorities must try very hard at all of these places in the early days to make them as human as possible and not talk as though everyone is serving time until the Golden Age that will arrive when the establishment is complete.

When all the facilities do come Sussex will be even more exciting than it is now, in the formative stages. The rewards of being here now are that one can play an active part in the development and lose nothing on the academic side. The emphasis on the tutorial system of teaching enables one to experience a degree of exchange with the faculty that must be far preferable to simple attendance at lectures. There is no standard attitude that one must learn; the stress is on individual response and responsibility in a way that cannot help but develop the undergraduate's potential. The openness of the faculty to questioning and complete disagreement is continued in the social life of the University, with shared common rooms, and so every opportunity exists for life at Sussex to be as organic as possible.

Very few people regret that they did not go to an older university. The benefits very largely outweigh the disadvantages, which one can fairly assume to be transitory anyway. One of the most marked effects of the Arts courses at Sussex is that it turns people out into the world around them; the campus could easily dominate one's entire life, were it not that the type of approach characterized by the Contemporary Britain paper goes a long way towards killing one's apathy and insularity. One is encouraged to think that learning for its own sake, without commitment, is useless. It is very significant that of my own year a large proportion of people wish to work in underdeveloped countries when they graduate.

For the undergraduate, Sussex is a demanding place to work in; its rewards and social opportunities have to be taken, they do not just come. No one is labelled according to what their schools expect them to do, or their A level results would suggest. One has to decide on one's own interests and capabilities – with guidance, of course – and then select the appropriate pattern of learning. Academically, this must make it one of the most terrifying, and yet thrilling, places of learning in the British Isles. I find it hard to believe that anyone who has put anything into a Sussex course can come out of it with an outlook and personality completely identical to what they were before he or she came here. For some people it could mean disaster, but for the vast majority it is, and will become in the future, an experience of the most compelling kind. It provides a course, and an environment, in which learning is being put to work on society and on the individual.

Perhaps the best analysis of what Sussex does to one has been provided by Professor Asa Briggs in his article 'Retrospect and Prospect' in *Bias*, one of the student journals:

> . . . My ideal is an independent student, helped to discover not only new knowledge but himself, becoming increasingly self-reliant (and self-critical) as he becomes more knowledgeable. . . .

12. *Building a New University: The First Phase*

The University site is near the village of Falmer, half-way between Brighton and Lewes; it consists of attractive parkland on what was formerly the estate of the Earls of Chichester. To be given a two-hundred acre site four and a half miles from Brighton in a beautiful downland valley, rich in mature trees, and then be asked to build a university on it – this must be the dream of every architect.

The only building to occupy the site when I first looked at it was a rather charming barn of boarded walls, tile roof with knapped flint and brick gables which was set on the flattest part of the ground in the hollow of an elongated valley stretching from the main Brighton-Lewes road deep in the two-hundred acres. A fine screen of tall trees masks the site from this road. At right angles to it another line of trees runs for about a mile right up the valley forming a dominant spine, even today with buildings built. The old barn used to cling to it in that sensitive, inevitable way that is peculiar to indigenous building. Rising from this emerald saucer are soft rolling hills decorated with casual clumps of trees between which one is afforded delicious glimpses of the surrounding downland country.

Fortunately, one enters the site from the main road looking due north with the sun at one's back; thus I was given the opportunity of planning the first buildings facing the light so that they could be seen fully revealed and not stand as the gaunt silhouettes that nearly always result when buildings are seen with the bright sky in one's eyes.

I was appointed architect in January 1959, and the excitement which always attends a challenge was there. The University Council asked for a master plan for a group of buildings to be built steadily from 1960 to 1965 so that the student population could grow to 800 in that time, but with ample provision for expansion.

Many questions of detail essential to the architect's brief had still to be worked out. One thing was known, however – the amount of money available from the University Grants Committee to reach this objective including all building, furnishing, roads, sewers, services and landscaping. The University Council was given £1·5 million, which sounds a lot but is no more than the funds allocated to a large technical college. It was made clear that the University would have to be planned for growth, that 800 students was only a beginning and in the early days a final population of 3,000 to 6,000 capacity was mentioned.

I shall never forget the first discussions with the newly appointed Vice-Chancellor, John Fulton. He gave me a clear idea of the University he wanted to see. It was not to be organized in colleges, but as an institution with its own identity; a University of Sussex that would have a strong 'esprit' not to be fragmented by secondary loyalties to colleges. It was small enough to do this, he argued. I was given the first practical programme of requirements which was to destroy the virginity of the white sheet of paper that confronted me.

First, 'College House' (later called 'Falmer House'); a building which should father and mother the undergraduates, be the genesis of the whole complex, a place where the student would meet with others from different faculties, where he would eat, argue, play, read, where he would meet his tutor in informal surroundings, where he could spend his waking hours. The vital process of cross-fertilization between members of differing faculties would take place here. My mind leapt to my native Edinburgh with the 18th century quad designed by Robert Adam, the nucleus of the great University of Edinburgh. This building arranged round a quadrangle appeared broadly to fulfil the same function. Moreover, it gave an air of completeness in itself which would be an essential in the new University with at least ten years of building activity lying ahead.

Next came Physics which was described only in principle with a global area to be simply divided into Teaching and Research, for there was no Professor yet appointed to give the architect detailed requirements.

Hard on the heels of Physics came the Library, Arts, Chemistry, Engineering and Administration with a site for a Great Hall and Chapel. Consideration had to be given to the sites for staff and students' residences, and also for playing fields.

An overriding consideration was provision for growth. While the

University Council found it difficult to give a clear brief for immediate requirements, they found it practically impossible to instruct on the future, with its undreamt-of mysteries of scientific development. The brief for each building was given to me simply in square feet areas and practically nothing else, as details were difficult to formulate without the professors to work them out. Nevertheless, it was sufficient to make a start with the preparation of the broad plan.

More than half the battle in designing buildings is to know exactly what is required. The next stage is to decide how to mould these requirements into efficient buildings.

In a university, architectural function has many facets. It is not sufficient just to afford shelter and provide rooms strung along in the correct sequence to satisfy the immediate requirement. The whole precinct should have the 'sense of a university' and should, if possible, grow out of the soil of Sussex to become a natural part of this beautiful site. The landscape should preferably be enhanced by the addition of the buildings, just as the English scene has so often been improved in the past. Bricks and mortar can provide a background that is sympathetic to young and energetic minds which are growing and developing apace. The buildings should help sixth-formers over the fence into manhood and womanhood. The gentle courtyards of Oxford and Cambridge have proved that an environment of a sensitive kind can add to human experience.

In the programmes approved by the UGC there is no place for what is called 'waste space' – the colonnade or cloister where friends can walk and talk, discussing the latest seminar or the last piece of research, or the distinguished lecturer. Yet the addition of spaces like these lifts a mere group of buildings to the level of a place of higher learning. Landscaping, with pools and sculpture, is just not accepted *per se* as a necessity by this authority, so pools have to be justified as static water tanks in case of fire and the cost of sculpture has to be found by outside donation.

With a sickening thud it is borne in on one that officially 'aesthetics' is a dirty word and any one who openly speaks of beauty as a necessity is to be treated with caution and, if possible, restrained. Beauty is only acceptable as a by-product not a necessity. Yet the level of aesthetic appreciation usually marks the standard of achievement of a civilization. It should not be necessary to emphasize this, for during the great civilizations of Greece, Rome and the Renaissance or our own 18th century, education was considered incomplete without a thorough grounding in aesthetics.

Beauty, then, must be accepted as a requirement.

About the time I was thinking of the basic idea for the University I visited Athens, where the Acropolis, that great monument to the first democracy, is even today still pregnant with vitality and powerful impact. The lugs of marble used for lifting the stones into position are still there at the entrance, signifying that work had not finished. It is true, of course, that as soon as a building is completely finished, it must begin to die. The idea of a living, growing thing made a deep impression, and in our University at Sussex this condition was bound to prevail for many years. This would be a period of planning, labour and achievement, with completion possible only in its parts. Though cranes and construction noises would be with us for many years, small cells of completion should be quite possible.

Also at this period I made a visit to Rome and the Colosseum made a special impact. I spent many hours wandering about this magnificent ruin which was, in its heyday, dedicated to the masses – mass enjoyment, mass hysteria, mass lust for blood. But I now saw it in a different light; centuries of decay had bared the structure, which was based on the arch. Many arches, covered with the spectators' terracing in Imperial times, were now exposed, framing the individual and reducing the scale to the single person. This was a great transformation and it interested me.

A very real necessity was some quick method of building as the time-table left little latitude for an elaborate or ambitious scheme. At the same time it was obviously wise to plan this University in units, allowing each unit to develop naturally and extend as circumstances demanded, for the future of scientific buildings cannot be foretold. Ground should be left for many alternatives permitting the greatest possible freedom for academic policy.

It was this reason which in my early discussions with the Vice-Chancellor decided the policy of the master plan. Though the budget was similar to that of a large technical college and the University might well have been designed as one large building, it was decided that interlocking courtyards fed by service roads with the possibility of adding more courtyards should be the basic idea for the plan form.

Because of the lovely site I was against building high; the trees should top the buildings and continue to form the skyline. The materials should be sympathetic to the location – a Sussex brick, concrete, knapped flint, copper, timber and white paint.

As time was an important factor, and flexibility another, a method of roofing was worked out with our engineer, Ove Arup, for a scheme of prefabricated concrete arches in three spans of 20, 15 and 10 feet, to be used for the first two buildings, College House and Physics. This was to be the pilot scheme. My associate, Gordon Collins, spent many hours working out the details with Paul Ahm, Ove Arup's associate, and Mr C. F. Neal of Modular Concrete who co-operated with us from the beginning and made some superb prefabricated units from a factory established on the site.

Our knapped flint panels were also made here and though this craft had been a thriving one in the district, the contractors found it best to enlist the services of a Pole who learnt his craft in a Soviet labour camp. After his escape to freedom he continued to break stones, but at least at Sussex he was well paid!

The English are probably the best bricklayers in the world. This may be an extravagant claim but there is much evidence to support it in my view. Many fine Georgian houses and earlier ones like Hampton Court bear witness, though I concede that some superb modern brickwork can be found in Scandinavia and Holland. Bricklaying is a living craft, and the brick is probably the best prefabricated building component ever invented. Sussex is famous for its bricks. This would be a red brick University.

The picture I had in my mind's eye was not an aggressive one of buildings thrusting themselves on the unsuspecting visitor but of brick enlivened by the white paint on window frames peeping through trees with a broad rhythm of arched frames, harmonizing, I hoped, with the rounded forms of the hills and trees. But the trees would dominate – even in winter without their leaves.

This peaceful pastoral scene could, of course, be destroyed by the intrusion of the motor car, especially the ancient variety favoured by undergraduates. In spite of the youth of undergraduates, the car population in universities continues to grow at an alarming rate. The plan must cope with this situation, but areas should be kept permanently free from vehicles so that the pedestrian could find peace with his visual, oral and nasal senses undisturbed.

Though College House (now known as Falmer House) would be the nucleus – the seed – it was clear to me that a great court bounded by the first buildings and free of motor vehicles should be a fundamental of the master plan. This would help to foster the 'Sussex esprit' which the Vice-Chancellor thought essential.

So it was decided to arrange the car parks near or adjacent to the service roads with the main one hidden in the trees near the first buildings. We decided to plan them in a casual way and not as has now been accepted as common practice in the American University Campus – where they have admitted great rectangular carpets of cars – or under cover, which was far too expensive. It may be that the status symbol of the automobile is not accepted here, whereas in America the automobile is established, with the one-, two- and three-car garage attached to houses fronting the highway.

As I have already said, College House, Physics, Chemistry, the Library, Arts, Engineering and Administration with sites for the Great Hall and the Chapel were the elements of the master plan. Detailed requirements were worked out for College House and Physics. Before the final arrangement was made we had decided that College House should be the gateway to the University and that it should be the first complete cell with Physics as the second. We had also decided that the method of growth should be by the addition of courtyards with the main buildings grouped round a great court free of all motor vehicles. The north-south spine of trees should, I felt, pass through this court so that the character of screening by trees could be maintained. We had decided on building methods and materials. I looked at my once white sheet of paper, now black with charcoal, the trees immovable, the buildings ever-changing in form.

Certain principles dominate during the design process when the broad disposition of buildings is being considered. First, it is essential to discard all secondary considerations and a decision must be taken at the outset on the question of major function – what the buildings had to do, their size and their future growth. This must be related to the terrain, lit as it is by the sun rising in the east, setting in the west and in the northern hemisphere shining from the south. Natural features, like trees in lines or clumps, are like decorations, and the ground itself, undulating and rolling, affords the opportunity to add and decorate further. I remember Frank Lloyd Wright talking on the siting of a house, saying that one should get to know the ground well, choose for preference a site of character – not flat – and from this point decide where the human being can look out of his house on to his favourite view, then design the house to take full advantage of these existing amenities. This is the humanist approach and I support it absolutely.

The buildings should, therefore, suit the ground selected for them and in a university they should be able to grow in many different ways. This was especially important for Science, but for Arts and the Library growth could be planned now as the present and future functions were known factors, and not subject to change as in the sciences.

The Library should be sited centrally since its function as a storehouse of knowledge is common to all faculties. This important fact determined the position of the broad masses of Arts and Library on one side and the Sciences on the other. For on the west side of the valley lay a fine sloping hillside ideal for the extension of the Science faculties which would be fed by a succession of service roads, whereas on the east, ground was limited but with a lovely view of a clump of trees which I thought ideal for the Library. Opposite our gateway was a ready-made site for Arts – on the axis of our main entrance archway – this view should, I felt, be terminated by the Arts lecture theatres in front of which, even on the earliest plan, I designed a symbol of incompleteness in raw concrete, breaking the skyline like two arms stretched skyward.

On the original plan the Great Hall was sited in the Great Court but I felt this would cramp the space and I suggested a new site so that it could be visible – just – from the main road. Also, on this early plan, Administration was sited where Arts is now located but this has been moved so that it is adjacent to the Great Hall, as both these buildings had a low priority on the timetable, and should be sited near each other so that the senate room could be used with the Great Hall on important occasions.

The Vice-Chancellor was against temporary accommodation in the shape of huts. (How many universities have been cursed by these awful shacks which become indispensable eyesores!) But we had to construct a small range to be used first as temporary accommodation for Arts and, later, when Arts was built, to be a general purpose 'decanting' block which would be suitable only for non-scientific purposes, because the expensive item of services was not planned for these temporary buildings. The temporary huts occupy the site reserved for the Great Hall and Administration, which will ensure their inevitable demolition when the construction of these buildings commences. In the meantime, Administration was placed in Stanmer House, a Georgian mansion adjacent to the main site.

Presentation drawings were now produced showing the master plan, with many sketches to give a general idea of the development but without committing any building specifically. I felt that this should be approved before we went into any detail.

On the 10th of July 1959 I presented the scheme to the University Council in Stanmer House. It was just before our usual summer holiday and I felt exhausted. I didn't know how this scheme would be received, for one can get little indication from members of a large committee before they come together. It was approved unanimously.

We now turned our attention to detail. In my view it is better in a large scheme involving many buildings to work one out thoroughly so that the principles developed in the first building can be applied to the ones which follow. In designing a first building the fact that this basic thinking can be applied to later developments should never be forgotten and when considering alternatives the choice can be made easy as the alternative to seek and apply is the one to satisfy all needs. Already the basic idea of prefabricated concrete vaults was established, with brick and the other materials already mentioned. With this in mind and on a metric grid of five foot squares we set to work on College House.

One of the most interesting and absorbing design exercises I have ever undertaken was the design of College House. I have already explained the function of this building; the task now was to relate the accommodation, details of which had been compiled by the University, to this function and to the basic quadrangle plan form. With the structure already decided, the building gradually took shape.

The accommodation programme fell into two sections: the areas used by students and that part of the building reserved for the faculty. Again the main elements of the students' section were divisible into two: where the student eats, and the accommodation for other activities.

There had to be a large refectory where important dinners could be held and minor dining-rooms to make up the required area. I was against a large cafeteria-type eating space as such a vast area devoted to student feeding with all its clatter presented a most unattractive picture to my mind. I was aiming at a refectory of character supported by the small cells which should not compete with it, but rather support it. We had to find dining space for a total of 820 students.

The next important space to be included was the Junior Common Room where all would meet. This I felt should be space of generous dimensions (height as well) placed in a prominent position.

The other interesting requirement was a small debating chamber which should be correctly laid out with a strangers' gallery – a chance here, I thought, for a change of architectural mood.

The remainder of the accommodation to be provided was minor in character, but varied and interesting: games rooms for indoor activities like table tennis (noisy), a small library (quiet), a room for women undergraduates (set apart), offices for the students' union, and a flat for a warden. A coffee room was also on the list, and there would have to be the usual entrance hall with its porter's desk and staircase, and with cloakrooms and lavatories. To feed the dining rooms an efficient kitchen with stores, goods entrance, and the usual staff offices had to be provided.

It was considered desirable to arrange the faculty part of this building adjacent to the students' part, though both should be capable of being made private on occasions. Faculty requirements were simple: a senior common room and library with a small bar and private dining rooms which could act as a buffer between the faculty and the students' section of the building. The faculty had to have their own staircase and entrance.

As I read the accommodation schedule and digested it, vague shadows of the final building flitted through my imagination. I had, of course, to keep in mind the provision for extensions which could not be detailed at this stage, a most difficult task for a building arranged round a courtyard, complete in form from the beginning.

The necessity for expansion both for dining (with kitchen) and other rooms, was the most important planning consideration. I was aiming at the apparently inconceivable objective of completeness at *all* stages, even if the university should wish to add say two or three rooms at a time.

As I have already said, accommodation not set out on the officially approved schedule is sometimes of vital importance. At the outset I imagined a large portion of the ground floor of this building as being devoted to a colonnade roofed by the concrete vaults and supported by pillars of Sussex brick – a small after-dinner promenade; and in order to cope with the possible future expansion I was certain that the frame of the whole building should be erected at the outset with flat roofs which could be used as terraces until they were required for future accommodation. On the rigid basis of a square this seemed at first quite impossible. But if the system of vaulted spaces could be applied in an informal way to a rigid form, it seemed that the answer might lie there.

Was this not the true character of the Colosseum in its ruined state? The geometric form of this Roman monument in its heyday could not have been more rigid and was almost symbolic in its unity, but now it was casual, informal and, as I have explained, cosseted the individual in spite of its vast size.

The concept taking form in my imagination was rather like four chests of drawers arranged round a square space with some of the drawers taken out. Quite a nice design exercise, I thought, setting within a rigid frame an abstract informal design. I had practised this before and found it fascinating, for in the Sea and Ships Pavilion on the South Bank Exhibition in 1951 I had used a framed cage of steel girders from which I hung floors, staircases and roofs.

This turned out to be the basis of the idea and I illustrated it with the first sketch I made of this building. The character is rather like that of the sequence of rooms one usually finds in the country house built during the first half of this century with one space leading to another, each of generous proportions. First the ground floor, with the dominant element being the courtyard itself, a true square of 120 feet. With so much green grass and so many trees about I was certain this courtyard should not have grass or shrubs, but should be a hard material related to the walls. (Remember, too, that I was aiming at a complete unity as a first step.) It was conceived as entirely paved, but a strip of water divorces this hard square from the vertical planes of the buildings. I arranged two 'bridges' to connect this paved square to the building – one at the entrance arch, and another on the opposite side to the students' entrance, leading to the main axial spine of the campus which was to terminate with the Arts Theatres.

To the east of this courtyard and partly to the south and north is the colonnade, separated from the court by the moat. This moat comes into its own at twilight with the points of artificial light and arched forms reflected in the water, but at all times, even during rainy periods, the moat gives a unique character to this building, and in my opinion all temptation to fill it in and plant flowers as has been suggested by outside critics should be resisted. Water requires a little maintenance, but amply repays the small outlay of care and attention.

To the west and accessible from the main entrance to the university is the goods yard to the kitchens which occupy the major part of this side of the building. The way in for students is on the northwest corner and the staircase is situated here. I emphasized this externally with a strong architectural form probably without precedent and difficult to describe. Students, ever ready to oblige, have referred to it as the 'pig's ears'. Nevertheless, the 'pig's ears' break the skyline in an interesting way and are not out of character with the trees that normally provide this service.

Taking the stair to the first floor, one reaches one of the most dominant chambers, the Junior Common Room, which rises through two floors and is on the main axis affording views through huge windows of the entrance arch and of the arts complex to the north.

Since this building will have to stand up to hard wear by the students, the same brick is used inside as on the outer walls. This gives a sense of unity with the exterior. The ceiling is vaulted in concrete and floors are oak. In the spandrels of the vaulted forms run all the electrical services. To avoid cutting chases in the brick walls all switches and hot water pipe runs are placed in a kind of boxed out skirting which also functions as a kerb to prevent the backs of chairs from rubbing against the hard brick walls. All radiators are off the floor and form natural handrail guards across the windows.

Beyond the Junior Common Room is the little debating chamber which is almost square on plan with walls especially constructed to give the correct acoustic result. Here the roof is a timber framework forming a lantern while the floor, moulded in concrete to form a terraced saucer, is finished in oak. Students can sit on the steps and argue or listen to music (the acoustics were found to be especially suitable for this secondary function of music, which is provided by a high fidelity gramophone).

Beyond the debating chamber are the games rooms, the library and other small rooms, some of which are approached from a secondary staircase from the Junior Common Room. This stair was a special design study from many designs worked out by Gordon

Collins. The final design aims at an abstract screen which is at once decorative as well as functional as a staircase.

On the west side of the square is the next dominant element, the Refectory. Approached from the first floor landing of the main staircase, through the coffee room, it rises to more than two floors and is roofed in a barrel of timber planks. Huge windows look inwards to the court and outwards to the Sussex landscape. One of the smaller dining spaces takes the form of a bridge floating across this room in a position off centre about two thirds down from the west window. This connects with the other dining rooms on the second floor.

The Refectory now has a magnificent mural by Ivon Hitchens who, after visiting the university during its construction, rang me on the telephone offering this painting as a gift. His generosity was prompted by his enthusiasm for the way he thought the buildings were seated in this Sussex valley. He said that if he was an undergraduate he would have liked to study here.

The faculty dining rooms had to be supplied from the central kitchen so this determined their location adjacent both to the Refectory and to our service stack which rises from the kitchens. On the south an ideal space existed for the Senior Common Room and from here a bridge under the entrance arch leads to the faculty library. On the south-east corner I placed the Students' Union Offices and the Warden's flat.

The result in three dimensions was unusual and informal, but it would be difficult for a committee fully to understand the intention without many perspective drawings and a model so I set to work to prepare these. I was asked to present this scheme along with the designs for the Physics Building and I determined to treat Physics in the same way as College House. These two buildings were of vital importance as the acceptance of these designs by the University Council would settle the design policy for all that followed.

The Physics Building started growing in my mind after the visit to Athens. When Mies van der Rohe came to London to receive the Royal Gold Medal, he made a significant remark to me. He said, 'I never look at modern buildings, only old.' This great architect, known for his pure, classical approach to a modern architecture which he has fathered, and also for his economy of statement (e.g. 'less is more'), was expressing a deep fundamental truth. By looking at old architecture of great quality one can begin to discern architectural truth. 'Architectural truth' is too complex a subject to discuss fully here, but let us define it as that constant quality of great architecture distilled by history. How much better it is to be stimulated in this field by historical study than to be seduced by some slick and flashy contemporary effort which may be disproved by time!

So the Stoa of Atticus influenced the Physics Building. The Stoa has recently been most faithfully restored by the Americans. This long building, which forms the most important element in the Athenian market place, has an extensive colonnade where perhaps the Greek philosophers, and even Archimedes, may have once walked. It is low, horizontal, repetitive and extremely simple. A row of shops screened by a colonnade is not a Physics building, but it is the essence of architectural simplicity; that sense of unity which transcends all function was what I wanted to achieve.

The programme approved by the UGC was for a building of 56,000 sq. ft. split into two sections – Teaching and Research. As I had built several physics buildings already I had learnt two things. First, that the rooms devoted to teaching were generally laid out to a constant pattern, provided there was space for special service ducting (for electricity, water, gas, vacuum, air). Second, that no two physics professors agreed on the layout of a research laboratory. As we had not had the advantage of a professor to draw up his own specification for research, for no appointment had yet been made, I suggested a completely open space with a mesh of services on a constant grid, feeding it. This would allow a professor, and indeed his successors, to alter and adapt the space without much trouble. We even cut out windows so that the wall so beloved by the research physicist was available for his festoons of wires and abstract arrangements of vessels. We gave him a lot of top light fitted with blackout blinds.

From past experience I had also learnt another thing, that the Lecture Rooms should be near the cloakrooms and entrance so that the crowds that attend lectures would not disturb the teaching and research laboratories. The position of faculty rooms varies from one University to another, but generally the most convenient arrangement would appear to include a certain aloofness: quiet but convenient proximity to the teaching and research laboratories.

As I have already said, I wished to arrange this accommodation round a courtyard and introduce a colonnade which was in any case almost a necessity here, for the ground rises to the east and one of the ways of arranging the laboratories could be to lift the main floor off the ground on the campus side so that it could catch the ground level at the back where the stores, workshops, and research departments could be placed adjacent to the service road.

The plan was now taking shape. By entering through the colonnade from the campus, the student would find himself in a courtyard like that of College House, completely devoid of grass and trees, being constructed of paving and gravel, but on several levels, with a magnificent hammer dressed concrete retaining wall running from north to south through it. From the entrance hall the lecture rooms would be readily accessible on the north side of the courtyard, while over the colonnade and overlooking the Great Court all the teaching laboratories were planned.

As I have already mentioned, Research, the Workshops and Store should be near the service road for convenience in handling heavy equipment, so these departments fell into position on the west side flanking the service road. This left the south side of the building connecting Teaching and Research, which seemed ideal for the faculty, and this is where they came to rest.

Scientific buildings are like submarines – riddled with pipes which should be accessible for repair, maintenance or extension. I often think these buildings should be cellular so that complete flexibility for services can be achieved. With our arched construction, which leaves ample space in spandrels and between floors, this is almost achieved. All our vaults run one way – from east to west – and the conception of this building is different from that of College House, which contains voids. Physics is solid, making runs of pipes easy.

The extension was planned to the east further up the slope on the other side of the service road, but connected with the original building by bridges.

Presentation plans were drawn up, perspective drawings prepared and a model of each building was made. Our surveyors, Reynolds & Young, gave estimates of these buildings which compared fairly accurately with the amounts allowed by the UGC and I was ready to present the schemes to the University Council.

This was done on 13th January 1960. I remember driving to Brighton in the snow. Under the kind control of Mr Stone, the Director of Education, I was manœuvred into the Committee Room at Old Steine, complete with models and a huge perspective I had drawn during the Christmas holiday.

Committees do not know the feeling of tension that always exists after a concerted effort to get a series of drawings together, especially when one observes the expressions on the faces of the members – some shocked, surprised, puzzled, distasteful, some hostile, some even amused. Harsh material to mould into enthusiastic acceptance.

I worked hard and was grilled, in a not unkindly way, by Lord Shawcross; and the scheme was accepted. I heard Lord Shawcross whisper to his neighbour 'A good show!'

So Falmer House and the Physics Building were now ready to move from the architect's dream to the practical realization. They were completed in time for the University to move to its own site in October 1962, with these two buildings constituting the operational centre of the institution. Month by month more buildings develop and one by one they become ready for occupation. Building will continue for many years yet. But the architectural tone and physical presence of the University, and the general character of its future building development, were determined – and, I am convinced, happily determined – when the Council approved the plans for College House and the Physics Building. And for one generation of students, at least, these two buildings will always be the University of Sussex.

The University Curriculum[1]

THE PRELIMINARY EXAMINATION

All undergraduates will take a preliminary examination after two terms' study. For Arts undergraduates this will be held at the end of the Spring Term; for Science undergraduates it will be held at the beginning of the Summer Term. It is necessary to satisfy the University's requirements in respect of this examination before proceeding to work for the final degree examination. Honours will not be awarded in this examination and a candidate will be adjudged solely to have passed or failed. A candidate who fails will be given a second opportunity to take the examination at the end of the third term of the first year.

Candidates for the preliminary examination will be examined in three fields. Both in the Arts preliminary examination and the Science preliminary examination two of the three fields will be common to all undergraduates. The third will be chosen according to the interests of the undergraduate and, in the case of the Arts preliminary examination, according to the undergraduate's likely choice of School. There will be an additional paper in Translation to be taken only by undergraduates proposing to enter the School of European Studies.

A. ARTS AND SOCIAL STUDIES

I. LANGUAGE AND VALUES (*Common to all candidates*)

The aims of this paper are to investigate certain immediately relevant philosophical problems as they arise in deliberations about personal conduct, in the making of social and political decisions, and in the study of the arts and sciences. To be considered will be such topics as the nature and justification of moral and other value judgements, free will and political liberty, responsibility and punishment, and the meaningfulness of religious language. Emphasis will be placed upon the value judgement, of which both historical and contemporary accounts will be studied.

[1] This is the curriculum as it stood in 1963, with the addition of the proposed curriculum for the School of African and Asian Studies which opens in October 1964. The curricula of other schools opening in 1964 or soon after are not shown.

2. AN INTRODUCTION TO HISTORY (*Common to all candidates*)

With what problems is the historian concerned and how does he define and investigate them? Why do historians disagree in the answers they give? What is the relationship between the motives and purposes of individuals and sequences of social change? These and related questions will be considered in terms of two historical works:

> J. Burckhardt   *The Civilization of the Renaissance in Italy*
> R. H. Tawney   *Religion and the Rise of Capitalism*

3. CRITICAL READING: ENGLISH POETRY, DRAMA AND FICTION (*For candidates proposing to study in the School of English and American Studies*)

This paper will require the careful critical reading of the works listed below. The objective is to provide both a training in literary understanding and discrimination that will be permanently valuable and useful and an opportunity of getting to know well some of the major works of English literature.

> Chaucer   *Troilus and Criseyde*
> Shakespeare   *Hamlet*
>   *Troilus and Cressida*
>   *King Lear*
>   *The Winter's Tale*
> Ben Jonson   *Volpone*
> Milton   *Paradise Lost*
> Jane Austen   *Persuasion*
> George Eliot   *Middlemarch*
> Henry James   *Portrait of a Lady*
> Joseph Conrad   *Under Western Eyes*
> Pope
> Wordsworth   } A representative selection of poetry
> Yeats

4. CRITICAL READING: EUROPEAN TRAGEDY AND FICTION (*For candidates proposing to study in the School of European Studies*)

This paper has three aims. It confronts the student with a number of seminal works of the European imagination which are vital in the sense that they still illuminate moral experience, refine sensibility, and embody important conceptions of artistic form. It tries to identify the characteristic modes of thought and feeling of certain national literatures. Finally, through close critical reading of the texts, it seeks to provide an introduction to the idiom and concerns of literary criticism. The paper is organized around a small core of texts common to all undergraduates in the School, whatever the language they choose, in combination with a strictly limited number of additional texts chosen to reflect the distinctive character of the various national literatures.

(*a*)   *TRAGEDY*

   Common texts:

> Sophocles   *Oedipus Rex*
> Shakespeare   *King Lear*

Common texts—continued

Ibsen	*Hedda Gabler*

Additional texts:

French

Racine	*Phèdre*
Musset	*Lorenzaccio*
Giraudoux	*Electre*

German

Goethe	*Iphigenie auf Tauris*
Schiller	*Wallenstein* (trilogy)
Brecht	*Mutter Courage*

Russian

Pushkin	*Boris Godunov*
Ostrovsky	*Groza*
Chekhov	*Tri Sestry*

(b) THE NOVEL

Common texts:

Homer	*Odyssey*
Boccaccio	*Decameron*
Jane Austen	*Emma*
Flaubert	*Madame Bovary*

Additional texts:

French

Mme de Lafayette	*La Princesse de Clèves*
Stendhal	*Le Rouge et le Noir*
Zola	*Germinal*

German

Goethe	*Werther*
Kleist	*Michael Kohlhaas*
Fontane	*Effi Briest*

Russian

Lermontov	*Geroy nashego vremeni*
Tolstoy	*Anna Karenina*
Nilin	*Zhestokost'*

All candidates proposing to study in the School of European Studies must also take a fourth paper in Translation in French or German or Russian.

All candidates proposing to major in a modern language other than English will be required to translate

(a) a passage of English prose into the language of their choice, and
(b) two shorter passages of prose from the language of their choice into English.

All other candidates will be required to translate two longer passages of prose from the language of their choice into English.

5. THE ECONOMIC AND SOCIAL FRAMEWORK (*For candidates proposing to study in the School of Social Studies*)

This course is concerned with the principles of economics and their relation to social problems, with reference mainly to the British economy.

Students are expected to become familiar with the sources of basic statistical data.

Population, labour force, occupations; growth and structural change in the economy; economic circulation and the concepts of income, consumption, saving and investment; factors influencing economic growth, productivity, income, consumption, saving and investment; economic fluctuations and unemployment; inflation; the formation of relative prices and of incomes; the selection of investment projects; monopoly and restrictive practices; inequality of income and wealth; social services; government intervention in price and income formation; international trade and payments; the problems of underdeveloped areas.

B. PHYSICAL SCIENCES

6. THE STRUCTURE AND PROPERTIES OF MATTER[1] (*Common to all candidates*)

The atomic structure of matter and inter-atomic forces; interpretation of the mechanical and thermal properties of matter in terms of the atomic picture; elementary kinetic theory and the Boltzmann distribution. Internal energy and temperature; the first law of thermodynamics and its applications.

Electrostatic phenomena and the nature of dielectrics. Elementary classical electron theory of conduction. Magnetic effects of a current. Forces on moving charges in magnetic and electric fields; origin of the magnetic properties of matter. Electromagnetic radiation and light quanta; diffraction of light and particles.

The Bohr atom and spectral lines; atomic orbitals; orbital hybridization; molecular orbitals and the structure of simple molecules; properties of δ and π bonds. Interpretation of the Periodic Table in terms of atomic structure; ionization potential and electron affinity; electronegativity; ionic, covalent and hydrogen bonds.

Properties of the nucleus; qualitative aspects of nuclear structure; nuclear forces. Radioactivity.

Structure and origin of the universe. Composition of the earth and its geological evolution.

7. MATHEMATICS WITH PHYSICS[2] (*Common to all candidates*)

Differentiation and integration. Logarithmic and exponential functions. Simple differential equations. Easy inequalities. Symmetric functions of roots of equations. Elementary plane co-ordinate geometry. (*No formal lectures will be given on the foregoing topics which may, however, be examined.*) Induction. Complex numbers. Three-dimensional geometry of lines,

---

[1] In 1965, when the School of Biological Sciences comes into being, this subject will be expanded to include a section dealing with the biological properties of matter.

[2] Undergraduates majoring in the School of Biological Sciences will be encouraged to take this subject, but for those with an inadequate mathematical background, an alternative mathematical paper will be available in 1965.

planes and spheres using vector methods. Partial differentiation. Introduction to limits and convergence of series. First mean value theorem and applications; Taylor's theorem.

Vector algebra with simple applications. Systems of forces; statics of particles and rigid bodies; relation between force and potential. Mechanics of particles and rigid bodies. Simple Harmonic Motion. Elasticity. One-dimensional waves on strings and in elastic media; use of Fourier series; standing waves; Doppler effect; phase and group velocity; energy transfer. More rigorous mathematical treatment of those topics in the field of physics covered in subject 6.

Either

8. FURTHER MATHEMATICS

Vector spaces; linear transformations; algebra of matrices; systems of linear equations; rank; determinants; quadratic forms; latent roots and latent vectors; canonical forms of matrices.

Inequalities. Rational and irrational numbers; enumerability; sequences; limits of functions of an integral variable. Infinite series with simple tests for convergence and absolute convergence. Limits of functions of a continuous variable; continuous functions; derivatives. Introduction to the idea of integral. Continuity and differentiability of functions of two variables.

Or

9. CHEMISTRY

The first law of thermodynamics; Hess's law and thermochemistry; heat capacity. The second law of thermodynamics; entropy; Gibbs-Helmholtz equation. Equilibrium criteria; Clausius-Clapeyron equation; Van't Hoff isotherm. The third law of thermodynamics. Structure of organic compounds; hydrocarbons; functional groups; elucidation of structure; interconversions of simple organic compounds; conjugation and resonance. Stereochemistry. Effects of structure on physical properties and reactivity. Types of organic reactions.

PRACTICAL WORK

The practical course will be an integral part of the teaching for subjects 6 and 9, and although there will be no practical examination, a candidate's performance during the class work will be assessed and taken into consideration.

C. COMBINATION OF SOCIAL STUDIES AND PHYSICAL SCIENCES

An undergraduate in the School of Physical Sciences who wishes to transfer to the School of Social Studies may, with the approval of the Deans of the School of Physical Sciences and the School of Social Studies, offer subjects 6 and 7 as common subjects together with paper 5 in the preliminary examination.

THE FINAL B.A. EXAMINATION

The final examination will be taken in the third term of the undergraduate's third year, except in the case of Modern Language specialists, who will be required to spend their third year abroad, in a country appropriate to the language they are studying, and who will take the final examination at the end of their fourth year. It is hoped that opportunities will be developed for specialists in Economics, Politics and Sociology, and Geography in the School of European Studies to spend their third year abroad in the same way.

Between the completion of the preliminary examination and the taking of the final examination, undergraduates will be attached to one of the three Schools of Study. They may major in a particular subject within the School of their choice, but they will also do a number of contextual papers common to all undergraduates in the School. Some of these contextual papers may be common to two or more Schools. All undergraduates will be required to offer, as one of their contextual subjects, a paper on Philosophy and a wide range of philosophical options is provided.

Some major subjects (e.g. History) may be studied in each of the three Schools. There are opportunities for studying Economics, Politics and Sociology, and Geography both in the School of Social Studies and in the School of European Studies.

1. THE SCHOOL OF ENGLISH AND AMERICAN STUDIES

Note: Where the same paper appears in more than one context, a reference is given in brackets after the title of the paper.

COMMON PAPERS

101 AN ESSAY
Candidates will have a choice of a literary, historical or philosophical subject.

102 THE MODERN EUROPEAN MIND (202)
The paper will be divided into two parts: (a) Expression. The ways in

which the literary imagination has responded to the problems of modern industrial society. (*b*) Diagnosis. Some of the major diagnoses of this situation.

(*a*) *Expression*. The books to be read will include works by Dostoievsky, Joyce, Lawrence, Kafka, Mann, Malraux, Camus and Pasternak and some French symbolist and modern English poetry.

(*b*) *Diagnosis*. The books to be read will include works by Marx, Nietzsche, Kierkegaard, Arnold, Ruskin, Morris, Freud and Jung.

103 ENGLISH HISTORY (*4311*)
One period to be chosen from the following:

1460–1612	1509–1660	1559–1713	1612–1760
1660–1783	1688–1815	1783–1914	1815–1945

Candidates majoring in American Studies must choose the period 1688–1815.

104 PHILOSOPHY
One paper to be chosen from the following list:

1041 ETHICS
This paper will deal both with recent ethical thought and the works of certain major moralists, to be prescribed from time to time. The former part will include the study of particular theories of moral judgement, such as emotivism and prescriptivism, and of such topics as free will and moral responsibility, religion and morality, and the role of imagination in morals. Candidates will also be given the opportunity to discuss related problems of aesthetics.

1042 LOGIC AND THEORY OF MEANING
Such topics will be considered as the theories of logical inference, logical paradoxes, the theory of descriptions, the problem of sense and reference, the problems of identity and individuation, existence, sentence and statement, the justification of empirical hypotheses, the problem of induction, theories of truth and probability.

1043 PHILOSOPHY OF MIND
The paper will consider general theories of the mind, such as those of Descartes, the behaviourists and Ryle, and such theories of perception and experience as phenomenalism and realism. There will also be study of particular mental concepts, for example those of emotion, feeling, motive, intention, self-knowledge, intelligence and the unconscious. The implications of relevant non-philosophical inquiries, such as cybernetics, will be considered.

1044 PLATO AND ARISTOTLE
This paper will be directed mainly to studying the development of the Theory of Ideas, the criticisms of the theory to be found in the later dialogues and in Aristotle, and the Aristotelian theory of substance. These problems will be discussed in the light of their connection with contemporary philosophical issues.

1045 DESCARTES TO KANT

The paper will be divided into parts dealing with Descartes and Locke, Spinoza and Leibniz, Berkeley and Hume, and Kant. Candidates will be required to answer questions from at least two of these parts and to show detailed knowledge of the writings of the philosophers in question, but they will also be given the opportunity to discuss important philosophical issues that arose elsewhere in the period.

1046 MARXISM AND EXISTENTIALISM

The development of Marxist and Existentialist thought, from their Hegelian origins to the present, and a critical and comparative study of the fundamental ideas of the two movements.

1047 SOCIETY AND HISTORY

This paper will bring together a number of topics sometimes dispersed under the headings of political philosophy and the philosophies of society, law and history. Some of these topics will be: political obligation, equality, individualism and holism, theories of legal responsibility and punishment, the process of history, the nature of historical explanation.

1048 SCIENTIFIC THOUGHT

Scientific inquiry, its character and relations to other forms of thought; logical analysis of scientific concepts and theories; the mechanist world-picture; philosophical issues of contemporary science – the indeterminacy principle, statistical and causal laws, space and time, alternative cosmologies. Some general questions on the historical development of science will also be set.

1049 FORMAL LOGIC

Boolean logic, the axiomatic method, paradoxes, theory of classes, logical syntax and semantics, elementary proof theory. An outline knowledge of the historical development of the subject will also be required.

105 A TOPIC IN HISTORY AND LITERATURE
One paper to be chosen from the following list:

1051 POETRY, SCIENCE AND RELIGION IN THE SEVENTEENTH CENTURY

1052 LITERATURE AND SOCIETY IN THE AUGUSTAN AGE

1053 THE FRENCH REVOLUTION AND THE ROMANTIC MOVEMENT

1054 THE INDUSTRIAL REVOLUTION AND THE ENGLISH LITERARY IMAGINATION

1055 THE LATE VICTORIAN REVOLT IN LITERATURE, POLITICS AND CULTURE

1056 THE GILDED AGE IN AMERICAN LITERATURE AND SOCIETY (1870–1910)

106 One paper to be chosen from the following list:

   1061   CONTEMPORARY BRITAIN (*Normally to be taken by candidates majoring in English Literature or History*) (*444*)

Contemporary British culture and society; demographic and social change; social problems and social policies; the instruments of communication and their control; social judgements in contemporary thought and writing; British approaches to the outside world.

   1062   CONTEMPORARY AMERICA (*Normally to be taken by candidates majoring in American Studies*)

A similar paper, with an exclusively American content.

   1063   PHILOSOPHY

A further paper chosen from list 104.

   1064   THE HISTORY OF CRITICAL THEORY

A study of some of the major contributions to the study of the nature, value and means of assessment of imaginative literature from the Greeks to the present day.

PAPERS IN MAJOR SUBJECTS

(a) English Literature

111   SHAKESPEARE (*1421, 212*)

112   PRACTICAL CRITICISM (*1422, 213*)
   The paper will include tests in the evaluating and dating of anonymous poems.

113   TRAGEDY (*135, 141, 214*)

114   THE ENGLISH NOVEL (*1423, 215*)

(b) History

121 One of the following:

   1211   A further period in ENGLISH HISTORY chosen from list 103.

   1212   A period of EUROPEAN HISTORY chosen from list 2031.

   1213   AMERICAN HISTORY SINCE 1783 (*131*)

122 A GENERAL SUBJECT in History (*253, 4331*)

123 ⎱ Two papers on a SPECIAL SUBJECT, to be chosen from the following
124 ⎰ list:

   1231   THE ITALIAN RENAISSANCE, 1475–1525 (*2541, 4341*)

   1232   LUTHER AND ERASMUS, 1515–1535 (*2542, 4342*)

   1233   THE HENRICIAN REFORMATION, 1525–1547 (*4343*)

   1234   THE ENGLISH REVOLUTION OF THE SEVENTEENTH CENTURY (*4344*)

   1235   THE ZENITH OF LOUIS XIV, 1680–1702 (*2543, 4345*)

   1236   THE FRENCH REVOLUTION, 1789–1795 (*2544, 4346*)

   1237   CHARTISM (*4347*)

   1238   THE DREYFUSIAN REVOLUTION, 1893–1906 (*2545, 4348*)

1239 IMPERIALISM, 1870–1914 (4349)

1240 THE AMERICAN RESPONSE TO INDUSTRIALISM, 1890–1914 (1331, 4350)

1241 SOCIETY AND POLITICS IN EDWARDIAN BRITAIN (4351)

1242 THE NAZI REVOLUTION (2546, 4352)

1243 THE AGE OF FRANKLIN D. ROOSEVELT (1332, 4353)

The first paper will demand detailed knowledge of set sources and critical comment on them. The second paper will consist of essays.

(c) American Studies

131 AMERICAN HISTORY SINCE 1783 (1213)

132 AMERICAN LITERATURE

Either

133 ⎫ Two papers on a SPECIAL SUBJECT, to be chosen from the following
134 ⎭ list:

    1331 THE AMERICAN RESPONSE TO INDUSTRIALISM, 1890–1914 (1244, 4350)

    1332 THE AGE OF FRANKLIN D. ROOSEVELT (1243, 4353)

Or

135 TRAGEDY (113, 141, 214)

136 One paper on a SPECIAL SUBJECT (1331 or 1332)

(d) Philosophy

Either

141 TRAGEDY (113, 135, 214)

142 One paper from the following list:

    1421 SHAKESPEARE (111, 212)

    1422 PRACTICAL CRITICISM (112, 213)

    1423 THE ENGLISH NOVEL (114, 215)

143 ⎫
144 ⎭ Two further papers on PHILOSOPHY chosen from list 104

Or

141 TRAGEDY (113, 135, 214)

143 ⎫
144 ⎬ Three further papers on PHILOSOPHY chosen from list 104
145 ⎭

N.B. Candidates offering four or more papers in Philosophy are required to include papers 1042 (LOGIC AND THEORY OF MEANING) and 1045 (DESCARTES TO KANT).

THE SCHOOL OF EUROPEAN STUDIES

COMMON PAPERS

201 THE FOUNDATIONS OF CULTURE

    Either

    2011 THE EUROPEAN FOUNDATIONS

This paper is designed both to examine the European traditions of moral and political thought before the sixteenth century, and to approach the civilizations of classical antiquity and medieval Christendom through the study of one or two of their outstanding literary works.

The following books are prescribed for detailed reading and criticism:

Either	Plato	*Apology; Phaedo*
	Virgil	*Aeneid*
	Dante	*Divine Comedy*
Or	Plato	*Republic*
	Aquinas	*Selected Political Writings* (ed. A. P. d'Entreves, Blackwell, 1954)
	Machiavelli	*The Prince*

These will be studied in translation, but candidates will be expected to recognize quotations from Dante in the original.

Or

2012 THE RUSSIAN FOUNDATIONS

This paper will be taken instead of 2011 by those majoring in Russian. It will examine the culture of pre-Petrine Russia and its Byzantine roots. Not only the literature, but also the art, religion and political theory of Byzantium and Old Russia will be studied.

The following books are prescribed for reading:

Baynes and Moss (ed.)	*Byzantium*
Constantine Porphyrogenitus	*De administrando imperio*
Mavrogordato (ed. and transl.)	*Digenis Akritas*
From *Penguin Book of Russian Verse*	*Slovo o polku igoreve*
	Byliny
	Dukhovnye stikhi

From N. K. Gudziy: *Khrestomatiya po drevney russkoy literature* the extracts from:	*Russian Primary Chronicle* *Life of the Archpriest Avvakum*

202 THE MODERN EUROPEAN MIND (*102*)

203 HISTORY

Either

2031 EUROPEAN HISTORY (*4312*)

One period to be chosen from the following:

478 B.C.–362 B.C.	78 B.C.–A.D. 14	1492–1598	1545–1648
1598–1715	1616–1727	1648–1760	1688–1789
1713–1815	1768–1871	1815–1919	1871–present

Or

2032 WORLD HISTORY SINCE 1900

This paper will be primarily concerned with the extension of the society of states from being confined to Europe until it is coterminous with the whole world, and with the consequent problems and conflicts. Undergraduates majoring in International Relations will be

required to take this paper; others may choose it with the consent of
the Dean of the School.

204 PHILOSOPHY
One paper to be chosen from list 104.

205 TRANSLATION
A paper in French, German or Russian.
Candidates majoring in a modern language other than English will be
required to translate
(*a*) a passage of English prose into the language of their choice, and
(*b*) two shorter passages of prose from the language of their choice
into English.
All other candidates will be required to translate two longer passages
of prose from the language of their choice into English.

PAPERS IN MAJOR SUBJECTS

(a) English

211 *Either* a paper chosen from the following, in conformity with the
language of the candidate's choice:
2111 THE GERMAN TRADITION
Selected reading from the works of Goethe, Hölderlin, Nietzsche,
Rilke and Mann.
2112 THE FRENCH IMAGINATION
Selected readings from the works of Pascal and Voltaire and from any
two of the following: Racine, Balzac, Hugo, Proust.
2113 THE RUSSIAN TRADITION
Selected works of the great 19th-century novelists and of the poets
Derzhavin, Pushkin, Tyutchev, Blok, Mayakovsky and Pasternak.
Or A TOPIC IN HISTORY AND LITERATURE chosen, in conformity
with the language of the candidate's choice, from paper 221, 231 or
241. A candidate may, with the consent of the Dean of the School,
offer instead a Topic in English History and Literature chosen from
paper 105.
212 SHAKESPEARE (*111, 1421*)
213 PRACTICAL CRITICISM (*112, 1422*)
214 TRAGEDY (*113, 135, 141*)
215 THE ENGLISH NOVEL (*114, 1423*)

(b) French

221 A TOPIC IN FRENCH HISTORY AND LITERATURE chosen from the
following:
2211 POLITICS AND RELIGION IN THE AGE OF PASCAL
2212 THE WRITER AND SOCIETY IN 18TH CENTURY FRANCE
2213 FRENCH ROMANTICISM AND THE SOCIAL QUESTION,
1830–48
2214 VICHY: OCCUPATION AND RESISTANCE, 1940–44

222 FRENCH MORALISTS
This paper will deal with the tradition of moral discourse in France. It will centre on Montaigne, Pascal and Rousseau, but candidates will also be able to offer a further 'special interest' within this general field.

223 FRENCH POETRY
This paper will combine questions about both individual poets and poetic movements. Candidates will be expected to show exact knowledge of some representative French poetry from Villon to the present.

224 FRENCH DRAMA
The emphasis will be on representative plays by major dramatists from Garnier to the present and candidates will be expected to show some knowledge of the drama of other European playwrights.

225 FRENCH FICTION
Candidates will be expected to show exact knowledge of some representative French fiction from Madame de Lafayette to the present and to be acquainted with the work of some other European novelists.

226 All candidates majoring in French will be required to spend their third year in a French-speaking country, and to prepare a short dissertation in French which will be submitted as part of the final degree examination.

227 A searching oral test will form an integral part of the final degree examination.

(c) German

231 A TOPIC IN GERMAN HISTORY AND LITERATURE chosen from the following:
2311 GERMAN ROMANTICISM AND THE FRENCH REVOLUTION
2312 NATURALISM AND THE INDUSTRIALIZATION OF GERMANY
2313 CONTEMPORARY GERMANY
A paper similar to CONTEMPORARY BRITAIN (*1061, 404*) with a German content.

232 GOETHE
Goethe's work will be studied as a whole (and will not be included piece-meal in other papers). Some knowledge will be expected of Goethe's life, of his interests outside the field of literature, and of the relation between his development as a man and as a writer.

233 GERMAN POETRY
Candidates will be expected to distinguish between the poetic styles of different periods from Luther's hymns to the present day. Detailed and extensive knowledge will also be required of the work of *either* Hölderlin *or* Rilke.

234 GERMAN DRAMA
The emphasis will be on representative plays of the major dramatists from Lessing to Brecht. Candidates must study in detail the complete dramatic works of *either* Schiller *or* Kleist.

235 GERMAN FICTION IN THE AGE OF REALISM
Candidates will be expected to have some knowledge of novels by
other European writers, in order to be able to show the distinctive
character of German fiction, of which representative texts will be
prescribed from the 18th to the 20th century. Candidates will be
required to make a special study of *one* of the following:
    (*a*) The German 'Novelle'
    (*b*) The 'Bildungsroman'.

236 Candidates majoring in German will be required to spend their third
year in a German-speaking country, and to prepare a short dissertation
in German which will be submitted as part of the final degree
examination.

237 A searching oral test will form an integral part of the final degree
examination.

(d) Russian

241 HISTORY
Either

    2411 RUSSIAN HISTORY
        One period chosen from the following:
        Up to 1682; 1682–1861; 1861 to the present.
    Or

    2412 A TOPIC IN HISTORY AND LITERATURE, to be chosen from
        the following:
        24121 FREEDOM AND REPRESSION FROM CATHERINE
        THE GREAT TO NICHOLAS I (with a study of Radischiev,
        Pushkin, Griboyedov, the Decembrists)
        24122 WRITERS AND REVOLUTION, 1905–1930

242 PUSHKIN AND HIS CONTEMPORARIES
The works of Pushkin, Gogol, Griboyedov, Lermontov and the
'Pleiad' will be studied as a whole in this paper, with particular refer-
ence to Pushkin's longer poems. A knowledge of Byron and of
Western European Romanticism will be expected.

243 RUSSIAN POETRY
Candidates will study the chief writers and tendencies in Russian
poetry from the seventeenth century to the present, and will be
expected to comment in detail on representative passages.

244 TWENTIETH CENTURY RUSSIAN LITERATURE
In this paper certain important themes from modern Russian literature
will be studied in depth. Candidates will offer *three* special interests
chosen from the following list:
    (*a*) Drama since the 1880's
    (*b*) Satire, ornamentalism and grotesquerie
    (*c*) Futurism and its aftermath
    (*d*) The *poema* since Blok
    (*e*) 'Socialist Realism' in theory and practice, 1932–53
    (*f*) Literature of the 'Thaw'.

245 RUSSIAN FICTION
This paper will centre on the major works of the great 19th century
novelists: Goncharov, Turgenev, Dostoievsky, Tolstoy, Leskov, Chekhov, Gorky.

246 A dissertation to be written in Russian on the year spent abroad.

247 An oral test.

(e) History

251 LITERATURE
One of the papers 2111, 2112 or 2113, to be chosen in conformity with
the language of the candidate's choice.

252 EUROPEAN HISTORY
A further period to be chosen from list 2031.

253 GENERAL SUBJECT
This paper will be concerned with a theme or aspect of European
History, capable of being studied in relation to a wide range of European countries, including the British Isles, so as to illustrate the unity
in diversity of European civilization. Each theme or aspect is also
capable of being traced through modern history down to the present
day, so that it may be considered either as a historical development
with contemporary relevance or as a contemporary problem seen in
historical perspective. One of the following will be chosen:

25301 CHURCH AND STATE
25302 THE BALANCE OF POWER (*45441*)
25303 ARISTOCRACIES AND BOURGEOISIES (*45442*)
25304 BRITAIN AND EUROPE (*45443*)
25305 EUROPE AND THE WORLD
25306 ECONOMIC PROGRESS, IDEOLOGY AND SOCIAL CHANGE
25307 LABOUR MOVEMENTS (*45444*)
25308 SCIENCE, TECHNOLOGY AND SOCIETY
25309 UNIVERSITIES
25310 CULTURE AND SOCIETY (*45445*)
25311 CONSERVATISM AND REACTION (*45446*)
25312 ARMIES AND POLITICS (*45447*)

With the consent of the Dean of the School, a candidate may choose,
instead of this paper,

Either A TOPIC IN HISTORY AND LITERATURE, to be chosen from
paper 221, 231 or 241, in accordance with the Translation paper that
is being offered;

Or a paper in REGIONAL HISTORY, to be chosen from:
  RUSSIAN HISTORY (*241*)
  AMERICAN HISTORY SINCE 1783 (*1213, 131*)
  ASIAN HISTORY SINCE 1800 (*4314*)

254 ⎫ Two papers on a SPECIAL SUBJECT, to be chosen from the following
255 ⎭ list:
  2541 THE ITALIAN RENAISSANCE, 1475–1525 (*1231, 4341*)
  2542 LUTHER AND ERASMUS, 1515–1535 (*1232, 4342*)

2543 THE ZENITH OF LOUIS XIV, 1680–1702 (*1235, 4345*)
2544 THE FRENCH REVOLUTION, 1789–1795 (*1236, 4346*)
2545 THE DREYFUSIAN REVOLUTION, 1893–1906 (*1238, 4348*)
2546 THE NAZI REVOLUTION (*1242, 4352*)

A candidate will normally be expected to choose a Special Subject whose authorities are in the language of his choice. The first paper will demand detailed knowledge of set sources and critical comment on them. The second paper will consist of essays.

(f) Philosophy

261 LITERATURE

One of the papers 2111, 2112 or 2113, to be chosen in conformity with the language of the candidate's choice.

Candidates must further choose *one* of the following combinations:

Either

262–265 Four further papers on PHILOSOPHY to be selected from list 104.

Or

262 A second paper chosen from list 203, or a paper chosen from 221, 231 or 241 in conformity with the language of the candidate's choice.

263–265 Three further papers on PHILOSOPHY to be selected from list 104.
N.B. Candidates offering four or more papers in Philosophy are required to include papers 1042 (LOGIC AND THEORY OF MEANING) and 1045 (DESCARTES AND KANT)

Or

262–263 Two further papers in HISTORY or LITERATURE, chosen with the approval of the Dean of the School.

264–265 Two further papers in PHILOSOPHY to be selected from list 104.

(g) Economics

271 ECONOMIC THEORY (*411*)
272 THE ECONOMICS OF DEVELOPED COUNTRIES (*412*)
273 THE ECONOMIC AND POLITICAL HISTORY OF EUROPE SINCE 1945 (*283, 4141, 4541*)
274 EUROPEAN INSTITUTIONS AND THE ECONOMICS OF INTEGRATION (*284, 3051, 4142, 4542, 4651*)
275 THE ECONOMY OF ONE EUROPEAN COUNTRY
276 Candidates majoring in Economics and spending a year abroad will be required in addition to submit a dissertation on the economics of the country where they have spent their year.

(h) Politics and Sociology

281 COMPARATIVE GOVERNMENT (*451*)
282 SOCIAL STRUCTURE AND SOCIAL CHANGE (*452*)
283 THE ECONOMIC AND POLITICAL HISTORY OF EUROPE SINCE 1945 (*273, 4141, 4541*)

284 EUROPEAN INSTITUTIONS AND THE ECONOMICS OF INTE-
GRATION (*274, 3051, 4142, 4542, 4651*)

285 THE POLITICS AND SOCIETY OF ONE EUROPEAN COUNTRY

286 Candidates majoring in Politics and Sociology and spending a year
abroad will be required to submit a dissertation on the politics and
society of the country where they have spent their year.

(i) Geography

291 THE PHYSICAL BASIS OF GEOGRAPHY (*421*)

292 HUMAN GEOGRAPHY (*422*)

293 THE GEOGRAPHY OF EUROPE (*423*)

294 ⎱ Two papers on a SPECIAL SUBJECT, to be chosen in pairs from the
295 ⎰ following list:

    2941 ECONOMIC GEOGRAPHY (*4153, 4241*)

    2951 ECONOMIC GEOGRAPHY OF AN APPROVED EUROPEAN
    REGION

    2942 SOCIAL GEOGRAPHY (*4242*)

    2952 SOCIAL GEOGRAPHY OF AN APPROVED EUROPEAN
    REGION

    2943 POLITICAL GEOGRAPHY (*4243*)

    2953 POLITICAL GEOGRAPHY OF AN APPROVED EUROPEAN
    REGION

    2944 HISTORICAL GEOGRAPHY (*4244*)

    2954 HISTORICAL GEOGRAPHY OF AN APPROVED EUROPEAN
    REGION

296 Candidates majoring in Geography will be required, as a necessary
part of their education in the subject, to attend field classes both in
their local area and in other European regions. They are expected to
acquire and demonstrate a knowledge of the cartographic techniques
appropriate to the subjects studied, and will be required to submit
evidence of satisfactory practical and field work, some part of which
should relate to an area of continental Europe.

(j) International Relations

301 INTERNATIONAL SOCIETY (*461*)
The economic bases of international power; the diplomatic system;
international institutions – political, economic and juridical.

302 INTERNATIONAL THEORY (*462*)
The chief traditions of political theory relating to foreign policy and
international society; the general principles of international law and
diplomacy; nationalism; Communist international theory; neutralism;
etc.

303 ⎱ Two papers on SECURITY AND STRATEGY (*463* and *464*)
304 ⎰ The balance of power and collective security; nature and kinds of
alliances; regional pacts, especially N.A.T.O.; the relation of defence

policy to foreign policy; weapons development; nuclear-missile strategy; mutual deterrence; the arms race; the economics of defence and disarmament.

305 *Either*

3051 EUROPEAN INSTITUTIONS AND THE ECONOMICS OF INTEGRATION (*274, 284, 4142, 4542, 4651*)

Or

3052 A SPECIAL TOPIC to be chosen from the following list:

30521 INTERNATIONAL COMMUNISM (*46521*)
The Comintern, relations of states and parties within the 'Socialist camp', Warsaw Pact, Russo-Chinese relations

30522 RACE RELATIONS (with special reference to Africa) (*46522*)

30523 THE ARAB WORLD SINCE 1945 (*46523*)

30524 TRADE AND AID (*46524*)
Economic relationships between advanced and developing economies.

N.B. Not all these options may be immediately available.

Or

3053 A SPECIAL HISTORICAL TOPIC to be chosen from the following list:

30531 THE ETHIOPIAN CRISIS, 1935–6 (*46531*)

30532 THE BERLIN QUESTION SINCE 1945 (*46532*)

30533 THE SUEZ CRISIS, 1956 (*46533*)

30534 THE CUBA CRISIS, 1962 (*46534*)

N.B. Not all these options may be immediately available.

3. THE SCHOOL OF SOCIAL STUDIES

COMMON PAPERS

401 CONCEPTS, METHODS AND VALUES IN THE SOCIAL SCIENCES
A general introduction to the different procedures followed in different branches of the social studies; concepts, theories, procedures; the use of mathematical models; social studies and natural sciences; value judgements implicit and explicit.

This course will be preceded by a terminal course on statistical methods. Subject to the approval of the Dean, candidates majoring in History may offer paper 1047 (SOCIETY AND HISTORY), and candidates majoring in Philosophy paper 1048 (SCIENTIFIC THOUGHT) from the Philosophy options in list 104, in place of this paper.

402 PHILOSOPHY
One paper to be chosen from list 104.

403 THE CONTEMPORARY WORLD
Either
4031 INTERNATIONAL POLITICS
The nature of the international community and of international law;

the diplomatic system; the balance of power and other concepts in international politics; small powers, great powers and super powers; the problems of security and aggression; the League of Nations and the United Nations; current problems of strategy, deterrence and disarmament.

Or

4032 WORLD POPULATION AND RESOURCES

N.B. Students choosing the major in Economics may take paper 4154 SOCIAL PSYCHOLOGY instead of paper 403. In this case they must also choose two further papers from papers 4141–4153. Candidates choosing the major in International Relations must take paper 4032.

404 CONTEMPORARY BRITAIN (*1061*)

Contemporary British culture and society; demographic and social change; social problems and social policies; the instruments of communication and their control; social judgements in contemporary thought and writing; British approaches to the outside world.

N.B. Candidates choosing the major in International Relations must take paper 2032 WORLD HISTORY SINCE 1900 *instead of* paper 404.

PAPERS IN MAJOR SUBJECTS

(a) Economics

411 ECONOMIC THEORY (*271*)

Consumption and demand; production and resource allocation; types of market situation; risk and uncertainty; the growth of the firm; value in economics; centralized and decentralized decision taking. Credit and money; interest and capital; the distribution of the national product; specialization, location, regional and international economics. Growth and structural change; business cycles; welfare and economic policy.

(The objects of this paper include the fuller exploration of some of the topics examined in paper 5 THE ECONOMIC AND SOCIAL FRAMEWORK. Mathematical techniques may be used but are not necessary for attaining the highest honours.)

412 THE ECONOMICS OF DEVELOPED COUNTRIES (*272*)

The economic systems of developed countries; the organization, policy and behaviour of producers, consumers and governments; the main problems confronting these countries; comparative rates of growth; causes and remedies of inflation; taxation, investment and the business cycle; other aspects of economic policy; the relations of these countries with each other and with under-developed countries.

413 THE ECONOMICS OF UNDER-DEVELOPED COUNTRIES

Concepts of 'backwardness' and 'development'; climatic, economic, social and political factors; the main problems confronting these countries; the colonial legacy; distribution of incomes and employment; population; comparative living standards; health and education;

subsistence agriculture; opportunities for economic growth; the control and development of economic policy; the relation of these countries with each other and with developed countries.

414 ⎫ In addition to the three papers described above (411, 412 and 413),
415 ⎭ candidates majoring in Economics must take two further papers in Economics from the following list. In general, candidates should choose papers which are related to each other or to the candidate's main interest in economics. Candidates attempting paper 4141 must also attempt paper 4142. These two papers taken together will provide a distinctive education in problems relating to contemporary Europe. Candidates attempting them must also take a further paper from the following list instead of paper 412.

4141 THE ECONOMIC AND POLITICAL HISTORY OF EUROPE SINCE 1945 (273, 283, 4541)
Reconstruction and recovery; the development of European economic co-operation; comparative European rates of growth; sectional, ideological and national differences; stages of European integration; the division of Germany; the fourth French Republic and de Gaulle; political parties; Britain's relations with Europe; problems of common defence.

4142 EUROPEAN INSTITUTIONS AND THE ECONOMICS OF INTEGRATION (274, 284, 3051, 4542, 4651)
The working of the main institutions created in Europe since 1945; their organization and role; debates about their future; the economic background of and the problems confronting the new institutions; progress towards and obstacles to further integration; the main economic and political factors involved.

4143 MATHEMATICAL STATISTICS
Students choosing this paper will take one of the courses offered in the School of Physical Sciences.

4144 ECONOMETRICS
The measurement of economic variables; quantitative models; testing of models; economic prediction; the relationship of econometrics to other approaches to economics.

4145 THE ECONOMICS OF SOCIAL POLICY
The meaning of social policy and social services; the economics of some particular social services (e.g., medical care, pensions, redundancy schemes, education); taxation and income distribution; the private sector and social policy. These topics will be studied with reference to past and future policies in various countries.

4146 LABOUR ECONOMICS
The composition of the labour force; industrial and occupational distribution; trade unions and employers' associations; the system of industrial relations in the United Kingdom and other countries; pay structure and determination; hours of work, fringe benefits and conditions of work; productivity; unemployment; measurement of

changes in the cost of living; the work of the I.L.O. and of trade union internationals.

4147 THE DEVELOPMENT OF ECONOMIC THOUGHT

How economics became a specialized field of enquiry; development in the 17th and 18th centuries; contributions of the classical economists; Marxian economics; marginal analysis; Alfred Marshall and neo-classicism in England; economic thought in 20th century Europe and America; Keynes and the 'new economics'; contemporary trends.

4148 ECONOMIC PLANNING

Central planning by governments and by large industrial firms; planning in Soviet-type, Western and under-developed economies; techniques of planning (social accounting, inter-industry analysis, mathematical programming, etc.); criteria for investment decisions; interrelated development projects; financial planning.

4149 THE ECONOMICS OF SOCIALIST COUNTRIES

4150 RECENT ECONOMIC HISTORY

This paper will be primarily concerned with the period since the late eighteenth century. Its principal emphases will be the economic evolution of the great powers and the national and international implications of economic growth and industrialization. More specifically it will deal with the following: the relevance of history to the economist and of economics to history; backwardness and growth in historical perspective; demographic trends; economic systems and fluctuations since 1815; changing patterns of enterprise and investment; the evolution of the international economy; government policy; nineteenth and twentieth century 'imperialism'; comparative trends in living standards.

4151 THE DEVELOPMENT OF THE BRITISH ECONOMY, 1760–1960

Trends in population, prices, production and trade; the Industrial Revolution; savings, investment and enterprise; the characteristics of long-term growth; government policy and economic performance; structural change; social and political aspects of economic change; Britain and the world economy; the use and limitations of theoretical analysis in history.

4152 CONFLICT, CO-OPERATION AND CHOICE (4559, 4654)

A study of the rational foundation of individual and collective decisions. Types of conflict; theory of games; decision-making under uncertainty; the calculus of democratic decisions; bargaining and persuasion; the dynamics of conflict. Applications will be drawn as far as possible from economics, or from the relevant major subject in cases where other candidates choose this paper.

4153 ECONOMIC GEOGRAPHY (2941, 4241)

4154 SOCIAL PSYCHOLOGY (4560)

N.B. Candidates may also take SOCIAL PSYCHOLOGY instead of paper 403. In this case they must also choose two further papers from papers 4141–4153.

(b) Geography

421 THE PHYSICAL BASIS OF GEOGRAPHY (*291*)
The broad features of the physical geography of land, air and oceans; an introductory study of soils and of biological distributions. The subject will be studied with particular but not exclusive reference to the local area.

422 HUMAN GEOGRAPHY (*292*)
The facts and concepts of the geography of society in the present and in past historical periods; an introduction to economic, social and historical geography. The subject will be studied with particular but not exclusive reference to the local area.

423 THE GEOGRAPHY OF EUROPE (*293*)
The broad geographical characteristics of Europe, including the British Isles; detailed and comparative studies of selected regions.

424 ⎫ Two papers on a SPECIAL SUBJECT, to be chosen in pairs from the
425 ⎭ following list.

4241 ECONOMIC GEOGRAPHY (*2941, 4153*)
The scope of economic geography; techniques of description and measurement, and methods of observation applied to the contemporary distributions of industry and agriculture; the geography of transport; land, and land-use competition; economic activities and the growth of regional specialization; geographical aspects of location and localization, economic region.

4251 ECONOMIC GEOGRAPHY OF AN APPROVED REGION

4242 SOCIAL GEOGRAPHY (*2942*)
The scope of social geography; techniques of description and measurement, and methods of observation applied to the regional differentiation of social groups; the demographic structure, social structure and organization of society in relation to environment; the distribution, type and function of rural and urban settlements.

4252 SOCIAL GEOGRAPHY OF AN APPROVED REGION

4243 POLITICAL GEOGRAPHY (*2943*)
Geographical aspects of the State; territorial organization; the geographical interrelation of states; political frontiers and boundaries; demographic considerations; strategic factors; the geographical bases of political strength; the interaction between geographical environment and the State.

4253 POLITICAL GEOGRAPHY OF AN APPROVED REGION

4244 HISTORICAL GEOGRAPHY (*2944*)
The scope and aims of historical geography; concepts of historical geography; the geography of man in past periods; man and environment in history; the changing geographical landscape.

4254 HISTORICAL GEOGRAPHY OF AN APPROVED REGION

426 Candidates majoring in Geography will be required, as a necessary part of their education in the subject, to attend field classes both in the local area and in other regions. They are expected to acquire and demonstrate a knowledge of the cartographic techniques appropriate to the subjects studied, and will be required to submit evidence of satisfactory practical and field work.

(c) History

431 NATIONAL AND REGIONAL HISTORY
432 Two papers to be chosen from the following list:

4311 ENGLISH HISTORY (*103*)

4312 EUROPEAN HISTORY (*2031*)

4313 RUSSIAN HISTORY (*2411*) *or* AMERICAN HISTORY SINCE 1783 (*1213, 131*)

4314 ASIAN HISTORY SINCE 1800
The stake of Europe in Asia in 1815; old societies and new pressures; British rule in India, its scope and its instruments; 1857; the development of Congress; the great powers and China; reaction and reform in China; political and economic change in Japan; the emergence of Japan as a world power; China's revolution and its consequences; the rise of communism in Asia; Gandhi, Nehru and the independence of India.

4315 WESTERN ECONOMIC HISTORY
(Candidates taking this paper must also normally take paper 4332 instead of paper 4331).
This paper will concentrate upon the comparative experience of, and the relationships between, the major powers of Western Europe and North America. One of the following periods will be chosen:

(*a*) 1450–1763
Trends in population, prices, production and trade; changes in agricultural organization and performance; the development of industry and finance; the emergence of capitalism and the significance of enterprise; social factors and economic change; international trade and communication; government policies; the rise of empires; the characteristics of colonial economies.

(*b*) 1700–1960
Trends in population, prices, production and trade; contrasting experiences of industrialization; innovation and enterprise; the international flow of commodities, capital, ideas and labour; the emergence of an international economy; economic imperialism; political and social aspects of economic change; government policies; western culture and economic growth; the characteristics of modern economies.

433 *Either*
4331 A GENERAL SUBJECT in History (*253*)

Or

4332 NATIONAL ECONOMIC HISTORY (Candidates taking this paper must also normally take paper 4315)
One of the following will be chosen:

    (*a*) English economic history, 1500–1750
    (*b*) British economic history, 1750–1960
    (*c*) American economic history, 1783–1960

Or

4333 WORLD HISTORY SINCE 1900 (*2032*)

434 ⎱ Two papers on a SPECIAL SUBJECT, to be chosen from the following
435 ⎰ list:

4341 THE ITALIAN RENAISSANCE, 1475–1525 (*1231, 2541*)
4342 LUTHER AND ERASMUS, 1515–1535 (*1232, 2542*)
4343 THE HENRICIAN REFORMATION, 1525–1547 (*1233*)
4344 THE ENGLISH REVOLUTION OF THE SEVENTEENTH CENTURY (*1234*)
4345 THE ZENITH OF LOUIS XIV, 1680–1702 (*1235, 2543*)
4346 THE FRENCH REVOLUTION, 1789–1795 (*1236, 2544*)
4347 CHARTISM (*1237*)
4348 THE DREYFUSIAN REVOLUTION, 1893–1906 (*1238, 2545*)
4349 IMPERIALISM, 1870–1914 (*1239*)
4350 THE AMERICAN RESPONSE TO INDUSTRIALISM, 1890–1914 (*1240, 1331*)
4351 SOCIETY AND POLITICS IN EDWARDIAN BRITAIN (*1241*)
4352 THE NAZI REVOLUTION (*1242, 2546*)
4353 THE AGE OF FRANKLIN D. ROOSEVELT (*1243, 1332*)

Normally the choice of Special Subject will be determined by the particular period and area covered in the papers chosen under 431 and 432 above. The first paper will demand detailed knowledge of set sources and critical comment upon them. The second paper will consist of essays.

(d) Philosophy

Candidates must choose one of the following combinations:
Either

441–444 Four further PHILOSOPHY papers chosen from list 104

445 One paper to be chosen from *one* of the following options:

    (*a*) Papers 411, 412, 4147, 4152, 4153, 4154
    (*b*) Papers 431, 432, 433
    (*c*) Papers 451, 452, 453

Or

441–443 Three further PHILOSOPHY papers from list 104.

445 ⎱ Two further papers to be chosen from *one* of (*a*), (*b*) and (*c*) above.
446 ⎰

Or

441 442 }Two further PHILOSOPHY papers from list 104.

445–447 Three further papers to be chosen from *two* of (*a*), (*b*) and (*c*) above.

N.B. Candidates offering four or more papers in Philosophy are required to include papers 1042 (LOGIC AND THEORY OF MEANING) and 1045 (DESCARTES TO KANT).

(e) Politics and Sociology

451 COMPARATIVE GOVERNMENT (*281*)
The methodological basis of comparative government; the study of major political forms – legislatives, executives, political parties, federal systems, etc.; the comparison of democratic, authoritarian and communist states; the mechanism of constitutional change; the study of one major political system in detail.

452 SOCIAL STRUCTURE AND SOCIAL CHANGE (*282*)
Social groups and sociological concepts; social institutions; culture and social character; modes of socialization; primary groups: the family; power and influence patterns in associations; social stratification; social mobility; factors, rates, and forms of social change; social change in selected contemporary environments.

453 POLITICAL SOCIOLOGY
Sociological approaches to politics; social groups and political behaviour; social and political institutions; élites, pressure groups and parties; opinion and its measurement; the sociology of elections, coups d'état and revolutions; the nature of political leadership; the sociology of bureaucracies.

454 455 }In addition to the three papers described above (451, 452 and 453), candidates majoring in Politics and Sociology must take two further papers in Politics *or* Sociology from the following list.
Candidates attempting paper 4541 must also attempt paper 4542. These two papers taken together (which are the same as papers 4141 and 4142 and thus are shared with specialists in Economics) will provide a distinctive education in the problems relating to contemporary Europe.

4541 THE ECONOMIC AND POLITICAL HISTORY OF EUROPE SINCE 1945 (*273, 283, 4141*)

4542 EUROPEAN INSTITUTIONS AND THE ECONOMICS OF INTEGRATION (*274, 284, 3051, 4142, 4651*)

4543 POLITICAL THEORY
The scope of political theory; political theory and political action; definitions of the state; the nature of sovereignty; power and authority; concepts of law; the variety of political ends; democracy and totalitarianism.

4544 A GENERAL SUBJECT IN POLITICS, to be chosen from the following list:

    45441 THE BALANCE OF POWER (*25302*)
    45442 ARISTOCRACIES AND BOURGEOISIES (*25303*)
    45443 BRITAIN AND EUROPE (*25304*)
    45444 LABOUR MOVEMENTS (*25307*)
    45445 CULTURE AND SOCIETY (*25310*)
    45446 CONSERVATISM AND REACTION (*25311*)
    45447 ARMIES AND POLITICS (*25312*)

4545 PUBLIC ADMINISTRATION

Politics, law and the administrative function; the scope of administration; administrative institutions; the appointment of administrators; administrative law; judicial review; the individual and government; nationalized industries; local, national and international administration.

4546 LOCAL GOVERNMENT

The main institutions of local government in Great Britain; the relationship between local authorities and central government; local elections; political and administrative processes in local government; the finance of local government; some foreign comparisons and contrasts.

4547 THE POLITICS AND GOVERNMENT OF NEW STATES

The colonial inheritance; the nature of modern nationalism and anti-colonialism; political problems confronting new states; modern and traditional hierarchies; democracy and parties in new states; the breakdown of democracies; the role of armies; political problems of economic growth; race and politics.

4548 HISTORY OF POLITICAL THOUGHT

The main developments in modern political thought since the Reformation; special attention will be paid to the writings of Hobbes, Locke, Rousseau, Burke, Bentham, Marx, John Stuart Mill; and examination of the historical context of these writings.

4549 THE HISTORY OF SOCIAL THOUGHT

The main developments in social thought; the notions of a society and a social science; how ideas about society were formulated, communicated and debated; the changing boundaries of social thought and changing views of the purposes of social science; the history of social thought and sociology.

4550 SOCIAL HISTORY

Social history and other branches of history; different approaches to its study; traditional societies and industrial revolutions; the main features of British social history since the industrial revolution; British experience compared and contrasted with that of other countries.

4551 URBAN SOCIOLOGY

The main features of urban life; theories of the city; the historical evolution of cities; the social investigation of cities; problems of growth and planning.

4552 THE SOCIOLOGY OF RELIGION

Church, sect, and denomination; religious institutions and practices and their evolution; social elements in religious allegiance; religion as a factor in social development.

4553 SOCIAL POLICY-MAKING AND ADMINISTRATION

Poverty and affluence; social contingencies; the pattern of social services; how they are administered and by whom; education and the social services, recent trends and future policies.

Much of the work for this paper will be done along with economists (see paper 4145).

4554 INDUSTRIAL SOCIOLOGY

Economics and Sociology; economic action; the division of labour and specialization; exchange and markets; industrial organization; the sociology of work; management, labour unions and interest groups; cultural effects of industrial organization and change.

4555 SOCIAL CONFLICT AND SOCIAL CONTROL

Collective behaviour; custom and public opinion; religion and morality; law; integration and disturbance; class conflict; minorities; social pathology; education.

4556 THE SOCIOLOGY OF LAW

Economic, political, religious, cultural factors in the evolution of law; legal order and law consciousness; the social field of the application of law; the functioning of the courts; law in the system of social control; social effects of the legal order; styles and classification of law; social and cultural factors in the creation and interpretation of law; clashes of legal orders and unification; schools of legal sociology.

4557 IDEOLOGIES AND THE SOCIOLOGY OF KNOWLEDGE

Socio-cultural factors associated with thought and its forms of expression; adaptation of behaviour to reality; culture and personality; traditional obstacles to empirical knowledge; social structures, mentalities, and ideologies; conservative and revolutionary ideologies; the manipulation of mentalities; the sociology of art and literature; the Intellectuals and the University; science and the social order; the history of the sociology of knowledge.

4558 RURAL SOCIOLOGY

Occupational and demographic structure of rural society; socio-economic groupings; the structure and role of the family and the household; income and expenditure; kinship and neighbourhood consciousness; class, status and leadership in the rural community; the provision of services and amenities in rural areas (housing, education, transport, local institutions); the impact of urban values and social change on rural communities; mobility and migration; the use of leisure and community participation; studies of rural life in contrasting environments and societies.

4559 CONFLICT, CO-OPERATION AND CHOICE (*4152, 4654*)

4560 SOCIAL PSYCHOLOGY (*4154*)

(f) International Relations

461 INTERNATIONAL SOCIETY (*301*)
The economic bases of international power; the diplomatic system; international institutions – political, economic and juridical.

462 INTERNATIONAL THEORY (*302*)
The chief traditions of political theory relating to foreign policy and international society; the general principles of international law and diplomacy; nationalism; Communist international theory; neutralism; etc.

463⎫
464⎬ Two papers on SECURITY AND STRATEGY (*303* and *304*)

The balance of power and collective security; nature and kinds of alliances; regional pacts, especially N.A.T.O.; the relation of defence policy to foreign policy; weapons development; nuclear-missile strategy; mutual deterrence; the arms race; the economics of defence and disarmament.

465 *One* of the following:
    4651 EUROPEAN INSTITUTIONS AND THE ECONOMICS OF INTEGRATION (*274, 284, 3051, 4142, 4542*)
    4652 A SPECIAL TOPIC, to be chosen from the following list:
        46521 INTERNATIONAL COMMUNISM (*30521*)
        The Comintern, relations of states and parties within the 'Socialist Camp', Warsaw Pact, Russo-Chinese relations.
        46522 RACE RELATIONS (with special reference to Africa) (*30522*)
        46523 THE ARAB WORLD SINCE 1945 (*30523*)
        46524 TRADE AND AID (*30524*)
        Economic relationships between advanced and developing economies
    N.B. Not all these options may be immediately available.
    4653 A SPECIAL HISTORICAL TOPIC, to be chosen from the following list:
        46531 THE ETHIOPIAN CRISIS, 1935–6 (*30531*)
        46532 THE BERLIN QUESTION SINCE 1945 (*30532*)
        46533 THE SUEZ CRISIS, 1956 (*30533*)
        46534 THE CUBA CRISIS, 1962 (*30534*)
    4654 CONFLICT, CO-OPERATION AND CHOICE (*4152, 4559*)

4. THE SCHOOL OF AFRICAN AND ASIAN STUDIES

COMMON PAPERS

501 CULTURES AND SOCIETIES
Distinctive characteristics of indigenous non-western cultures and

societies, particularly in Africa south of the Sahara and South Asia. Societies: their variety and diversity; kinship; economic organization; politics and law. Cultures: belief systems; religion and philosophy; art. Social and cultural change. Small-scale and large-scale social and cultural complexes: their historical development and characteristics; civilization.

502 WESTERNIZATION AND MODERNIZATION
The interaction of current changes in Africa and Asia, with special reference to Africa south of the Sahara and South Asia. Western influences; demographic trends; recent social changes; economic backwardness and economic growth; urbanization; political and administrative patterns; problems of cultural identity.

503
504 } Two papers to be chosen from the following list:

    5031 WORLD POPULATION AND RESOURCES (4032)
    5032 SOCIAL MICROCOSMS
    Critical study of selected monographs on African and Asian societies.

    5033 IMPERIALISM AND NATIONALISM
    The concept of empire; critiques of imperialism. The expansion of empire; the nature of imperial authority; the imperial 'mission'; imperial social, economic and administrative policies and practices, and their consequences; native states. Native rebellions; the new nationalisms; the struggle for independence; the transfer of power; the aftermath.

    5034 ENVIRONMENT
    The physical environment of inter-tropical and arid lands: climatic types; landforms; water resources; soil types and soil erosion; vegetation communities. Resources conservation; disease and environment.
    Society and environment: the adjustment and adaptation of human groups to the changing possibilities of the natural environment; the broad distribution of population; the forms of occupance; farm, village and town; land tenure systems.
    Land utilization in relation to the physical and social environment; land-use systems; shifting cultivation; padi; permanent dry-land cultivation; irrigation; pastoralism.

    5035 CONCEPTS, METHODS AND VALUES IN THE SOCIAL SCIENCES (401)

PAPERS IN MAJOR SUBJECTS

(a) Economics

511 ECONOMIC THEORY (271)

512 THE ECONOMICS OF DEVELOPED COUNTRIES (272)

513   THE ECONOMICS OF UNDER-DEVELOPED COUNTRIES (*413*)

514   THE ECONOMY OF AN APPROVED AFRICAN OR ASIAN COUNTRY
OR REGION

515   One further paper in Economics to be chosen from papers 4143–4154

(b) Geography

521   THE PHYSICAL BASIS OF GEOGRAPHY (*421*)

522   HUMAN GEOGRAPHY (*422*)

523   *Either*

5331   THE GEOGRAPHY OF AFRICA SOUTH OF THE SAHARA
Or
5332   THE GEOGRAPHY OF SOUTHERN ASIA
Major geographical characteristics, including natural resources,
economic activities, population distribution and settlement patterns.
Detailed and comparative studies of selected regions.

524   ⎫
525   ⎬ Two papers to be chosen from the following list:

5341   ECONOMIC GEOGRAPHY (*4241*)
5342   ECONOMIC GEOGRAPHY: REGIONAL APPLICATIONS
5343   SOCIAL GEOGRAPHY I (*4244*)
5344   THE PHYSICAL ENVIRONMENT OF TROPICAL LANDS
The climate, hydrology, soils, vegetation and geomorphology
of tropical lands; the natural resource potential afforded by
these environmental factors; the utilization and conservation of
resources.

(c) History

531   AFRICAN AND ASIAN HISTORY
One paper to be chosen from the following list:
5311   AFRICAN HISTORY SINCE 1750
5312   ASIAN HISTORY SINCE 1800 (*4314*)
5313   SOUTH ASIAN HISTORY SINCE 1750

532   EUROPEAN AND AMERICAN HISTORY
One paper to be chosen from list 431–432

533   *Either* a further paper in History to be chosen from the following list:
5331   HISTORY OF PRE-COLONIAL AFRICA
5332   HISTORY OF MUGHAL INDIA
5333   A GENERAL SUBJECT in History to be chosen from list 253
Or a further paper from list 531 or 431–432.
Candidates may not offer both 5312 and 5313. If they choose two
papers from 531 they may not choose 5033 (IMPERIALISM AND
NATIONALISM) but they may then offer in place of 5033 one paper
from lists 253 or 431–432.

534 Two papers on a SPECIAL SUBJECT, to be chosen from the following
list:

    5341 BUGANDA AND ITS NEIGHBOURS, 1862–1962

    5342 RURAL SOCIETY IN WESTERN AND UPPER INDIA,
          1875–1922

    5343 INDIA'S ATTAINMENT OF INDEPENDENCE, 1906–1950

(d) Politics

541 COMPARATIVE GOVERNMENT (281)

542 *Either*

    5421 POLITICAL THEORY (4543)
  Or
    5422 HISTORY OF POLITICAL THOUGHT (4548)

543 POLITICAL SOCIOLOGY (282)

544 THE POLITICS AND GOVERNMENT OF NEW STATES (4547)

545 One paper to be chosen from the following list:

    5451 THE POLITICS AND SOCIETY OF ONE AFRICAN OR
          ASIAN COUNTRY

    5452 A GENERAL SUBJECT in Politics to be chosen from list 4544

    5453 A SPECIAL TOPIC to be chosen from list 5551.

(e) International Relations

551 INTERNATIONAL SOCIETY (301)

552 INTERNATIONAL THEORY (302)

553 ⎫
554 ⎬ Two papers on SECURITY AND STRATEGY (303–304)

555 *One* of the following:

    5551 A SPECIAL TOPIC, to be chosen from the following list:

        55511 INTERNATIONAL COMMUNISM (30521)

        55512 RACE RELATIONS (with special reference to Africa) (30522)

        55513 THE ARAB WORLD SINCE 1945 (30523)

        55514 TROPICAL AFRICA SINCE 1945

        55515 SOUTH AND SOUTH-EAST ASIA SINCE 1945

        55516 TRADE AND AID (30524)

    5552 A SPECIAL HISTORICAL TOPIC, to be chosen from the
        following list:

        55521 THE ETHIOPIAN CRISIS, 1935–6 (30531)

        55522 THE SUEZ CRISIS, 1956 (30533)

        55323 THE KASHMIR DISPUTE SINCE 1947

        55524 THE SINO-INDIAN BORDER QUESTION SINCE 1958

        55525 THE CONGO CRISIS, 1960–1962

(f) Social Anthropology

A Major Subject in Social Anthropology will be offered in the School in the near future.

(g) Philosophy

A Major Subject in Philosophy will be offered in the School in the near future.

THE FINAL B.Sc. EXAMINATION

5. THE SCHOOL OF PHYSICAL SCIENCES

In this School an undergraduate will, in general, major in one of the subjects *Physics, Chemistry* or *Mathematics*, but it will also be possible to major in *Philosophy*. In addition, he must make a study of specialist topics either in another science or in mathematics. As an alternative for those majoring in mathematics, a limited number of undergraduates may study *Economics*.

The study of a supporting science will not be confined to its elementary aspects. On the contrary, the main concern will be with advanced topics at the borderlines between it and the major subject. To obtain maximum benefit from such an arrangement, the study of the supporting subject will take place at intervals throughout the full three years of the course.

In addition to the specifically scientific and mathematical subjects, an undergraduate will be required to follow a course of study dealing with the role of science and scientists in the life of the twentieth century and to write a short dissertation *either* on a topic in this field, *or* on any other topic which can be adequately supervised by a member of the Arts Faculty.

The main papers for the final examination will be taken in the third term of the undergraduate's third year. An undergraduate will be required to state the subject in which he wishes to major immediately after passing the Preliminary Examination, although in special cases changes may be allowed later on in the course. In particular it is possible for an undergraduate to delay the decision whether he should major in Physics or Mathematics until his second year. The choice of subjects available and the allowed combination for those majoring in the different subjects, together with their syllabuses, are set out below.

APPENDIX A

(i) Physics Major

COMPULSORY SUBJECTS
PHYSICS

ELECTRICITY AND MAGNETISM
Elementary vector treatment of the electric and magnetic fields due to charges and currents, including the effects of dielectrics and magnetic materials, leading finally to the derivation of Maxwell's equations and simple applications. Units and fundamental measurements.

ELEMENTARY ELECTRONICS
Alternating current theory; resonance in L, C, R circuits; coupled circuits; elementary treatment of valve and transistor circuits.

THERMODYNAMICS
Cyclic processes; second law of thermodynamics; reversibility; Carnot's theorem and its generalization; entropy; thermodynamic relations. Change of phase; vapour pressure equation. Joule and Joule-Kelvin effect. Thermodynamic potentials; Gibbs-Helmholtz relations. Third law.

WAVES AND PHYSICAL OPTICS
Huygen's principle; wave propagation in isotropic media. Interference and diffraction of sound, microwaves, light and particles; applications of interference and diffraction; limit of resolution. Circular and elliptic polarization; wave propagation in anisotropic media; applications of polarized light. Semi-classical treatment of the interaction of light with matter.

RADIATION AND QUANTUM THEORY
Classical and quantum theories of radiation in an enclosure. Photoelectric effect. Quantum theory of specific heats. The uncertainty principle and the foundations of quantum mechanics; Schrödinger's equation and simple applications; perturbation theory. Transition probabilities; selection rules. Scattering theory. Angular momentum and spin. Exclusion principle.

STATISTICAL MECHANICS
Ensembles. Ensemble averages; relation to thermodynamic properties. Partition function. Fermi-Dirac, Bose-Einstein and Boltzmann statistics. Classical ideal monatomic gas. Fermi-Dirac gas; electrons in metals. Bose-Einstein gas; photon gas; monatomic crystals.

RELATIVITY
Experimental basis of the special theory of relativity. Lorentz transformation including electro-magnetic field. Collisions in centre of mass and laboratory systems.

ATOMIC SPECTROSCOPY
The hydrogen atom and the quantization of atomic states; periodic table; vector model of the atom and its applications; X-ray, optical, infra-red and radio-frequency spectra of atoms and molecules.

SOLID STATE PHYSICS

Interatomic forces; crystal structure; X-ray and neutron diffraction. Lattice vibrations; lattice specific heats. Metals; Fermi-Dirac statistics; electronic specific heat; conductivity; band structure. Insulators and semi-conductors; electrons and holes; donors; carrier injection; transistors. Magnetism; the main varieties of magnetism; spin waves. Applications of nuclear and electron spin resonance to solid state physics. Dislocations; application to strength of materials and to crystal growth.

NUCLEAR PHYSICS

Measurement of nuclear sizes, masses, spins and moments. Neutron and proton as constituents of the nucleus. Nuclear forces and nuclear binding; energy levels; elementary description of the nuclear shell and collective models. α, δ and γ decay of nuclei. Nuclear reactions. Elementary particles.

METHODS OF EXPERIMENTAL PHYSICS

All candidates reading Physics will be expected to carry out experimental work and candidates offering physics in the final B.Sc. examination will receive credit for work carried out during the preceding years. There will be no practical examination, but a written paper will be taken dealing with the more experimental and applied aspects of topics covered in Physics, including the treatment of errors and ultimate limits of accuracy, the estimation of fundamental constants, vacuum technology and elementary electronics.

MATHEMATICS

MATHEMATICAL METHODS

Multiple and curvilinear integrals; vector operators; theorems of Gauss, Green and Stokes, and simple applications.

Linear ordinary and partial differential equations; separation of variables, singular points, solution in series. Bessel and Legendre functions; spherical harmonics. Eigenvalue problems; Sturm-Liouville system. Orthogonality and completeness; expansion in eigenfunctions. Fourier series and integrals. Types of partial differential equation.

CLASSICAL MECHANICS

Generalized co-ordinates; holonomic systems; Lagrange's equations; normal modes. Hamilton's equations and Poisson brackets; elementary mechanics of rigid bodies.

LINEAR ALGEBRA

Vector spaces; linear transformations; matrices; determinants; applications.

COMPLEX VARIABLE THEORY

Regular functions. Cauchy's theorem; contour integration.

STATISTICS

Probability; frequencies; binomial, normal and Poisson distributions; simple tests of significance.

NUMERICAL ANALYSIS
Introduction to standard techniques for handling numerical problems, including practical work.

MECHANICS OF CONTINUOUS MEDIA
Simple mathematical theory of wind tunnels, shock waves, river bores, viscous flow, Reynolds number.
Stress–strain relations for elastic media with theory of simple elastic waves.

OPTIONAL SUBJECTS

Candidates will take *one* of the following options:

(1) CHEMICAL PHYSICS

CHEMISTRY OF SOLIDS
Relation between physical properties and chemical bonding; anisotropy. Chemical crystallography. Close packing; molecular compounds; metals and interstitial compounds. Ionic and covalent radii; bond energies; gradation from ionic to covalent bonding in crystals. Hydrates and hydrogen bonding. Lattice defects. Crystal field theory (electrostatic model) and its applications to colour, magnetic effects and stereochemistry.

CHEMICAL SPECTROSCOPY
Rotational spectra of diatomic and polyatomic molecules; vibrational and vibration-rotational spectra of di- and tri-atomic molecules; group frequencies in polyatomic molecules; electronic spectra of molecules; radio-frequency spectroscopy.
Practical techniques, including those of microwave, infra-red, Raman, ultra-violet, nuclear magnetic resonance, and electron spin resonance spectroscopy. Applications.

(2) FURTHER MATHEMATICS

A more advanced knowledge of the compulsory mathematical subjects will be required, together with the following:

DIFFERENTIAL AND INTEGRAL EQUATIONS
Laplace and Fourier transforms.
Differential equations – existence theorem, linear equations; variation of parameters, contour integral solutions, hypergeometric equation.
Introduction to Integral equations.
Either

INTRODUCTORY GROUP THEORY
Group axioms; subgroups; cosets; Lagrange's theorem. Permutation groups; Cayley's theorem. Normal subgroups. The isomorphism theorems. Abelian groups.
Or

TENSORS AND ELASTICITY
Elementary tensor theory, with particular application to elasticity.

Candidates will be required to take a Special Subject selected from the following list, or from such other subjects as may be arranged from time to time:

Probability and Statistics
Numerical Analysis
Relativity (and Differential Geometry)
Electromagnetic Theory
Hydro- and Aero-Dynamics
Quantum Mechanics
Group Representations
Functional Analysis

(ii) Chemistry Major
COMPULSORY SUBJECTS
CHEMISTRY

KINETICS OF REACTIONS
Order and molecularity of reactions. Collision theory; transition state theory. Unimolecular processes. Termolecular processes. Chain reaction; explosion limits; photochemical reactions; flash photolysis. Heterogeneous and zero order reactions. Reactions in solution.

PROPERTIES OF SOLUTIONS
Conductance of solutions of strong and weak electrolytes. Activities and activity coefficients of strong electrolytes. Standard electrode potentials; oxidation-reduction potentials. Proton theory of acids and bases; pH; theory of indicators. Thermodynamic treatment of colligative properties of ideal and non-ideal solutions of non-electrolytes.
Structure of solutions of strong electrolytes; Debye-Huckel theory; theories of conductance; Debye-Falkenhagen effect; Wien effect.

RADIATION AND QUANTUM THEORY
Classical and quantum theories of radiation in an enclosure. Photoelectric effect. Quantum theory of specific heats. The uncertainty principle and the foundations of quantum mechanics; Schrödinger's equation and simple applications; perturbation theory. Transition probabilities; selection rules. Scattering theory. Angular momentum and spin; exclusion principle.

STATISTICAL MECHANICS
Ensembles. Ensemble averages; relation to thermodynamic properties. Partition function.
Fermi-Dirac, Bose-Einstein and Boltzmann statistics. Classical ideal monatomic gas. Fermi-Dirac gas; electrons in metals. Bose-Einstein gas; photon gas; monatomic crystals.

ATOMIC SPECTROSCOPY
The hydrogen atom and the quantization of atomic states; periodic table; vector model of the atom and its applications; X-ray, optical, infra-red and radio-frequency spectra of atoms.

APPENDIX A

MOLECULAR SPECTROSCOPY

Rotational spectra of diatomic and polyatomic molecules; vibrational and vibration-rotational spectra of di- and tri-atomic molecules; group frequencies in polyatomic molecules; electronic spectra of molecules; radio-frequency spectroscopy.

Practical techniques, including those of microwave, infra-red, Raman, ultra-violet, nuclear magnetic resonance and electron spin resonance spectroscopy. Applications.

PHASE EQUILIBRIA

Thermodynamic treatment of equilibria between phases. Allotropy. Fractional distillation. Eutectics; solid solutions; alloys; fractional crystallization.

SURFACE CHEMISTRY

Physical adsorption. Chemisorption. Heats of adsorption. Langmuir and B.E.T. adsorption isotherms. Gibbs adsorption equation. Surface films on liquids. Zetapotential; electrophoresis; electro-osmosis. Ion-exchange. Chromatography.

STRUCTURE OF SOLIDS

Relation between physical properties and chemical bonding; anisotropy. Chemical crystallography. Close packing; molecular compounds; metals and interstitial compounds. Ionic and covalent radii; bond energies; gradation from ionic to covalent bonding in crystals. Hydrates and hydrogen bonding. Lattice defects. Crystal field theory (electrostatic model) and its applications to colour, magnetic effects and stereochemistry.

CHEMISTRY OF NON-TRANSITION ELEMENTS

Stability and separation of isotopes. Hydrogen, deuterium, tritium; ionic and covalent hydrides. Alkali metals and their compounds. Alkaline earth metals. Oxidation-reduction in inorganic chemistry. Compounds of the inert gases.

Trends within the boron, carbon, and nitrogen groups; properties of the elements, halides, oxides, and oxy-acids. Electron-deficient compounds and addition compounds; boron hydrides and related topics. Graphitic compounds. Silicates and condensed oxy-acids. Nitrogen and phosphorus hydrides. Liquid ammonia and non-aqueous solvents. Trends in physical and chemical properties in the oxygen group and in the halogens; peroxy compounds, hydrides, oxides, halides, and oxyacids; oxidation-reduction relationships. Interhalogen compounds and pseudo-halogens.

CHEMISTRY OF TRANSITION ELEMENTS

Electronic configurations of transition elements; ionization potentials, sizes and oxidation states. Binary compounds and salts. Co-ordination compounds and complex ions. Ligand field theory (including molecular-orbital treatment) and its applications to the mechanisms of electron-transfer and ligand substitution reactions.

Solution chemistry of transition elements. Relation of structure of complexes and stability of oxidation states to position in the periodic table.

π-Complexes; hydrides, carbonyls and related compounds. Lanthanides and actinides.

ORGANIC REACTIONS AND MECHANISMS

The chemistry of the main classes of organic compounds discussed in terms of functional groups and reaction types.

Mechanisms of ionic reactions (substitutions, additions, eliminations and rearrangements) of free radical reactions, and of reactions of biochemical importance.

ORGANIC STEREOCHEMISTRY

Geometrical and optical isomerism. Conformation. Steric effects on physical properties and chemical reactivity. Applications to natural product chemistry.

SYNTHESIS AND DEGRADATION OF ORGANIC COMPOUNDS

Chemical methods of determining the structures of organic molecules. Principles involved in the synthesis of organic compounds with examples drawn from natural products and chemicals of technical importance (including dyestuffs).

COMPOUNDS OF BIOLOGICAL IMPORTANCE

Outline of the chemistry of alkaloids, terpenes, steroids, hormones, natural colouring matters, carbohydrates, vitamins, polypeptides, proteins and nucleic acids.

POLYMER CHEMISTRY

Properties of macromolecules. Kinetics and mechanisms of polymerization processes. Types of organic polymers. Types of inorganic polymers.

PRACTICAL ELECTRONICS

Alternating current theory; resonance in L, C, R circuits; coupled circuits; elementary treatment of valve and transistor circuits.

EXPERIMENTAL CHEMISTRY

All undergraduates reading Chemistry will be expected to carry out practical work, and students offering Chemistry in the final B.Sc. examination will receive credit for work carried out during the preceding years.

MATHEMATICAL METHODS

Multiple and curvilinear integrals; vector operators; theorems of Gauss, Green and Stokes and simple applications.

Linear ordinary and partial differential equations; separation of variables; singular points, solution in series. Bessel and Legendre functions, spherical harmonics. Eigenvalue problems, Sturm-Liouville system. Orthogonality and completeness, expansion in eigenfunctions. Fourier series and integrals. Types of partial differential equation. Vector spaces, linear transformations; matrices; determinants; applications.

Generalized co-ordinates; Lagrange's equations; normal modes; Hamilton's equations and Poisson brackets.

Statistical treatment of experimental results.

OPTIONAL SUBJECTS

Candidates may, with the approval of the Dean of the School of Physical Sciences and the Professors of Chemistry and Mathematics, substitute further mathematical topics for some of the above chemical topics.

(iii) Mathematics Major

COMPULSORY SUBJECTS
MATHEMATICS

The mathematics of the Preliminary Examination studied in more detail and greater depth, together with:

REAL AND COMPLEX ANALYSIS

Sets of points in one and two dimensions; uniformity; Riemann integration; convergence and uniform convergence of sums, products and integrals; double limit problems.

Functions of a complex variable; analytic functions; Cauchy's theorem and applications to contour integration.

MATHEMATICAL METHODS

Multiple and curvilinear integrals; vector operators; theorems of Gauss, Green and Stokes and simple applications.

Linear ordinary and partial differential equations; separation of variables, singular points, solution in series. Bessel and Legendre functions; spherical harmonics. Eigenvalue problems; Sturm-Liouville system. Orthogonality and completeness; expansion in eigenfunctions. Fourier series and integrals. Types of partial differential equation.

CLASSICAL MECHANICS

Generalized co-ordinates; holonomic systems; Lagrange's equations; Hamilton's equations and Poisson brackets; examples including application to motion of a top, small oscillations and normal modes.

Calculus of variations; Euler's equation, Hamilton's Principle and derivation of Lagrange's equations from Hamilton's Principle.

MECHANICS OF CONTINUOUS MEDIA

Simple mathematical theory of wind tunnels, shock waves, river bores, viscous flow, Reynolds Number.

Stress-strain relations for elastic media with theory of elastic waves.

DIFFERENTIAL AND INTEGRAL EQUATIONS

Laplace and Fourier transforms.

Differential equations – existence theorem, linear equations; variation of parameters, contour integral solutions, hypergeometric equation.

Introduction to Integral equations.

STATISTICS

Probability; frequencies; measures of location and dispersion; binomial, normal and Poisson distributions; sampling distributions; simple tests of significance; correlation.

ALGEBRA AND NUMBER THEORY
Euclid's algorithm for integers and polynomials; highest common factor; decomposition into primes; congruences; theorems of Fermat and Wilson; finite fields.

INTRODUCTORY GROUP THEORY
Group axioms; subgroups; cosets; Lagrange's theorem.
Permutation groups; Cayley's theorem.
Normal subgroups. The isomorphism theorems.
Abelian groups.

TENSORS AND ELASTICITY
Elementary tensor theory, with particular application to elasticity.

SPECIAL SUBJECTS
Candidates will be required to take Special Subjects selected from the following list, or from such other subjects as may be arranged from time to time:

> Real Analysis
> Complex Analysis
> Partial differential equations
> Algebra
> Projective Geometry
> Differential Geometry
> Topology
> Probability and Statistics
> Numerical Analysis
> Relativity
> Electromagnetic Theory
> Hydro- and Aero-Dynamics
> Elasticity
> Quantum Mechanics
> Group Representations
> Functional Analysis
> Measure Theory

OPTIONAL SUBJECTS

Candidates will take *one* of the following options:

(1) MATHEMATICAL PHYSICS I

Candidates will be required to study the theoretical aspects of the following subjects:

ELECTRICITY AND MAGNETISM
Elementary vector treatment of the electric and magnetic fields due to charges and currents, including the effects of dielectrics and magnetic materials, leading finally to the derivation of Maxwell's equations and simple applications.

THERMODYNAMICS

Cyclic processes; second law of thermodynamics; reversibility; Carnot's theorem and its generalization; entropy; thermodynamic relations. Change of phase; vapour pressure equation. Joule and Joule-Kelvin effect. Thermodynamic potentials; Gibbs-Helmholtz relations. Third law.

RADIATION AND QUANTUM THEORY

Classical and quantum theories of radiation in an enclosure. Photoelectric effect. Quantum theory of specific heats. The uncertainty principle and the foundation of quantum mechanics; Schrödinger's equation and simple applications; perturbation theory. Transition probabilities; selection rules. Scattering theory. Angular momentum and spin. Exclusion principle.

STATISTICAL MECHANICS

Ensembles. Ensemble averages; relation to thermodynamic properties. Partition function.
Fermi-Dirac, Bose-Einstein and Boltzmann statistics. Classical ideal monatomic gas. Fermi-Dirac gas; electrons in metals. Bose-Einstein gas; photon gas; monatomic crystals.

SOLID STATE PHYSICS

Interatomic forces; crystal structure; X-ray and neutron diffraction. Lattice vibrations; lattice specific heats. Metals; Fermi-Dirac statistics; electronic specific heat; conductivity; band structure. Insulators and semiconductors; electrons and holes; donors; carrier injection; transistors. Magnetism; the main varieties of magnetism; spin waves.

(2) MATHEMATICAL PHYSICS II

Candidates will be required to study the mathematical aspects of the following subjects:

ELECTRICITY AND MAGNETISM

Elementary vector treatment of the electric and magnetic fields due to charges and currents, including the effects of dielectrics and magnetic materials, leading finally to the derivation of Maxwell's equations and simple applications.

WAVES AND PHYSICAL OPTICS

Huygen's principle; wave propagation in isotropic media. Interference and diffraction of sound, microwaves, light and particles; applications of interference and diffraction; limit of resolution. Circular and elliptic polarization; wave propagation in anisotropic media; applications of polarized light. Semi-classical treatment of the interaction of light with matter.

RADIATION AND QUANTUM THEORY

Classical and quantum theories of radiation in an enclosure. Photoelectric effect. Quantum theory of specific heats. The uncertainty principle and the foundations of quantum mechanics; Schrödinger's equation and simple applications; perturbation theory. Transition probabilities; selection rules. Scattering theory. Angular momentum and spin. Exclusion principle.

RELATIVITY

Experimental basis of the special theory of relativity. Lorentz transformation including electro-magnetic field. Collisions in centre of mass and laboratory systems.

ATOMIC AND NUCLEAR PHYSICS

The hydrogen atom and the quantization of atomic states; periodic table; vector model of the atom and its applications; X-ray, optical, infra-red and radio-frequency spectra of atoms and molecules. Neutron and proton as constituents of the nucleus. Nuclear forces. Theories of nuclear structure. Radioactive decay of the nucleus. Elementary particles.

(3) ECONOMICS

With the approval of the Dean of the School of Physical Sciences, the Professor of Mathematics and the Professor of Economics, a limited number of undergraduates in each year will be allowed to study Economics. The following subjects will be taken:

ECONOMIC THEORY

Consumption and demand; production and resource allocation; types of market situation; risk and uncertainty; the growth of the firm; value in economics; centralized and decentralized decision taking.

Credit and money interest and capital; the distribution of the national product; specialization, location, regional and international economics.

Growth and structural change; business cycles; welfare and economic policy.

ECONOMETRICS

The measurement of economic variables; quantitative models; testing of models; economic prediction; the relationship of econometrics to other approaches to economics.

(4) NUMERICAL AND STATISTICAL MATHEMATICS[1]

Subjects to be taken will include Advanced Statistics and Numerical Analysis; calculating machines and programming.

(iv) Philosophy Major

COMPULSORY SUBJECTS

PHILOSOPHY

Candidates must take *four* PHILOSOPHY papers chosen from list 104 and approved by the Professor of Philosophy.

For those candidates taking Option (1) below, three such papers must be taken, together with

[1] May not be available for those entering in 1963-64;

APPENDIX A

Techniques of deduction in formal systems; Boolean algebras; propositional calculus; logical paradoxes; axiomatic set theory; problems and methods of proof theory; Godels incompleteness theorem. An outline knowledge of the historical development of the subject will also be required.

OPTIONAL SUBJECTS

Candidates will take *one* of the following options:

(1) MATHEMATICS

The subjects studied must include:

> Linear Algebra and Elementary Group Theory
> Real and Complex Analysis
> Set Theory and Transfinite Numbers
> Probability Theory and Elementary Statistics
> Foundations of Geometry

and a further geometrical subject chosen from

> Projective and Non-Euclidean Geometry
> Topology
> Differential Geometry and Relativity

The syllabus for the above subjects may differ in detail from the syllabus for similar subjects taken by candidates majoring in mathematics. For instance, more detailed attention will be given to the foundations of Real Analysis.

(2) MATHEMATICS AND PHYSICS

MATHEMATICAL METHODS

Multiple and curvilinear integrals; vector operators; theorems of Gauss, Green and Stokes and simple applications.

Linear ordinary and partial differential equations; separation of variables. Singular points, solution in series. Bessel and Legendre functions; spherical harmonics. Eigenvalue problems; Sturm-Liouville system. Orthogonality and completeness; expansion in eigenfunctions. Fourier series and integrals. Types of partial differential equation.

CLASSICAL MECHANICS

Generalized co-ordinates; holonomic systems; Lagrange's equations; normal modes. Hamilton's equations and Poisson brackets; elementary mechanics of rigid bodies.

LINEAR ALGEBRA

Vector spaces; linear transformations; matrices; determinants; applications.

COMPLEX VARIABLE THEORY

Regular functions. Cauchy's theorem; contour integration.

STATISTICS

Probability; frequencies; binomial, normal and Poisson distributions; simple tests of significance.

NUMERICAL ANALYSIS

Introduction to standard techniques for handling numerical problems including practical work.

MECHANICS OF CONTINUOUS MEDIA

Simple mathematical theory of wind tunnels, shock waves, river bores, viscous flow, Reynolds Number.

Stress-strain relations for elastic media with theory of simple elastic waves.

(3) PHYSICS

ELECTRICITY AND MAGNETISM

Elementary vector treatment of the electric and magnetic fields due to charges and currents, including the effects of dielectrics and magnetic materials, leading finally to the derivation of Maxwell's equations and simple applications.

WAVES AND PHYSICAL OPTICS

Huygen's principle; wave propagation in isotropic media. Interference and diffraction of sound, microwaves, light and particles; applications of interference and diffraction; limit of resolution. Circular and elliptic polarization; wave propagation in anisotropic media; applications of polarized light. Semi-classical treatment of the interaction of light with matter.

RADIATION AND QUANTUM THEORY

Classical and quantum theories of radiation in an enclosure. Photoelectric effect. Quantum theory of specific heats. The uncertainty principle and the foundations of quantum mechanics; Schrödinger's equation and simple applications; perturbation theory. Transition probabilities; selection rules. Scattering theory. Angular momentum and spin. Exclusion principle.

APPENDIX B

List of books and articles quoted and used in Chapter 3

COMMAND PAPER 2154, *Report of the Committee on Higher Education . . . under the chairmanship of Lord Robbins*. 1963

R. R. DALE, *From School to University*. 1954

R. R. DALE, 'Some non-academic factors influencing university studies'. *British Journal of Sociology* III (1952)

N. DEMERATH, 'Adolescent status demands and the student experiences of twenty schizophrenics'. *American Sociological Review*, VIII (1943)

A. EDEN, 'Social Life in a Provincial University'. *Brit. Jnl. Sociol.*, X (1959)

D. FURNEAUX, 'The Psychologist and the University'. *Universities' Quarterly* (Dec. 1962)

D. FURNEAUX, 'Some psychometric characteristics of university students seeking psychiatric help'. (Paper read before the British Psychological Society, 1956)

A. GIDDENS, 'Aspects of the social structure of a university hall of residence'. *Sociological Review*, VIII (1960)

A. H. HALSEY, 'University expansion and the collegiate ideal'. *Univ. Qtly.* (Dec. 1961)

E. HARTSHORNE, 'Undergraduate society and the college culture'. *Amer. Sociol. Rev.*, VIII (1943)

J. HOPKINS, 'Handicaps to success at the University'. *Educational Review*, XI (1959)

J. HOPKINS, N. MALLESON and I. SARNOFF, 'Some non-intellectual correlates of success and failure among university students'. *British Journal of Educational Psychology*, XXVIII (1958)

E. HUXLEY, 'Report from Redbrick'. *Punch* (12th Dec. 1962)

A. JENKINSON, 'Wastage; natural, built-in and imposed'. *The Vocational Aspect*, XXIII (1959)

R. KELSALL, *Application for admission to universities*. 1957

A. KERR, *Universities of Europe*. 1962

F. D. KLINGENDER, 'Students in a changing world'. *Yorkshire Bulletin of Economic and Social Research*, VI (1954)

N. MALLESON, 'Operational research in the University'. *British Medical Journal*, 18th April 1959

N. MALLESON, 'Treatment of pre-examination strain'. *ibid.* 7 Sept. 1959

N. MALLESON, 'Academic study and mental health'. See W.U.S. April 1961 *Report*

N. MALLESON, Evidence to the [Robbins] Committee on Higher Education. Duplicated; Nov. 1961

N. MALLESON and J. HOPKINS, 'University Student, 1953'. *Univs. Qtly.* (May 1959; Nov. 1959/Jan. 1960; Feb./April 1960; Dec. 1960)

P. MANN and G. MILLS, 'Living and learning at Redbrick: a sample survey at Sheffield University'. *ibid.* (Dec. 1961)

J. MOUNTFORD, *How they fared*. 1956

NATIONAL UNION OF STUDENTS, Memorandum to the . . . [Hale] Committee on University teaching methods. 1961

J. READ, 'Social problems and student mental health'. See W.U.S. April 1961 *Report*

A. H. SINCLAIR-GIEBEN, 'The concept of mental health in the context of higher education'. See W.U.S. Dec. 1961 *Report*

R. STILL, 'The incidence, variety and severity of symptoms of psychological ill-health occurring among university students'. See W.U.S. April 1961 *Report*

D. THODAY, 'Halls of residence'. *Univs. Qtly.* (Nov. 1957)

D. THODAY, 'Residence and education in civic universities'. *International Journal of Social Psychiatry*, IV (1958)

UNIVERSITY GRANTS COMMITTEE, *Report of the sub-committee on halls of residence*. 1957

UNIVERSITY GRANTS COMMITTEE, *Interim report of the [Hale] Committee: The use of vacations by students.* 1963

UNIVERSITY OF LEEDS, *Report of a committee on student accommodation.* 1962

UNIVERSITY OF LEEDS: DEPT. OF STUDENT HEALTH, 'A study of the academic performance of 751 first year students'. Duplicated: Sept. 1952

WORLD UNIVERSITY SERVICE, *Report of a conference held at Campbell Hall, London, 8th to 9th April, 1961*

Ibid. *Papers read at a conference on The Student and Mental Health held at B.M.A. House, London, 28th to 29th Dec. 1961.*

G. WORSWICK, 'Anatomy of Oxbridge; classifying the classes [of degree]. *Times Educational Supplement* (3rd May 1957)

F. ZWEIG, *The Student in the Age of Anxiety.* 1963

Immensely useful has been the duplicated Bibliography of operational research into University and Student Problems, produced by the Research Unit for Student Problems, University of London Institute of Education (July 1961 and Supplement, Nov. 1962).

Index